With Her
Own Hands

With Her Own Hands

WOMEN WEAVING THEIR STORIES

NICOLE NEHRIG

W. W. NORTON & COMPANY
Independent Publishers Since 1923

For information about permission to reproduce selections from
this book, write to Permissions, W. W. Norton & Company, Inc.,
500 Fifth Avenue, New York, NY 10110

For information about special discounts for bulk purchases,
please contact W. W. Norton Special Sales at
specialsales@wwnorton.com or 800-233-4830

Manufacturing by Lakeside Book Company
Book design by Anna Knighton
Production manager: Gwen Cullen

Library of Congress Cataloging-in-Publication Data is available.

ISBN 978-1-32407-485-4

W. W. Norton & Company, Inc., 500 Fifth Avenue,
New York, NY 10110
www.wwnorton.com

W. W. Norton & Company Ltd., 15 Carlisle Street,
London W1D 3BS

10 9 8 7 6 5 4 3 2 1

For Eleanor & Ari

Contents

Introduction

When I was twenty-six, I picked up a knitting kit at a hobby store, with big plastic needles and a skein of chunky blue yarn. It was a tumultuous time in my life. I was ending a long-term relationship that had culminated in a brief marriage followed swiftly by divorce, while ambivalently beginning a career as a qualitative market researcher. I really wanted to go to graduate school but was torn between studying literature and psychology. As I mourned the loss of a future I had imagined and began shaping a new one, I learned to knit from books and online videos. I made a lot of mistakes along the way and had to rip out rows of stitches to get back on course—a fitting metaphor for what was happening in my life at the time. But from that skein of blue yarn, I made a wonky garter- and stockinette-stitch scarf and sewed a garter-stitch square into something resembling a hat shape. I put the scarf and hat on a pumpkin as a gift for my friend's October birthday.

When I finally made the decision to go to graduate school for psychology, I found myself knitting more than ever, in part because I had so much assigned reading for school that I could no longer read for pleasure, but mostly because it provided an antidote to my work as a therapist. Knitting is tangible; you can see your progress, you can unravel stitches and fix mistakes as though you're turning back time, and you can trust what you see. It was something I could ground myself in to counter the intangible, multilayered work of therapy.

It also provided a way to connect with people. I joined a knitting circle that met in a Brooklyn pub and included a number of psychologists, all of us knitting for our own sanity in some way. When one of the members had her first baby, several of us knit a blanket using leftover bits of yarn that the group contributed. We knitted mitered squares and gathered one Saturday to sew them all together into a rainbow blanket. Knitting made us a community.

Once, I sat down on a subway train and pulled out my knitting and noticed that the woman sitting next to me was also knitting. The shared activity offered an easy icebreaker of "what are you working on?" which led me to invite her to join my knitting circle. I taught her Fair Isle knitting, and she taught me how to sew. We've been friends ever since.

I found myself returning to knitting to find moments of calm amid chaos time and time again. As I was finishing my doctoral dissertation, I decided to knit myself a dress to wear at my defense. Having the same deadline both for the dress and the dissertation helped me take breaks from writing and create balance during that busy time—I finished the dress, defended my dissertation, got married and pregnant all in the same week! When I had my first child, I realized I was spending nearly eight hours a day either breastfeeding or trapped under a sleeping baby. So I rigged a sling to free up my hands to knit during this time. I recalled seeing women weaving with babies strapped to their backs in Central America—effective and necessary multitasking to meet domestic and economic needs.

When the world locked down in March 2020 during the COVID-19 pandemic, the boundary between my work and home life dissolved. I was working at a VA hospital as a clinical and research psychologist. Research studies were put on hold, and I was quarantined with a three-year-old and a five-year-old, coordinating work and childcare schedules with my husband. I just barely managed my responsibilities to my patients and students, who were similarly struggling with this drastic reorientation of the world as we knew it. So many aspects of life that had supplied its dimensions and textures went by the wayside.

Yet, I could still knit. Despite the fact that it was one of the busiest, most stressful years of my life, or perhaps because of it, I knitted even more than I had in graduate school. Knitting occupied my hands and my mind while the kids played outside and during their school Zoom meetings. After the kids went to bed and I could no longer string words together on clinical notes or research papers, I could still string stitches together and often fell asleep with my knitting in my hands. I had Zoom knitting dates with friends and participated in virtual knit-a-longs online. I completed the International Sweater-a-Month Dodecathlon (#IntSweMoDo), a challenge in which participants must knit twelve adult-sized sweaters in twelve months. I also took custom orders from my kids—a pair of swordfish socks, a narwhal stuffy, and a tiny mouse named Nibbly. More than ever before, life felt like it was about survival, and knitting was an important part of my survival strategy. It gave me a sense of control, an escape, an emotional release, and an outlet for the creative and intellectual energy I had previously channeled into my research. It also connected me to the long history of women who have made cloth. Like my female ancestors knew, making textiles by hand is compatible with childcare (unlike writing research grants). I had found a source of meaning through textile crafts in a way that I imagined women might have for thousands of years.

During the forced break from research, I was surprised to find that I didn't miss it—I had found other activities to stimulate my mind and a more sustainable balance between professional and personal pursuits. I decided to leave the academic career I was building and reenvision my life. I realized how much of my identity was entwined with the institution where I worked and the roles I played as a therapist, teacher, and researcher. I felt like I had been a tightly wound ball of yarn and all the threads were coming out in a tangled mess. I had to pull at the different strands to liberate the yarn so it could be transformed into something more functional and beautiful. I thought a lot about how to make meaning during times of struggle, how to be creative within constraints, how to locate yourself when suddenly under radically different circumstances, how to unravel old identities and knit them anew. As a mother in a caregiving profession who was knitting daily for sanity and a sense of self, I wondered how women throughout history had overcome the challenges they faced in life and what role textile work played in the process. I started a small private practice to continue working as a therapist and began researching these questions. This book is the result of my exploration.

Women's roles in society have been intertwined with textile work to such a large extent that the tools of textile production have served as a metonymy for female. In ancient Greece, a tuft of wool was hung on the door of a family's home when a daughter was born (a crown of olive leaves was hung for the birth of a son). The distaff, a traditional handspinner's tool used for holding raw fibers as they are spun into thread on a spindle, became shorthand for "women's work" in the English language. By the sixteenth century, the "distaff side" was a common way of referring to the mother's relatives. Making textiles has essentialized the differences between men and women and served as a means of inculcating the virtues associated with femininity—patience, obedience, silence. Yet, throughout history, it has also been a way for women to exercise agency.

Textiles have been used to express political protest, convey coded messages, record historical events, transmit cultural ideology, process traumas, earn an income, celebrate, and mourn. That may explain why, for millennia, women went well beyond what was necessary for survival, to dye yarn, create complex designs, and make textiles that are beautiful, expressive, and personal. Even when textile work was compulsory and tedious, the repetitive nature allowed space for women's minds to wander—to daydream, process emotions, find comfort in the familiar, and ground themselves in the tangible while creating something of value, often in the company of other women. Today, many women carry on this legacy and continue to take an interest and find meaning in textile crafts. A National Endowment for the Arts survey found that in the United States, fiber arts were the most common form of craft for women of nearly all ages and ethnic groups.[1] I am fascinated by how these women, in the past and present, have used textile work to create meaning in their lives.

While we may have little choice regarding our life circumstances, we can choose to find value and significance in the experiences available to us. The psychologist Viktor Frankl wrote that a wide array of life's activities, if approached creatively, may be imbued with meaning. His ability to make meaning of his suffering while imprisoned at Auschwitz maintained his will to live. Psychoanalyst Carl Jung observed, "Meaning makes a great many things endurable—perhaps everything."[2]

Throughout history, finding meaning amid constraints was particularly important for women living in oppressive societies. French philosopher Simone de Beauvoir argued that women's subordinate roles in patriarchal societies do not permit the freedom needed to make a meaningful life. However, her focus on the condition of all women may have caused her to overlook the possibility of self-realization for each individual woman.[3] Philosopher and psychoanalyst Julia Kristeva suggests that although women have often been oppressed collectively, each woman had her own individual capacity for creativity and freedom. While it is critical to strive to collectively free women from the binds of the patriarchy, and whatever other oppressive systems they have been up against, it is also meaningful to explore the ways each woman could overcome the challenges of her particular situation. Women did not wait for the "feminine condition" to change in order to exercise their freedom—if we did, we'd still be waiting.[4] In any given place, on any given day, women have had more control over their individual lives than over cultural norms and institutional restrictions.

Carolyn Heilbrun, a feminist literary scholar, poses the problem and a solution in *Reinventing Womanhood*. She writes:

> Men have monopolized human experience, leaving women unable to imagine themselves as both ambitious and female. If I imagine myself (woman has always asked) whole, active, a self, will I not cease, in some profound way, to be a woman? The answer must be: imagine, and the old idea of womanhood be damned. . . .
>
> Let us imagine ourselves as selves, as at once striving and female. Womanhood can be what we say it is, not what they have always said it was.[5]

But Heilbrun also highlights the difficulty of imagining new ways to live; we can only live by the stories we have already heard. "We live our lives though text,"[6] she writes, and the stories we have are what we must use to make new narratives.

We have relatively few texts to work with, especially ones with stories written by women or that provide an enticing model to follow or adapt. Women's writing was rarely published, their art was often for private audiences only or overlooked entirely, and their music was often sung among themselves as they worked. Their daily work—cooking, cleaning, making clothes—got used up and worn out. Women were often excluded from census data or classified only as someone's wife or daughter, without a name of her own. Women's lives, their identities, their internal experiences have historically been hidden from public view. But the textiles they created offer a glimpse into their world. It is with thread that women wrote.

The meaning women made from their experiences with textiles certainly varied, depending on personal and cultural factors. In a presidential address in the journal *American Anthropologist*,[7] archaeologist Elizabeth Brumfiel presented three images of women weaving on backstrap looms in Mesoamerica—a ceramic figurine from the Late Classic Maya from eleven hundred to twelve hundred years ago, an illustration from the Aztec *Florentine Codex* written around five hundred years ago, and a photograph of a woman weaving in Guatemala in 1992. Brumfiel observed that at first glance these images suggest a striking continuity in women's work as weavers across over a millennium of Mesoamerican history. Then she asked the question, "But are these women engaged in a single, uniform activity?" The similarities on the surface mask differences that archaeologists and cultural anthropologists ignore at their peril. Often all we have to study is the material record of previous societies. We may know what they did, but we can only speculate about why they did it, being careful to investigate our own cultural and temporal biases.

Brumfiel argued that despite the similar outward appearance of their weaving practice, the women in these images are engaged in three very different activities. Among the Classic Maya, weaving defined class—a skilled craft that marked one's elite status; in Aztec Mexico, weaving defined gender; and in twentieth-century Meso-america, weaving defined ethnicity. The women weaving in these images are performing virtually the same movements on virtually the same loom, perhaps even creating virtually the same fabric, but the cultural context radically changes the meaning of the activity of weaving.

As I explore the role of textile work in women's lives throughout history, I endeavor to keep Brumfiel's argument in mind and to situate women's textile practice in its cultural and temporal setting; not to ascribe an exact meaning to any woman's work unless stated by her but to wonder about the possibilities of this meaning. I also keep in mind that whatever the cultural meaning of making cloth might have been, each woman had her own reasons for making cloth and found her own unique meaning in it. In any cultural context, she may have done it out of necessity, as a dreaded chore, or because her body and mind craved it and her thoughts on what she would make next kept her up at night.

To gain insight into the meaning of "women's work" to individual women, I read biographies, diaries, and accounts of historians and anthropologists. I also conducted in-depth interviews with artists, scholars, designers, and textile makers of all kinds, which form the foundation of this book. While my focus is on the long history of women as principal textile creators, I by no means wish to convey that cisgender men, transgender men, or non-binary people do not connect in meaningful ways to textile work. There are places where making cloth has been primarily the domain of men, like the weavers of *kente* cloth in Ghana, or where the work is divided as it is among the Kuba of Zaire, where men weave raffia cloth and women embroider it. Anyone who engages in textile work can find meaning and purpose in it, and I hope this book resonates with them all.

I focus each chapter of the book on a potential source of meaning in life and explore how textile work can contribute to that meaning. These include the ability to fully engage in the life cycle, to develop and express intellectual abilities, to craft a self through creative practice, to experience and process complex emotions, to have meaningful relationships and a sense of belonging, to feel that your contributions are valued by others and that you have some ability to improve your circumstances, and to stand up for what you believe in. The boundaries between chapters are not always clearly defined: maintaining a social connection through textile work can include the intergenerational processing of trauma; creative work is often intellectual work; and standing up for your convictions often involves social, cultural, and emotional elements and could reflect a fight for selfhood or a life-or-death struggle. By necessity, I've also had to leave some sources of meaning out. The connection between textile work and religion and spirituality, for example, could fill an entire book on its own.

Stitched together like pieces of a patchwork quilt, this book is a synthesis of archaeological, anthropological, historical, literary, and personal accounts of the meaning women have made through their textile work. The overall pattern reflects, as the title of the book suggests, women's ability to take matters into their own hands and make the best life they can out of the materials they have to work with.

CHAPTER I

To Live and Dye

On a hill high above the city of Cusco, Peru, Marcela Salas Calcina, a master weaver of ceremonial textiles from the remote village of Q'eros, and her husband Lorenzo, a shaman, make the vertical warp by passing a ball of yarn back and forth as each one wraps the thread on their end of the loom, staked into the ground by four posts. Woven fabric consists of the warp threads, which are attached vertically to the loom and remain fixed throughout the weaving process, and the weft threads, which are woven horizontally in and out of the warp threads. My guide and translator, Juan Carlos Auccapuma Ccorqhua, an expert in Andean religion, explains the importance of mixing masculine and feminine energies in the creation of ceremonial textiles, just as Pachamama and Pachatata, Mother and Father Earth, together created the Incan cosmos. From spinning to weaving, the process gives birth to a textile in an act of creation that symbolically mirrors reproduction. Calcina explains that she spins a single strand of yarn and gives it to her husband to twist together to create a two-plied yarn. She says it is "female to male, always. After I create it, he plies it."[1] The intermingling of male and female energies brings the yarn to life and gives it a soul. As Calcina and her husband warp the loom, their energies further imbue the cloth with masculine and feminine energies. Calcina does the weaving once the loom is warped, in a parallel with gestation. From this integration of the warp and weft, a textile is born. In the Andean tradition, textiles have a life of their own. Just like passing one's genetic material to a child, weavers put their life, knowledge, and emotion into their textiles.

Creating life and creating cloth have been two of women's most critical contributions to human societies, and many parallels have been drawn between them. On a practical level, women's ownership over textile work was likely due to its compatibility with pregnancy and childcare.[2] Although labor intensive, textile work is relatively safe and can be readily interrupted and combined with other tasks like breastfeeding and watching over children. On a more figurative level, as a second skin, cloth signifies an extension of the human body and evokes ideas of reproduction, birth, and death that relate to women's procreative and destructive power.[3] The process of making textiles serves as a metaphor for the life cycle—from the conception and creation of a fabric to the slow unraveling of a life.

The Tree of Life

In Norse mythology, Yggdrasil, the tree of life, connects the nine realms of the Norse universe, including the world of the gods, the world of humans, and the world of the dead. The three Norns—Urdr, Verdandi, and Skuld, powerful deities who control human destiny—are responsible for tending to Yggdrasil. They carry water from the well of Urd and pour it over the tree to maintain its life and, consequently, life in all worlds, since the tree sustains all of existence. The Norns also appear at the birth of children to measure their lifespan, determine their fate, and spin the thread of their life. Urdr translates to "what once was," Verdandi to "what is coming into being," and Skuld to "what shall be." Their names, reflecting past, present, and future, construct the very fabric of time. Most of the threads the Norns spin are coarse and gray, but every now and then they spin a colorful or, even more rarely, a golden thread signifying an exceptional destiny. The Norns were revered among the Norse for the great power they hold over the destinies of gods and humans, neither of whom can change their fate after their thread is spun.

Many mythological traditions share a tale of fate similar to the Norns, suggesting a shared Indo-European origin for these stories. The ancient Greeks had the Moirai, often referred to as the Fates: Clotho, who spun the thread of life, Lachesis, who measured its length, and Atropos, who cut it to determine the precise moment of death. In *The Republic*, Plato described the Moirai as the daughters of Ananke, the personification of necessity and inevitability who was often depicted holding a spindle, and her partner Chronos (Time). It naturally follows that their daughters would use the tools of cloth production to determine the length of time each person lives. In modern English, the term *lifespan* comes from the word *spin* and encapsulates this mythological concept of the thread of life and women's symbolic connection to it through textiles.

While Atropos's metaphorical cutting of the thread indicates the time of death, the midwife's cutting of the umbilical cord reflects the separation of the baby from the mother, with the midwife acting as the human version of these mythological female figures. In Greek and Roman antiquity, midwives were responsible for examining an infant at birth, before the umbilical cord was cut, to determine its viability. During this exam, the baby was in a liminal territory between life and death. If the midwife lifted the child from the ground and cut the umbilical cord, it was given a future; if not, it was left to die.[4] According to Aristotle, the cord was tied with a "fillet of wool" near the baby's abdomen and cut above the tie.[5] In some North African traditions, when weavers cut the last threads of a completed cloth, they recite similar blessings as is done when cutting the umbilical cord of a newborn child.[6] Navajo weavers often add a small line to their weaving in a different color that travels to the very edge of the work, called the "weaver's path" or "spirit line." It is a sort of exit from the fabric and signifies a way to free the weaver's mind from the confines of the woven cloth, which is viewed as a living being itself. The weaver's path, like the umbilical cord, is a way of freeing the creator from its creation to create anew.

Creation stories and procreative powers are often associated with weaving in mythological traditions. One of the oldest Egyptian goddesses, Neith, whose representations date back to nearly 3000 BCE, was the goddess of creation, wisdom, weaving, and war. She was thought to be the creator of the universe and everything in it. Other accounts say she is the virgin mother of Ra, the sun god who created the rest of the world—the creator of the creator. She was thought to weave and reweave the world on her loom daily so that all that she conceived of in her heart came into being. In Incan mythology, Mama Ocllo, the personification of Pachamama or Mother Earth, is a fertility goddess who taught the Incans to spin, weave, and sew. The Mayan goddess Ixchel presides over fertility, physical love, childbirth, and weaving. In the Germanic tradition, Holda, also known as Mother Holle, is the source of women's fertility and the patron of spinning and was said to be the first to make linen from flax. And Saulė, a Baltic sun goddess considered the mother of all planets, spins the sunbeams on her wheel, generating light like thread. Like the sun, she is associated with fertility and growth.

Textiles themselves have also carried symbolic and ceremonial purposes related to childbearing and the life cycle. String skirts, a garment dating back to the Paleolithic era (which lasted from roughly 2.6 million years ago until 10,000 BCE), were likely a symbol of women's fertility or readiness to conceive.[7] Some of the string skirts found in archaeological digs would have hung just over the pelvis and included metal details at the bottom of the strings that would have sparkled in the light, attracting attention to the region of women's procreative power. These skirts are our earliest known connection between textile work and women's reproductive function in society. Similarly, baskets have been used as a symbol for fertility in many traditions. Like a womb, they can hold and let go, protect and restrict, making them a meaningful symbol of the creation of life.[8] Navajo ceremonial wedding baskets, called *ts'aa'*, are often woven with sumac shoots dyed in red, black, and white to create a pattern that includes a direct pathway in white from the center of the basket outward. This is comparable to the "weaver's path" and, while it has several interpretations, is often considered to portray the birth canal of the female deity, Changing Woman, who represents girls' transition to womanhood.

For the Kodi, who live on the island of Sumba in Eastern Indonesia, "cloth is a master symbol for the transitions in a woman's life."[9] Textile production reflects the creation of female identity over time.

Among the Kodi, "womanhood" is not given at birth or assumed at the onset of menstruation but rather is created through stages that parallel women's roles in textile work. They use indigo dye and the ikat technique for dyeing yarn, in which threads are tightly bound to resist the dye in certain areas, creating a predetermined pattern in the final woven cloth. Kodi women keep secret their method of indigo dyeing as part of a cult of knowledge. Young, unmarried girls, as they are first initiated into this cult, learn to chew up the herbal preparations used to make the dyes, but when they reach sexual maturity, they are no longer allowed to participate in the dyeing process until they reach menopause. The dyebath is thought to be dangerous to pregnant women, able to dissolve the contents of their wombs, and endangered by menstruating women, since the power of their blood flow could make the dyes run irregularly. Women in their childbearing years instead weave and tie warp threads in ikat patterns, preparing them for dyeing, but are not allowed near the dye pot. The binding of threads is symbolically equated with sexual restraint and the production of healthy children because women are seen as dangerous when they are "open," their procreative energies not properly channeled or contained. So, like the threads, their reproductive capacities must be tightly bound to not let anything unwanted seep in and ruin the intended pattern.

Kodi women who are past menopause and have acquired the traditional tattoos on their forearms and legs that mark their achievements as wives and mothers may again begin to dye the cloth with indigo. The tattoos that signify these life passages for women are often the same patterns that are used in ikat weaving and give women enhanced status in society—their permanence on the skin reflecting a more permanent position of the woman in the patrilineage. Notably, many young Kodi women are now eschewing the practice of tattoos and reject having what they view as signs of male ownership carved into their bodies, but the power of being skilled in indigo dyeing persists and provides an opportunity for older women to distinguish themselves in the community.[10] As anthropologist Janet Hoskins explained, indigo dyeing is "still a specialty and there are basically only a few women in each region who are known for this. . . . It is a way of getting respect for knowledge you've accrued. And it's like your hidden recipe, like a really good cook . . . , a mark of accomplishment that is still culturally significant."[11] Hand-dyed indigo cloth is used as a form of social currency—worn for special occasions and gifted at funerals—so while younger Kodi women often opt for more financially lucrative, modern jobs like working in an office, older women typically fill the demand for these fabrics.

Status for older women in Kodi society is gained through their knowledge of the "blue arts," or *moro*, occult practices that include herbal preparations for childbirth recovery, fertility, abortion, contraception, and a hastening of menopause. These practices are closely tied with the art of ikat dyeing; for instance, the same herbal preparation used to stop bleeding after childbirth is used to stop the indigo dye from bleeding when it is washed.[12] Notably, the health benefits of indigo (and many dyestuffs used medicinally in other cultures) have been borne out through scientific study. Natural indigo dye has significant anti-inflammatory, antioxidant, antibacterial, antiviral, and analgesic properties that likely do aid in health and healing.[13] Because of these links between dyeing and herbal medicine, developing skill in the dyeing process may also qualify a woman to practice as a midwife and healer known as *tou tango moro*, literally "person who applies blueness," allowing her to continue her participation in the life cycle beyond her childbearing years.

Indigo dyeing is a specifically female practice and even considered dangerous for men. Hoskins believes that it represents an independent female creation, akin to childbirth, that is outside male control.[14] A Kodi midwife and herbalist, Gheru Wallu, explained: "Men will never know women's secrets about these things, and they will always think that we can control even more than we can."[15] Kodi women's secrecy and control of the dye process mimics their secrecy and control over female reproduction. Men are typically unaware of women's fertile times, menstruation, and even pregnancy until it becomes difficult to conceal. Women's efforts to manage their fertility might be viewed as surreptitious or even duplicitous, as they may work counter to their husband's aims. Given the importance of women's roles in reproduction and textile production, it is perhaps not surprising that both roles are regarded with some ambivalence— venerated as gifts from the heavens and feared as a potential threat to the social order.

Sex, War, and Witchcraft

Cloth's symbolic connection to concepts of fate, birth, creation, and death makes it material that both sustains life and poses threats to it. As in the Kodi practice of the "blue arts," women's powers for creation were often interwoven with their powers for magic, duplicity, and death. Many of the goddesses related to fertility and spinning or weaving have a dark side, alluding to the idea that with powers for creation also come powers for destruction. Neith, the Egyptian creator of life, was also worshipped as a funerary goddess and the goddess of war. Mayan goddess Ixchel was thought to have both healing and destructive powers; she is often depicted as a fearsome warrior with a sword and shield or with the claws of a jaguar.[16] Germanic goddess Holda's connection to the spirit world through spinning became associated with witchcraft in Catholic Germanic folklore, where she was depicted as riding with witches on distaffs.

The Hindu goddess Māyā, who also figures prominently in Buddhism, encapsulates this complex relationship between creation, magical powers, and danger. The term *māyā* is associated with the "maker's power" and therefore with art and procreation, "the wondrous and mysterious power to turn an idea into a physical reality."[17] Māyā is thought to be the manifestation of *shakti*, the dynamic feminine energy responsible for the creation, maintenance, and destruction of the universe. Often depicted as a spider, Māyā is the spinner of magic, fate, and earthly appearances. Around her she spins the complex web of the universe. She created the world alongside Brahma; while Brahma created the world of reality, Māyā created the world of illusion, which we cannot see. She creates a disjuncture between what is and what appears to be, and only by unveiling these illusions can we understand reality. Because of Māyā's association with illusion, her web also becomes one of deceit, trapping people into thinking they can find happiness in worldly pleasures rather than through transcendence of the senses and connection to a higher power.

Textiles can serve as a vehicle for supernatural forces, both good and bad. Part of the impetus for decorating cloth was to imbue it with symbols that expressed a wish or warded off a fear. But what happens when things do not go well? If people can bestow a blessing, they can also deliver a curse. If women could weave magic into their cloths to impart fertility and protection from evil spirits, perhaps they could also weave in harmful elements.

In a Seneca myth called "The Quilt of Men's Eyes," we see

how women's creative work was imbued with deadly power.[18] Twin brothers, known as Younger and Driven, leave their home to play among the hills. They must pass by a lodge where women are gathered singing and dancing. The elder brother, Driven, tells his brother not to look at the women as they pass, warning that a single glance could be fatal. Although the women exclaim "Look up and behold us!" the brothers refuse. As they continue, Driven explains that they must submit to one more danger: "A company of women is making a quilt of young men's eyes. They gouge out the men's eyes and sew them into a quilt. The eyes live and wink as in life for the skins of the eyelids are with the eyes. Now we must pass through their lodge, and if we can do so without looking at the awful quilt, we will be safe." As they enter the lodge, the women entreat them: "Look up and see the beautiful quilt we are making. It is beautiful. Look up!" The brothers continue through the room, keeping their eyes down, but when they near the exit, a woman holds the quilt right in front of Younger and his eyes jump onto it, leaving him blind. Driven disappears, and the blind Younger makes his way to a cornfield, where he is discovered by two sisters who take him in and nurse him to health. Eventually, he marries the younger sister, who gives birth to another set of twin boys. When they grow older, these twins find their lost uncle and bring him home. They borrow eyes from a deer so that their father can temporarily see. They then embark on their own adventure to retrieve their father's eyes and succeed in restoring their father's lost sight.

In this myth, the quilt of men's eyes brings power to the gathered women, but at the direct expense of the power of men.[19] The women are depicted as seductive, tempting men by the power of their works, and succeeding even when the man has great resolve, like the sirens in *The Odyssey* who use their alluring voices to hypnotize men into shipwrecking their boats on a rocky cliff.[20] The Seneca myth reflects a fear that women hold power over men that can make men act against their rational judgment, even when they know that harm may come to them.

Men may have felt the need to control the source of women's power over life and death in order to manage their own fears and sense of powerlessness against these controllers of fate. In a paper called "What Do Men Fear?," psychoanalyst Eugene Goldwater writes that while men have, on average, been assured of their superior size and strength, they may have feared that "what women lack in might, they sometimes make up for in magic."[21] Thus, the very aspects of life that gave women power (namely, reproduction and cloth production) have also served as reasons for it to be taken away. At times, women may have been able to wield this power as a double-edged sword, using both the beneficial and potentially detrimental properties of their creativity to their advantage. As Kodi midwife Gheru Wallu alluded, it may be advantageous to let men think women can control even more than they can—the mystery around the extent of their power is itself a source of power. Women may have played into men's fears by embracing the perception of their magical potential for both creation and destruction. At other times, this perceived magical potential severely restricted women's freedom and safety in society.

During the Viking era, Icelandic women wove in *dyngjas*, small pit houses that were separate from the main house. Men were barred from weaving houses, and legend has it that they would be punished by death for peeking in or entering. Dyngjas became associated

with witchcraft and were considered dangerous places where mysterious rituals and processes occurred. This may have derived from
women's seemingly magical ability to transform wool into cloth as
well as the songs, chants, and stories that the women sung while
weaving, sometimes as ways of recalling patterns, that may have
been interpreted as invocations or spells.

The *Njáls saga*, a thirteenth-century account of blood feuds that
raged in Iceland between the years 960 and 1020, depicts dyngjas as
places where life and death decisions were made.[22] In the battle song
"Darraðarljóð," a soldier peers into a dyngja at the start of a battle
and witnesses twelve Valkyries weaving a gruesome cloth. In Norse
mythology, the Valkyries, like the Norns, are powerful controllers
of fate, but they specifically preside over battles and usher the souls
of worthy soldiers to Valhalla, the afterworld of those slain in battle.
The Valkyries sing to narrate their actions:

> Blood rains
> from the cloudy web
> on the broad loom
> of slaughter.
> The web of man
> grey as armor
> is now being woven;
> the Valkyries
> will cross it
> with a crimson weft.
>
> The warp is made
> of human entrails;
> human heads

are used as heddle-weights;
the heddle rods are blood-wet spears;
the shafts are iron-bound
and arrows are the shuttles.
With swords we will weave
this web of battle . . .[23]

As the "choosers of the slain," the Valkyries foretell who will fall in battle, weaving the soldiers' destinies on the warp-weighted loom.[24] In "Darraðarljóð" they use the loom as an engine of war and death, bringing about the destruction of lives through their creation of cloth. Like the thread of life that the Norns cut, soldiers' fates are sealed in this bloody fabric hanging from the loom. When the weaving is finished, the Valkyries tear up the fabric, a practice thought to release the spiritual energy accumulated through making it, and ride off with their shares in different directions. What is woven comes to pass.

The scene brings to life the parallel between creating cloth and creating human life, as they weave a cloth made of human bodies. It also speaks to the danger of women's collective and creative actions carried out behind closed doors; the story is known only because the soldier peered in and witnessed this gory business where he wasn't allowed. In the seventeenth century, the practice of weaving in dyngjas was eradicated and looms were moved into the main house, perhaps to decrease the perceived threat posed by women's private spaces.[25]

For the Vikings, powerful female deities Freya and Frigg oversaw textile work. Freya is the Norse goddess associated with love, beauty, sex, fertility, war, and magic. Frigg is the goddess of marriage and motherhood and believed to have prophetic powers. In Scandinavia, the constellation often called Orion's Belt is known as Frigg's Distaff. Both Frigg and Freya were believed to practice *seiðr*, a form of ecstatic magic related to the telling and shaping of the future, often by symbolically weaving events into being—another connection between textiles and fate. Seiðr involves achieving a trancelike state through the meditative process of spinning or weaving and chanting. In these rituals, the loom is a symbolic doorway that allows women to pass into alternate realms.

Men did not take part in seiðr, fearing *ergi*, unmanliness or effeminacy, by association. Because of the potential for spinning tools to be used as phalluses in the practice of seiðr, men's involvement in both seiðr and cloth production was linked with adopting a receptive sexual position in penetrative sex. It is also possible that women used spinning tools to achieve orgasm in rituals involving masturbation.[26] Ambiguous gender roles were common among gods, and Frigg taught her husband, Odin, the most powerful of the Norse gods, the magic of seiðr so he could practice it without being emasculated. However, for mortal humans, transgressing against traditional gender roles was associated with witchcraft.

Despite the fact that men feared being emasculated through women's work, women were not considered powerless. The distaff was a source of power for women—her weapon. Depictions of women dominating men with a distaff or using a distaff in place of a spear to battle against a man were popular misogynistic themes in medieval and early modern Europe, suggesting a shameful role reversal.[27] Men feared losing their status as warriors, a status based on their ability to dominate and destroy, not their ability to create. This shame may be embedded in the fact that children, regardless of gender, initially identify with their mothers as the primary caregiver, and therefore masculine identity is born through the renunciation of the feminine, not only through the affirmation of the masculine.

Boys must learn to actively separate their identity from their mothers and may reject traditionally feminine traits in themselves and others as a way to cope with the loss of this identification.[28]

For women, the disruption of gender norms and social behaviors was often associated with witchcraft. Today it is still all too common that in countries such as Ghana, Nepal, India, and Papua New Guinea, women may be branded as witches if they singly own property or have outstayed their welcome as financial dependents in their family home.[29] These women—often widowed or never married—are either too independent or not independent enough. Either way, they do not neatly fit into the social order.

At times, men's ambivalence about these women's level of independence has been reflected through the customs or language of textiles. The early modern European witch craze was bound up with anxiety about what place women had in society at a time when Europe was undergoing fundamental social and economic transformations. By the end of the sixteenth century, marriage rates had declined, and up to 20 percent of women remained single, compared with only 5 to 10 percent in the fifteenth century.[30] Unmarried women were crucial to the economy, often contributing to household labor as servants in other peoples' homes.[31] However, there was always the question, conscious or not, about what happened to women's sexuality when it was not directed toward reproduction in a marriage. It was threatening to imagine that women's sexual desire could exist apart from men and be satisfied without them. That is likely why widows and "spinsters" were accused of witchcraft in numbers far out of proportion to their representation in society.[32] These women were often self-supporting, many through textile work, and therefore operated outside a traditional woman's role in society. The sexual symbolism of spinning, particularly the distaff as a phallic representation, linked women's financial independence through textile production to women's independent sexuality, which was seen as a dangerous force. Women who were not under the direct control or protection of a man were both threats to the social order and vulnerable targets.

This perception led both to the persecution of women as witches and to efforts to regulate spinning rooms, which were the center of village nightlife and a place for rural courtship in early modern Europe. Women gathered together to spin yarn at night so they could socialize and conserve energy by sharing the light and warmth of the fire. Men often visited to mingle and work on their own projects in wood and leather. Yet, representations of these spaces in German and Dutch art reflect the turbulence of a world turned upside down where women held the upper hand and men helped with the spinning and winding, sometimes even depicting sexual debauchery. It was clear that these spaces were primarily women's domain and men were visitors. One Dutch emblem from the early seventeenth century portrays a woman with snakes in her hair spinning while a devil holds the spun thread and a man winds the yarn. The inscription reads, "This is how things turn out when the threads of life are tangled."[33] Sebald Beham's *Spinning Bee*, a German woodcut from 1524, shows overt sex acts taking place, sometimes with the use of spinning tools.[34] At the time, "spindle" was slang for a penis, and metaphors for copulation based on textile tools (for example, needles filling holes with thread) were common. In the woodcut, men are shown being dominated by women wielding distaffs and being made to spin and wind yarn. This perceived threat to gender roles led to the formation of a German council in Nuremberg tasked with regulating village activity; the council addressed the issue by barring men from spinning rooms.[35]

In the 1800s, the rise of the middle class in Europe led to an increase in marriage rates and a corresponding decrease in women's paid labor. In the Victorian era, women's embroidery became increasingly entwined with aristocratic femininity and an abundance of leisure time for women of the upper classes. As described by psychotherapist and art historian Rozsika Parker in her book *The Subversive Stitch*, "Once [embroidery] was equated with a lifestyle that necessitated female dependence, it quickly became synonymous with feminine seductiveness. Female dependence was flattering but fearful to men. The helpless, leisured lady affirmed a man's social and economic standing, but simultaneously produced the image of a woman as a self-interested, subtle seductress."[36] Notably, during this time, embroidery patterns were increasingly created by men for women to faithfully copy. Even in their leisure activities, women were often not permitted free license for creativity, further reinforcing their dependent position. In this context, men's efforts to control women's reproductive and creative capacities through economic and social dependence led to suspicion about women's intentions and fears that women would entrap men to ensure their own economic and social survival.

It was against this backdrop of Victorian female dependency that Sigmund Freud developed his model of psychosexual development. His theories of women's identity development included the idea of "penis envy." He went so far as to propose an absurdly unfounded claim that women's invention of weaving was modeled after some shame-driven practice of braiding their pubic hair to conceal their lack of a penis.[37] According to Freud, women can only resolve their penis envy by having a (preferably male) child of their own. Freud's concept of penis envy has been heavily criticized, even in his own time by psychoanalyst Karen Horney, who first developed feminist psychology. Horney reasoned that Freud's theory of penis envy made sense when taken as a metaphor for the social prestige and economic power that men wielded; but she proposed that it was more likely that men experienced "womb envy" because of their inability to bear children, which they attempt to compensate for through economic and social achievements. Without a strong sense of the role as creator and sustainer of life, men must seek other accomplishments to bring them satisfaction and esteem. And because men generally are of superior size to women and have greater physical strength, men can achieve such status through hunting, building, farming, and fighting.[38]

Among the Iban of Borneo, men distinguish themselves as warriors and women as weavers, and their status is gained by demonstrating skill in headhunting and creating cloth, respectively. Headhunting, collecting enemy heads as trophies, was largely eradicated by the 1920s, but weaving and other rituals around the practice continue among the Iban today. A weaver's stages of social development paralleled those of a headhunter. Before marriage, a woman was expected to weave a *pua* (a ceremonial blanket), and a man was expected to take a head. Women could gain prestige by creating new weaving patterns and mastering the process of dyeing with *Morinda*, a plant that produces a rich, red color. Only a few women whose dyeing skills have distinguished them as leaders of the community dare to conduct the *Ngar* ceremony, which is also known as the *kayau indu*, or "warpath of women," and involves the application of the mordants used to fix the color prior to dyeing with *Morinda*. Leading the Ngar represents a weaver's highest possible achievement, and her position is likened to that of a leader of headhunting parties, the highest achievement for a warrior. The two were equated because both were seen as carrying the risk of injury and death. A woman needs the support of helping spirits and powerful charms to perform the Ngar; otherwise she can be "defeated" in the process, resulting in sickness or even death.[39] No doubt, dyeing with particular mordants and dyestuffs has at times led to health problems and perhaps even proved fatal, but it is also possible that the risks associated with weaving and dyeing actually symbolize the risks of childbirth, which has been dangerous throughout history, not unlike war. As Medea indicated in Euripides's play, "I would rather stand three times with a shield in battle than give birth once."[40]

Powerful patterns such as the *rang jugah*, or trophy head pattern, a lozenge shape motif, are the most technically difficult and must be dyed a deep maroon with *Morinda*. This cloth was used for the reception of trophy heads as they were brought into the longhouse and was thought to protect the community from the potentially damaging power of the head. Only women who had mastered this powerful and complex pattern were accorded the honor of ritually receiving enemy heads in their *pua kumbu*. The lozenge motif dates to the Neolithic and Paleolithic periods (the time before about 2000 BCE) in eastern Europe as a female fertility symbol, representative of a vagina. Could it be that this Iban tradition suggests that a woman's procreative powers are what combat the threat of death and destruction represented by the taken head? If so, then life and death battle each other within the cloth.

If women have the power to give and nurture life, then they also have the power to take life away by denying their nurturing gifts. These dual powers for creation and destruction set up a binary for women's roles in society reflected in the saint/sinner, Madonna/

whore, submissive/dominating dichotomies that have long constricted women's expression of self and their roles in society. Rather than integrating women's powers into a unified persona that women can fully inhabit in all their complexity, society limits them to only appropriately "female" traits while others are the domain of men or the province of witches, women who must be dominated or destroyed.

Death and Rebirth

Prior to the nineteenth century, the words *die* and *dye* were used interchangeably to refer to both the end of life and the process of coloring cloth. Though the words do not appear to be linked etymologically, there is a connection conceptually in the power or feared powers of dyes to cause harm. Certain dyes contained arsenic and could prove fatal. The Greeks, Romans, and Egyptians used orpiment to make a gold pigment, also known as "king's yellow." It was so poisonous that mining it was essentially a death sentence. A related mineral, realgar, was used as both a rich orange pigment and rat poison during the Middle Ages. Scheele's green, a synthetic dye popular in the nineteenth century, was used in clothing, upholstery, and wallpaper and could cause dire symptoms ranging from vomiting and rashes to death.

Perhaps an allusion to the potential for deadly dyes, the Greek god Heracles was killed by a shirt soaked in the blood of the centaur Nessus, given to him by his wife, Deianira, to try to ensure his faithfulness after he took a new lover. Nessus had tricked Deianira into believing it contained a love potion, when in fact it was the venom of the Lernaean Hydra, which Heracles had used to poison the arrow that killed Nessus. When Heracles put the shirt on, the poison burned his body, cooking him alive, and he jumped onto a funeral pyre to escape the pain. Just as dyes have the power to heal, they also have the power to inflict harm and even death.

Analogous to women's connection to the life cycle through childbirth, women have often been charged with tasks pertaining to death and rebirth. Froma Zeitlin, a classics scholar specializing in Greek literature, wrote about women's role in death rituals in ancient Greece:

> Woman can never forget her body as she experiences its inward pain, and she is not permitted to ignore its outward appearance in that finely tuned consciousness she acquires with respect to how she might seem to the eyes of others. Bodiliness defines her in the cultural system that associates her with physical processes of birth and death and emphasizes the material dimensions of her existence. . . . Men too have bodies, of course, but in a system defined by gender, the role of representing the corporeal side of life in its helplessness and submission to constraints is primarily assigned to women.
>
> Thus, it is women who most often tend the bodies of others, washing the surface of the body or laying it out for its funeral. Theirs is the task to supply the clothing that covers the body. . . . She seems to know, whether consciously or not, how vulnerable, how open—how mortal, in fact—is the human body.[41]

Women served a critical social function in ancient Greece by weaving burial shrouds for their kin, as evidenced in the tale of

Penelope, who forestalls remarrying under the pretense that she must first fulfill her obligation of weaving a burial shroud for her father-in-law, Laertes. Each day, she spends hours dutifully weaving; then, after everyone has gone to sleep, she carefully unravels her work. Her true aim is to preserve her marriage to Odysseus in the continued hope of his return, or to earn herself additional time to process her grief over their lengthy separation, or to maintain her independence. Her suitors could not deny her request to finish the shroud because through it she demonstrates the ideal qualities they would seek in a wife. Penelope would not let a prominent man be buried without a shroud woven by a member of his household.[42]

Women's province over life and cloth reflects a connection between women and the ephemeral. Women cook a constant churn of meals that are gone soon after they are made, make the cloth that will be grown out of or worn to rags, and birth the children that will one day die. In contrast, in many cultures, men create work in metal and stone that can continue to exist hundreds or even thousands of years later.[43] Among the Kodi in Sumba, Janet Hoskins explained, "when they talk of women as textile workers, they compare it to men as metal workers. . . . They associate metal work with forming the hard parts of the body which come from the man—the skeleton—while the fleshy parts, the equivalent of the textile bundle, comes from the woman."[44] Perhaps women's role in shrouding the body is in some way compensation for the notion that their contribution to the body's creation is more ephemeral. Babies are wrapped in blankets when they are born, and the dead are buried in woven shrouds—both as a protective response to the vulnerability of life. But cloth is semidurable and thus can offer only a kind of protection that must ultimately be left behind, like a mother's womb and our bodies when we die.[45] Hoskins noted that dead people in

Sumba are arranged in the fetal position and wrapped up like babies in a kind of round textile bundle, creating a connection between birth and death. She said, "I think for them women's roles in textiles are associated with a process of decay that then gives life. From the dark gooey liquid (of the indigo dyebath) you're then able to make beautiful textiles that are somewhat like your children. You give birth to them. So, I think those metaphors are linked for them."[46] Women's role as the custodian of death parallels their role as the creator of life.

In Kodi society, it is understood that men dislike the messy business of handling bloody infants and decomposing corpses, so this work, like the messy business of indigo dyeing, falls to women. Their jurisdiction over the business of life and death becomes their source of power. In one Kodi myth, a young princess conceives a child but quickly miscarries. A wise old woman finds the embryo in a stalk of white millet and wraps it in a fine textile. The fetus grows into a beautiful young man. The cloth creates a substitute womb that allows this elderly woman to gestate life in such a way that parallels the dressing of a corpse in fabric in preparation for a rebirth after death.[47] While this cloth was able to bring someone back to life, indigo dye is also used among the Kodi to fix spirits in their graves. After someone dies what is known as a "blue death" through a violent accident, murder, or drowning, the soul of the victim is said to fly off into the sky and the body cannot be buried until a ceremony has been performed to bring it back. The smell of the body waiting for its soul to return is likened to the smell of the indigo dyebath—both pungent and evocative of decay. After the body is buried, a pot of indigo dye is poured on top of the burial to ensure that the spirit remains in its grave and to keep it from wandering.[48]

In many cultures, cloth is an essential part of mourning rituals. In early modern Europe, the linen bedsheets and underclothes that a person died in were often given to surviving loved ones. Sheets and clothing contained the life essence—the sweat and blood—of the dying person who convalesced in them. Therefore, they were imbued with the person who died and became one of the most valuable things a loved one could receive to hold onto the person after death.[49] Among the Hanunuo Mangyan in the Philippines, the *kutkot* ritual involves exhuming their dead and dressing them in cloth to bring them to life again, often several years after their death.[50] The cloth serves as a sort of skin to give the spirit form so they can remain among the living.

Cloth is also used to symbolically "untie" the dead from this life, cutting the ties between the living and the dead. In the Andean tradition, funerary *khipus* are used to help liberate the dead from this world and transition them to the next. Khipus are made of two threads twisted together into a rope, with a black or blue thread representing female energy and a white thread representing male energy, making it evenly balanced. The harmony between these energies is needed to ensure the strength and efficacy of this cord both materially, as plied threads are substantially stronger, and metaphorically, through the union of masculine and feminine energies. Since Incan times, khipus were knotted to record numerical information, such as the number of chickens you own or how many children you have, as well as processes, such as documenting the start and end of a project such as a harvest, building venture, or a woven fabric. Khipus were traditionally wrapped around the corpse's waist and interred with the body to animate the soul of the deceased so it could make its way to the afterworld. However, if someone is suspected of being a *condenado*, a lost soul who committed terrible crimes in life and is punished in death by being made to wander the earth devouring anyone they meet, the only way to disarm them is to take their khipu, symbolically cutting their tie to the living and causing them to collapse.[51]

Anthropologist Catherine Allen explains how the act of making a khipu expresses the Andean ontology of death through the concept of *raki*.[52] As a Quechua mathematical concept, raki denotes a particular kind of division that separates "one large, complex object or entity into several smaller, simpler ones," as when one separates the strands of a plied or braided thread.[53] In the community of Chinchero, Peru, a textile pattern called *raki-raki* provides a diagrammatic expression of this division in which the colored areas of the pattern are held apart by intervening white threads. For residents of Chinchero, this pattern evokes a feeling of sadness and loss and is likened to "when the husband is in one land and his wife in another, or a son is alive and his mother is dead."[54] If death is understood as the unwinding of threads that were once plied together, then we can see how the making of a khipu during the wake symbolically rectifies the dissolution of death. The different skeins of yarn that comprise the funerary khipu are provided by the relatives of the deceased, who help to twist and bind the threads together, making a long black and white rope reminiscent of an umbilical cord that allows for a type of rebirth, perhaps for

Raki-raki textile motif.

both the dead and the living.[55] Cutting this symbolic cord offers a way to move forward.

Weaving artist and textile scholar Deborah Valoma told me about a hooked rug that her ex-husband's Scandinavian grandmother had made using all the pieces of her children's outgrown clothing. The rug depicted the tree of life design with branches forming a circular, or Celtic, knot reflecting the never-ending cycle of life. "It took her forty years. She was a farm wife and had six sons—a super strong woman. You wouldn't know by looking at it but there was the history of her life and her accomplishments just in the material."[56] The rug consisted of all the clothes she had made for all the children she had made—clothes that had been grown into and out of, passed down from older to younger siblings. The pants got ripped, elbows got patched. If they scraped their knees, the blood is in the fibers. Cloth also contains the cells of the maker—our sweat, skin, and blood as it moves through our hands. As a result, the rug holds not just the story but the life essence of the family. Their lives are immortalized, at least for hundreds of years, in this hooked rug that provides a genetic and material link to the family's ancestral past. The maker of this rug was herself the tree of life—the creator and sustainer of her family.

CHAPTER 2

Webs of Knowledge

In the Navajo creation story, the holy ones told Spider Woman, a powerful deity, that she had the ability to weave a map of the universe and the geometric patterns of the spirit beings in the night sky. She had no idea what they meant or how this could be done, but curiosity drove her to find out. One day, while she was out exploring and gathering food, she wrapped her fingers around the branch of a small, young tree, and as she let go, a string streamed out of the center of her palm and wrapped around the tree branch. She shook her hand to release the string, but it did not break. Spider Woman wrapped the string around the branch to try to free herself, but she could not. She began to run out of space on the branch, so she started wrapping her string around another branch on the tree, and the strings began to form shapes and patterns. She realized that this was the weaving that the holy ones had told her about. She stayed by the tree all day wrapping the string into patterns on the branches. When she came home that evening, she told Spider Man about her new skill. The holy ones instructed Spider Man to make a loom and tools for Spider Woman so she could weave the universe at home.

Many thousands of years ago, women all over the world learned to weave through a process of experimentation much like Spider Woman's. Taking raw materials like plant and animal fibers and finding a way to make them into string is a feat of human ingenuity. Dyeing fibers using available materials—plants, bugs, mollusks— requires tremendous amounts of experimentation to make colors adhere to a variety of fibers. Creating textiles from these dyed strings with complex designs requires the ability to plan, problem-solve, and hold large amounts of information in one's memory. Far from being a simple domestic craft for practical necessity or to pass the time, activities like weaving, sewing, and knitting present intellectual challenges and give form to thought.

Today, young Navajo weavers are instructed to place the palm of their right hand on a spiderweb without damaging it to allow Spider Woman's gift of weaving to enter the young weaver's spirit, where it will live forever. Spider Woman, an ever-present teacher, is always available to help weavers, if they listen to the wind.[1]

THE TRANSMISSION OF KNOWLEDGE

Back on the hilltop above Cusco, Peru, enthralled by the speed and ease with which Marcela Salas Calcina and other weavers practiced their craft, I asked Calcina how she first learned to weave. Like most Andean weavers, Calcina considers her weaving skills as part of her heritage, genetically passed down from her Incan ancestors. She said, "In the Andes we have the memory in our cells. . . . Everyone learns very fast. It is in our DNA. You just need to activate it."[2] However, when asked for more specifics, she shared that her grandmother began teaching her to weave when she was eight years old. "I was really happy to learn to weave. Usually, we weave in the mountains when we tend to the alpacas and llamas. . . . Within one month I learned to make the basic iconography. In one year, you can learn to make this"—she gestured to the complex *pallay*, or pattern, she was currently weaving—"depending on how smart you are." This work takes considerable intellectual ability to learn, something that is very clear to me in watching Calcina's adroit handling of the warp threads as she creates this complex pattern from memory. Calcina noted that foreigners who come to live in the Andes have trouble learning to weave, even if they have lived there a long time, because it is not part of their heritage. She seemed to imply that this heritage is both cultural and innate. My translator elaborated, telling me about a ritual performed in the Andes when a baby is born in which the parents take the baby's hands and feet and breathe into them to transfer their power and knowledge to the baby. Just then, in a serendipitous moment of synchronicity, a baby's cry punctured the tranquility of the open-air studio.

Calcina was teaching her daughter-in-law, Anita Quispe Apaza, a new mother, to weave. Apaza got up from where she sat beside the loom to feed her infant son, who had been napping under an umbrella while the loom was being prepared. When she finished, she handed the baby to her husband and took Calcina's place at the loom. Apaza had not learned to weave from the women in her family and expressed gratitude for her mother-in-law's instruction, saying, "Now I have the best master and am learning all this knowledge from her." Calcina, too, was happy to be able to pass her knowledge along: "I have this capacity to teach others because I have this knowledge. Everything is in my hands. With all this power, I have the authority to teach. I feel very happy."

As Apaza wove, Calcina watched her and provided support, correcting her at times. Apaza, who is in her early twenties, explained that it had taken her a month to learn this particular pallay and she had already practiced it before beginning the ceremonial scarf they were currently working on. That pallay was especially difficult because it involved a lot of counting for each row, of which there were many before the pattern repeated, and Apaza had to hold all this in her mind as she worked.

Apaza was able to articulate the challenges of weaving differently than Calcina. Learning to weave for Apaza is akin to learning a second language in adulthood, which takes conscious effort and practice (explicit information processing), whereas the acquisition of a first language takes place largely outside of conscious effort (implicit information processing). Similar to learning a language, those who learn a complex skill like weaving in early childhood may experience it as arising naturally—hence Calcina's sense that it is part of her DNA and the Navajo concept that the skill is transferred through touching a spider's web.

In fact, there is a rather well-defined pathway to knowledge that is followed by Andean weavers, progressing from smaller and simpler projects to larger ones requiring more complex skills and designs. From the ages of three to five, girls typically learn to spin. Around age five, they begin to weave narrow straps or ties known as *jakima* and then move on to making belts, or *chumpi*, at age eight. In early adolescence, girls start making a mantle—*lillija*—which can also be used as a carrying cloth for babies. Making a lillija is a rite of passage as girls transition to adulthood and they learn increasingly advanced pallay to add to their designs.[3]

For those like Calcina, who grew up watching women weave all around them, the skill feels like second nature. They have observed the steps for setting up a loom, the movements of the hands, and the textiles that are created from them from birth. The ease with which they acquire and perform the skills obscures the real intellectual challenge of learning this work.

In the Shetland Isles, a group of islands scattered like skipping stones north of mainland Scotland, knitting is an important tradition passed down from generation to generation. I spoke with Hazel Tindall, an expert in Fair Isle colorwork knitting and a prominent knitwear designer, who has been knitting longer than she has been reading or writing. As a child growing up in Shetland in the 1950s, she does not remember learning to knit: "I would have been watching knitters since the time I could focus on movement, so I knew what it should look like. My only memory of learning to knit was looking at the stitches on the needle to recognize what was plain and what was purl."[4] Plain refers to a knit stitch, which makes a V shape on the front of the work, while a purl stitch has a bump.

Drawing a comparison to learning how to knit, Tindall recounted this memory: "Not long ago I was having a walk on a lovely calm day and I thought it would be nice to have a boat to go for a row, and then I thought I don't actually remember learning how to row. It was just something I always knew how to do and we were let loose in a rowing boat when we weren't very old, not able to swim and with no life jackets. We never fell in." Boating and knitting were the two primary activities of people in Shetland when Hazel was growing up in the 1950s and '60s, and she learned them very early in mind and body. So automatic is knitting for Hazel that she holds the title of the world's fastest knitter, knitting 255 stitches in three minutes. Out of curiosity, I timed myself knitting and managed only 178 stitches in the same span. While I am an experienced and avid knitter, I learned to knit in my mid-twenties, so I do not have the benefit of having it ingrained in my hands from early childhood. What many people call muscle memory is really embodied knowledge—a knowing that is deeply encoded and fluently enacted by the body.

The apparent ease with which knitting skills were assimilated by children who grew up surrounded by this work may have caused people to undervalue the skill as rote, easy to learn, and not intellectual. In Shetland, designing and knitting the multicolored Fair Isle sweater yokes was the province of women. Men, if involved in the process, often did the relatively simpler work of knitting the single-color stockinette bodies and sleeves using a knitting machine. In conversation with Tindall, I noted the specialized skills and intellectual challenges that went into creating the yokes. Knitters employ mathematical skills to determine the number of stitches and pattern repeats to make a sweater based on sizing and knitting gauge and have the challenge of choosing multiple coordinating colors—often upward of ten—to knit with. Tindall added that traditional colorwork patterns were often held in memory and not written down. So, in addition to knowing when to decrease in the yoke and change colors to achieve their desired effect, knitters had to recall each row of the colorwork pattern as they worked—and they did this all quite quickly and often while walking, socializing, or tending to children and other household tasks.

Mid-century American knitting icon Elizabeth Zimmermann said, "One tends to give one's fingers too little credit for their own good sense."[5] Embedded in these words is a call to trust one's embodied knowledge, maybe even above conscious mental effort when skills are so internalized. It also reflects a challenge to textile creators, like the knitters in Shetland, to recognize that the work of their fingers is the work of the mind, even if it feels automatic.

THINKING WITH OUR HANDS

The embodied knowledge evident in the work of our hands, or the "good sense" of our fingers, as Zimmermann put it, has not always been valued or understood. During the Italian Renaissance, artists tended to diminish the manual aspects of their work—a devaluation that has persisted and pervaded the distinctions drawn between art and craft that continue today. The artistry of sculptors was compared unfavorably with that of painters. Even Michelangelo, whose work elevated the field of sculpture, did not want to be referred to as a sculptor.[6] The Renaissance was under the influence of the philosophy of Neoplatonism, where the material world was considered a pale reflection of the vibrant world of ideas. Painting seemed closer to the world of ideas—the word *idea* comes from the Greek word *idein*, which means "to see." Painting is only accessible through the eyes, whereas sculpture has a tactile quality that made it seem further removed from the purity of thought. Those who sculpted in marble emphasized their work as a product of their brains rather than their brawn, as though the engagement of the artist's body degraded the art of sculpture—which, ironically, often depicted the ideal body as one that is well chiseled through physical exertion.[7]

Studio jeweler Bruce Metcalf, who writes about modern craft, argues that truly valuing craft requires "the return of labor to equal status with thought."[8] Like Cartesian dualism, which unnaturally separates mind and body, dichotomies that separate the work of our bodies and the work of our minds are inaccurate. When we craft, multiple areas of the brain work together to plan, problem-solve, process sensory input, understand spatial relationships, recall patterns and processes, and coordinate movement.

Research shows that the work of our hands is critical to optimal brain functioning. In fact, one-third of the motor cortex is devoted to our hands, indicating the intellectual importance of the work we do with them. A neuropsychiatrist at the Mayo Clinic found that women who engaged in knitting or quilt making in middle age or later life had a decreased risk of mild cognitive impairment and memory loss, which he attributed to the mental stimulation of these activities.[9] A survey of over three thousand knitters showed a significant positive correlation between frequency of knitting and perceived improvements in cognitive ability, such as the ability to organize thoughts and improvements in memory, concentration, and spatial awareness.[10] Experimental studies show that restrictions of physical activity also restrict our mental abilities. A study in which participants had their left hands temporarily immobilized with a splint for two days revealed a reduction of synaptic activity for the restricted limb as well as other areas of the motor cortex—so a hands-off lifestyle may ultimately atrophy existing neural networks or fail to build them in the first place.[11]

Philosopher Matthew Crawford, who left a job at a think tank to become a motorcycle mechanic, argues that our efforts to build a knowledge-based workforce may have produced less-challenging contexts for our brains than those afforded in a more traditional manual labor workforce. This is also true in our homes, where many of us no longer do our own home repairs, mend torn clothing, or prepare meals from scratch. He quotes a shop teacher who said, "Without the opportunity to learn through the hands, the world remains abstract and distant, and the passions for learning will not be engaged."[12]

Psychoanalyst Anna Freud, who was known to weave on her loom behind the couch as she saw patients, believed that people who work with their mind need a creative activity that involves their hands. So much of what happens in therapy is intangible: ideas are exchanged, theories are formed, emotions are felt, the unspoken hangs in the air, and progress is difficult to measure. Her weaving was different; there she could see the direct impact of her efforts, the textile growing and taking shape with each pass of the weft thread. In her writing, she used weaving as a metaphor to explain the usefulness of psychoanalysis for the human mind with its layers that can be woven and unwoven through experience. She often used her weaving time to think through her psychoanalytic ideas and compose lectures. Her thoughts also found expression in her work on the loom—influencing the structure of the warp and weft, the choices of colors, and how they interplayed in the fabric. What she did with her hands facilitated what she did with her mind, and vice versa.[13]

Knowing a skill at this deep, embodied level allows the mind freedom to work on other problems while the hands are engaged in their creation. It also allows for spontaneity based on a felt sense of the work, which is the foundation of improvisation and the invention of new techniques and technologies. Multimedia artist Ann Hamilton writes, "The motion of the hands working is a form of thinking" and "The interval between stitches seaming two surfaces together is thinking at the pace of the body. . . . Busy hands make a space that allows attention to wander. Productive wandering is how projects are made."[14] For much of history, thinking-by-hand characterized the intellectual life of women who spent so much of their time engaged in textile creation.

Working with materials that don't always behave the way we

would expect requires improvisation in the design and execution as the creation process unfolds. Sometimes, what we see taking shape in our hands tells us what to do next. We learn from this evolving process, which improves both the acuity of our minds and the precision of our hands. When I met with lacemaker and textile scholar Elena Kanagy-Loux, who specializes in the creation and study of intricate historical bobbin lace, she explained how the improvisational process of making bobbin lace requires the adroit handling of many bobbins that, like keys on the piano, are "played" to create the desired pattern. Each bobbin holds a strand of thread that must be moved and twisted together to create a design. She noted that you cannot label the bobbins to know what to do with each, and yet you must always make sure that as you cross the threads and move the bobbins, you have threads available to you when and where you need them. Moreover, there are rarely specific instructions provided on how to move the bobbins to create a pattern. The pattern is simply drawn out on a piece of paper that lacemakers work from, and they figure out the mechanics as they go. Kanagy-Loux explained how the design and execution of lace were divided tasks historically; the designers simply drew the designs—what the outcome should look like. The lacemakers had to work from that design and figure out how to move the bobbins and where to cross the threads to both realize the vision of the designer and create a functional textile that does not unravel once it is unpinned from the lace pillow.

Despite the lacemaker's complex knowledge, Kanagy-Loux noted that historically, "The pattern books for bobbin lace are so rudimentary and have such little technical information, but if you look at [the lace] being produced in the same time period, say in the sixteenth century, it is so much more elaborate [than what is in the books] because they didn't even know how to write this stuff down."[15] The process was largely improvised based on the lace-maker's experience and experimentation, which often becomes a felt sense of the right way to work out a pattern. Kanagy-Loux explained that she often does not look at her work as she is making lace except to periodically place a pin or check her work, so she usu-ally *feels* a mistake first: "Like if I cross or twist in the wrong direc-tion, I will go 'oh, that was wrong,' and then I'll look and see, yes, that was wrong."

Kanagy-Loux recalled a workshop on lace identification that she took at ModeMuseum (MoMu), a fashion museum in Antwerp, Bel-gium. The teacher, Tessy Schoenholzer, an expert in Flanders lace, encouraged her to see the story of the lacemaker in the lace—where is she happy, where is she sad? Kanagy-Loux was initially stumped by these questions, but after many years of studying and making lace, she learned how to read the lace. She explained:

> You can see where in a repeating pattern they've tried dif-
> ferent things to resolve a complicated part of the pattern
> in every single repeat. It's so rare that you find a historical
> piece of lace where every repeat is the same. Especially
> early on when lace was still an emerging technique. They
> were much more experimental then . . . if people wanted
> to make a more complex piece, they had to figure it out as
> they went along.

To the trained eye, the lace leaves a threaded trail to follow the thinking process of the woman who made it, to find where she had to make frustrating choices, gave up and left in an error, or made multiple attempts at problem-solving.

Learning Through Making

Growing up in the small village of Chinchero, Peru, Nilda Callañuapa Alvarez, an Indigenous weaver and textile scholar, was alarmed by how quickly traditional Quechua weaving and natural dyeing practices seemed to be dying out in her community. Threatened by the ease of imported acrylic yarns and aniline dyes and socially by discrimination against Indigenous people that had created shame around donning traditional dress, these textile practices were losing popularity. To counter these forces, Callañuapa Alvarez founded the Centro de Textiles Tradicionales del Cusco (CTTC), a nonprofit organization that partnered with Indigenous communities throughout the Andes to recapture traditional designs and their meanings, weaving techniques, and dye processes that the elder weavers had preserved so they could be passed down to younger generations. She worked with local residents to build a weaving center in each community, where women and men could come to weave together and share their knowledge.

I visited the CTTC, a shop of bright woven and knitted garments with a small textile museum attached, to meet with Callañuapa Alvarez. Outside the shop, protestors in similar woven garb made their way down the street. Our interview had been precariously scheduled due to the political crisis in Peru that had unfolded in response to the impeachment of President Pedro Castillo Terrones. Callañuapa Alvarez and I had hoped to connect in her hometown of Chinchero several days earlier, but I had been stuck for days in the Sacred Valley, where roads were blocked by felled trees, rocks, fires, and protesters. We managed to meet once I had made it through the blockades and back to Cusco, where I waited for the airport to reopen.

Callañuapa Alvarez founded the CTTC in the late 1990s. As we talked, she recalled the early days of building the organization: all the women she had spoken to, now deceased, about the materials and processes they recalled using to dye the different-colored yarns; the many trips people made into the jungle to gather plants and insects to prepare the dyebaths; the mistakes they made and the return visits to the jungle with new information. Callañuapa Alvarez explained: "That was the purpose of this project—to experiment. Many times it did not work because they misunderstood or they thought it [would] work in [a certain] way, but it didn't work. It's a complex system of information that we piled up and researched so finally we now have recipes for most of the colors that work out."[16] She added that she is not completely sure that they're dyeing in exactly the same way that their ancestors did a century ago—for one thing the weavers in the CTTC use pure citric acid instead of lemon juice—but they are able to obtain colors that match those of the older textiles. They prepare dye pots and dye yarn as a community at the local weaving centers a few times a year. This way, they can gather weavers together and maintain the knowledge of the dye process. Sharing in the labor also offsets the additional time that natural dyeing takes, which had prompted the shift to chemical dyes when they became available in the early part of the twentieth century.

Callañuapa Alvarez regularly holds challenges to re-create antique textiles among the weavers in this collective, which now number over seven hundred people across ten different regions, each with their own unique textile traditions. They have to figure out how to use techniques like discontinuous warp and ikat weaving, many of which have largely been lost. She told me, "When I brought that idea to the communities they said, 'you are crazy, where are these textiles coming from?' So I said, 'this is done by our people. . . .' Then they look and say, 'oh yeah, this is like this and this is like that,' and they figured it out. At the beginning they say this is crazy, but then they enjoy it . . . after two or so years, they become masters."

The CTTC aims to reconstruct traditional textile methods, empower weavers to practice them, and keep traditions alive through succeeding generations. At the same time, this work must meet the immediate financial needs of the weavers so they can dedicate their time to it and maintain a traditional lifestyle within their communities rather than seeking paid employment elsewhere. When reconstructing lost weaving methods, the first pieces are never going to come out right and can't be sold. The CTTC funds these endeavors, recognizing that weavers need to be compensated to allow them to devote their time to experimenting. In addition to financial compensation for these weaving experiments, Callañuapa Alvarez gathers the participating weavers of the community together, providing them not only with materials but also with food and chicha, a traditional Peruvian beer. Her approach is psychological: "You have to create that circle of joking, laughing, congratulating the first person who is starting, applauding the other ones. Next time you will have more people because they're watching and telling people."

Callañuapa Alvarez reflected on how far they have come over the last three decades in learning the traditional methods and building communities that can carry forward work that is both profitable and rewarding: "There's this full dedication of the weavers, and it's a community that interweaves with the scholars and institutions that believe in the cultural issues. Weavers have so much to give in terms of the intellectual meaning of the work that they do and the history that they carry. We don't have written language, so the knowledge is passed through oral histories. That put it in danger because the elders don't live forever, you know." Whether passed down or reconstructed, through Callañuapa Alvarez's efforts, the knowledge lives on.

The weavers in the CTTC learned and adjusted their methods as they worked to re-create textiles that were hundreds of years old. Through empirical methods—observation and experimentation—they figured out dye ingredients and recipes. Cochineal bugs, found on the prickly pear cactus common in the Sacred Valley, are dried and crushed to make brilliant red dyes that are particularly popular in Chinchero, Callañuapa Alvarez's hometown. Add citric acid to the cochineal dyebath, known by locals as *sal de limón* (lime salt), and you get a red orange. *Qaqa sunkha*, a lichen, can also be used to produce orange. It is boiled with yarn before roughly one cup of fermented urine, which has been stored for two weeks to one month, is added and then boiled for an additional ten minutes as a fixative. In the tropical region near Manu National Park, you can find the *yanali* tree, whose bark produces a yellow hue when fixed with salt. The leaves of the *ch'illca*, which grows near the edges of streams in the Cusco region, creates a green dye with the addition of *collpa*, a local form of copper sulfate found in the jungle that is boiled for at least an hour before the yarn is added. *Tara* pods make blue dye when mixed with blue collpa. The leaves from the *awaypili* plant, a rare mountain plant that is difficult to find in the Sacred Valley, are boiled to make a purple dye, which is then fixed with fresh urine to intensify the color.[17]

The various mordants used in the natural dye process help the yarns absorb the dyes and affect their vibrancy and colorfastness. The acidity or alkalinity of the mordant or dyebath will change the color. Citric acid has a pH level between 3.0 and 6.0 (acidic), salt has a pH of 7.0 (neutral), fresh urine typically has a pH between

6.0 and 7.5, and fermented urine has a pH around 9.0 to 9.5 (alkaline). The fermentation process that occurs as urine sits out changes the chemical structure, as urea decomposes into ammonia, which has a pH of 12.5, causing the rise in pH level. Research shows that pH levels of urine also drop with age, often falling below 6.0 by age sixty, with women's urine tending to have lower pH levels than men's.[18] Children's urine has a higher excretion of calcium, oxalate, and citrate.[19] One recipe in Peru creates a brilliant turquoise dye by adding baby's urine to a dyebath made from the *quinsaquchu* plant. Without testing pH levels or the specific chemical compounds of their dyestuffs, weavers in the CTTC and their ancestors many centuries ago learned through experimentation with natural materials. It is clear through these efforts how the human hand can alter and transform nature.

Academics have also adopted the practice of re-creating traditional textile practices, recognizing it as a way to understand early societies. At Columbia University, the Making and Knowing Project explores the intersections between artistic creation and scientific knowledge. Today these realms are generally regarded as separate, yet in the earliest phases of the Scientific Revolution, "making" was "knowing." Pamela H. Smith, founder of the Making and Knowing Project, explained:

> Craft can be investigative—like natural philosophy or "science"—and not just productive . . . its products are records of practices as well as repositories of knowledge. We might think of an object as the residue of an enormous number of cultural exchanges among individuals and their belief systems, organized practices, networks, and accumulated knowledge. Objects inscribe the mem-

ory of previous generations' innovations and cognitions, and their making requires very significant expertise.[20]

Reconstructing artisan practices in the Making and Knowing Project requires tolerance for ambiguity and patience with the iterative process. There are rarely measurements in the medieval and early modern "recipes" that the members of this lab attempt to re-create. It is difficult to quantify natural materials—more or less liquid may need to be added, depending on weather conditions; leaves and flowers vary in sizes, so specific numbers of them can't be used; and temperatures can be difficult to hold steady when using an open flame. Craftspeople learned to rely on qualitative descriptions to determine the proper proportions and conditions for their creations—consistency, smell, taste, and color are all indicators to gauge that the recipe or process is correct. Makers' senses became highly attuned to these attributes, often feeling that something is wrong without having exact data to inform them of a mistake. Many artisans didn't have instruments to tell time, so they devised strategies to determine the proper length for each step, such as a song or prayer that lasted just the right amount of time. Dyers have historically had a felt sense for preparing their dyebaths, relying on their sensory experience to tell them if it is on course. Kodi indigo dyers monitor the timing of chemical interactions through smelling, feeling, tasting, and examining their materials at every stage of the process. Each dye compound with its impurities is unique in its ability to bond or react with fibers, so as anthropologist Janet Hoskins writes, "the good traditional dyer, like the medieval alchemist, develops her own preferred materials and techniques, which become guarded secrets that often disappear upon the dyer's death."[21]

❖

"Of all the areas of human activities," writes French historian Dominique Cardon, "dyeing with plants is one of the best examples of the efficiency of the empirical acquisition of expertise."[22] However, in eighteenth-century Europe, dyeing was not considered a science because the practitioners usually self-identified as artisans, and their material products, rather than scientific principles, guided their investigation.[23] Because it was mercantile activity, the technical knowledge used in dyeing went unacknowledged in much the same way that the sculptors' use of their hands removed their art from the realm of the mind. Learning through the work of the hands was often devalued in Western academia in favor of reading and other activities of the mind, largely due to class distinctions between those who made things for economic benefit and those who had the leisure to think and write. Swiss physician and alchemist Paracelsus, who introduced chemistry into medicine in the sixteenth century, disagreed: "For who could be taught the knowledge of experience from paper? Since paper has the property to produce lazy and sleepy people, who are haughty and learn to persuade themselves and to fly without wings. . . . Therefore the most fundamental thing is to hasten to experience."[24]

Some educators in the nineteenth and twentieth centuries took up a similar idea, recognizing that needlework trained the eye and the hand and thereby developed the brain. In 1911, Ann Macbeth and Margaret Swanson, teachers at the Glasgow School of Art, published *Educational Needlecraft*, an instructional manual that advocated for needlework education to assist in the "development of intelligence and formation of character."[25] Most important for Macbeth, Swanson, and others at the Glasgow School of Art was freedom for play and experimentation in needlework—to allow children to follow their own curiosity, for "without curiosity, no conjecture is possible." They argued that "the boy or girl who uses material and needle freely in independent design . . . ranks on a plane with the scientist who makes a hypothesis, with the artist who makes an experiment" and "the craft of the needle becomes not merely a doing, but from this point it may become a personal development both of knowledge and experience."[26] When we are able to create our own patterns or work without a pattern, we learn about our minds.

Elena Kanagy-Loux declares, "The stereotype that always irks me is the sort of modern women in period dramas who hate needlework. Who talk like, 'I don't embroider. That's for idiot ladies who have frills in their brains.' "[27] In a witty twist on her deep intellectual engagement in lacework, Kanagy-Loux describes herself as "a sentient pile of doilies" on social media. Drawing on her work as a textile collections specialist at New York's Metropolitan Museum of Art, she continues:

> Embroidery was an educational tool. Half of the samplers we have in our collection taught literacy—you're learning to spell and write and you're learning geography. We have map samplers and globe samplers that were famously made by the Westtown School in Philadelphia. We even have algebra and mathematic equations on samplers. And this was a practical tool. . . . You need to know how to mend your clothes because you can't just throw them out and buy new ones.

Founded in 1799, the Westtown School was a Quaker boarding school twenty miles outside of Philadelphia. Both boys and girls were educated at the school, separately until 1840, but in many similar subjects. Sewing education was compulsory for girls until 1843 but continued as an elective or hobby for many years. Samplers from the first half of the nineteenth century include the commonly known alphabet and darning samplers as well as three-dimensional embroidered silk globe samplers, unique to the Westtown School. The globes are both terrestrial and celestial, indicating girls' understanding of not only the locations of continents and countries, stars and planets, but the relationship between the earth and the sky. They may have made the samplers to learn "mathematical geography"—latitude, longitude, and the movements of the earth in relation to the sun. A letter from a student to her parents in 1816 explains the usefulness of these globes "to strengthen [her] own memory, respecting the supposed shape of our earth, and the manner in which it moves."[28]

Maria Mitchell, the first female astronomer in the United States, also known as the "computer of Venus" for her work guiding sailors around the world, was also trained in needlework from an early age. Like many young women in the nineteenth century, she had a complicated relationship to the craft. As a young woman she called the needle the "chain of women" but later credited her skill as an astronomer to her early training in needlework:

> Nothing comes out more clearly in astronomical observations than the immense activity of the universe. . . . Observations of this kind are peculiarly adapted to women. Indeed, all astronomical observing seems to be so fitted. The training of a girl fits her for delicate work. The touch of her fingers upon the delicate screws of an astronomical instrument might become wonderfully accurate in

results; a woman's eyes are trained to nicety of color. The eye that directs a needle in the delicate meshes of embroidery will equally well bisect a star with the spider web of the micrometer. Routine observations, too, dull as they are, are less dull than the endless repetition of the same pattern in crochet-work. . . . The girl who can stitch from morning to night would find two or three hours in the observatory a relief.[29]

Textile work has provided young girls with valuable skills that are applicable to the pursuit of knowledge and skilled work in many areas of intellectual pursuit. While embroidery education supplanted learning in other subjects at times, textile work and its associations to femininity also permitted some girls to at least get an education. The inclusion of embroidery instruction in schools made formal education for girls more palatable to men by demarcating it from male education and ensuring that school would turn girls into proper ladies and not just "spoil their brains" with too much knowledge.[30]

Although needlework has been bound up with the inculcation of some of the worst traditionally "feminine" qualities, like docility, silence, and meekness, these associations with textile making are nothing more than social constructions. Feminist multimedia artist Kate Walker corrected this fallacy: "Passivity and obedience . . . are the very opposites of the qualities necessary to make a sustained effort in needlework. What's required are physical and mental skills, fine aesthetic judgment in colour, texture, and composition; patience during long training; and assertive individuality of design (and consequent disobedience of aesthetic convention). Quiet strength need not be mistaken for useless vulnerability."[31]

FINDING FORMS FOR THOUGHT

Su Hui, a female poet living in China in the fourth century, created a most unusual poem using silk thread on woven brocade fabric, which came to be known as "Xuanji Tu," or "Star Gauge."[32] It is structured as a square grid of twenty-nine rows of Chinese characters that can be read horizontally, vertically, and diagonally, resulting in 2,848 possible poems. Its structure relies on the fact that Chinese can be read in any direction and the characters can operate as any part of speech, depending on the context.[33] The poem's structure mimics that of an armillary sphere, an instrument used to gauge the movements of the stars made of multiple concentric rings of metal, which correspond to the important meridians of the celestial sphere. Readers must choose which direction to go as they encounter a junction of meridians, marked by lines that break the grid into segments, resulting in the many variations of the poem.

Although the text of the poem has been preserved, the original embroidery did not survive. Still, the story behind it is the stuff of legend and has been recounted in books and plays over the last sixteen hundred years. Su Hui was born in the city of Baoji in Shaanxi Province—the starting point for the northern route of the Silk Road. She was married at sixteen to a high-ranking government official. They were said to be quite happy together until her husband took a second wife, which infuriated Su Hui. Soon after, he was transferred to a post far away. Su Hui refused to go with her husband and his new wife, so he broke off all communication with her. She composed "Star Gauge" to express her pain through lines like "such countless star-glimmers, they contain all of your grief and love" and "sorrow swells such longing, longing—all this grief-wounded love."[34] According to retellings, when Su Hui's husband read the poem, he realized her great intelligence and sent his second wife away, more deeply committed to Su Hui than ever.

David Hinton, who translated "Star Gauge" from Chinese, cites writing that shows how proud Su Hui was of the difficulty presented by her complex composition. He notes, "It is clear that the poem is much more than a woman's plea for her husband's return. It is a complex philosophical statement, as well as an assertion of her own dignity and even superiority to the men who dominated her world."[35] To conceive of, plan, and execute this poetic puzzle is nothing short of brilliance.

In "Star Gauge," Su Hui found a literary, visual, and tactile form for her tortured thoughts about her husband's betrayal. The grid structure belies the tangled and meandering experience of creating poems from the characters that Su Hui laid out in such meticulous order. There is, in fact, much less order to "Star Gauge" for the reader than there would be had the poem been written in a standard linear format. Her thoughts, like the poem's structure, are circular. They get turned over and over and lead you wandering through an unending mental maze. Words and ideas repeat again and again, backward and forward, and while the thoughts may vary slightly, no path leads to resolution or peace—there is no way out. The embroidery itself has a similar obsessive quality. Stitch by stitch, Su Hui slowly realized each character—so different from writing, where each character could be completed in just a few strokes of a pen. As she stitched, the words would have been painstakingly repeated in her mind and by her hand. The visual form and materials communicate her feelings about her husband's betrayal and her longing for him in a way that words alone cannot.

This is the work of artists—communicating ideas, processes,

and experiences through visual media that are difficult to put into words alone. Artists use the material language of a culture to express themselves, and cloth is the material that was traditionally available for women. As art historian Janet Catherine Berlo says, "The work of our hands is our thought made manifest."[36]

The process of giving form to thought can be as informative as the final product. When representing a physical object, say a bowl of fruit, we must adapt the image to what we can represent in our chosen medium, which often means deciding which properties to highlight to simplify the image while still making it recognizable. Cross-stitch designer Haley Pierson-Cox is drawn to the intellectual challenge of translating images, objects, and ideas into the grid structure of a cross-stitch pattern that sets clear parameters for the design:

> I like that within a grid you can make so many differ-
> ent things happen and it's all just moving a pixel. So, I
> literally design pixel by pixel, stitch by stitch, and mov-
> ing something over one stitch can make all the differ-
> ence. . . . I love seeing how detailed and recognizable I
> can make something that is like nine pixels. It's possible
> to make recognizable images even when you're working
> on a scale like that. And I think that's such a fun puzzle
> to solve. . . . Playing with those formats gives your
> brain a workout that most day-to-day activities . . . sim-
> ply don't. It's math in the real world. I feel like it gives
> me something more than just the ability to make some-
> thing pretty or just the ability to make something that
> would outrage people. It is also an intellectual pursuit
> and it can be an intellectual pursuit in many different
> directions all at once.[37]

She noted that this grid structure is especially important for her as a person on the autism spectrum, because it provides a physical space with solid boundaries in which to organize her thoughts. She can give her ideas shape within the grid, breaking down complex figures, such as the mooning gnome that graces (or some might say disgraces) the cover of her book *Improper Cross-Stitch*, into their simplest forms while retaining enough of their character to be recognizable. Notably, her publisher asked her to remove a single stitch from the middle of the mooning gnome's behind for the cover image. That one line of thread crossed the line of propriety, even on a book that is, by its title, meant to be "improper."

As Pierson-Cox's description of working within a grid structure shows, math is embedded in the making of fabric. Anthropologist Carrie Brezine writes in "Algorithms and Automation" that "the existence of cloth is evidence of mathematics at work in the tangible world."[38] According to mathematician and handweaver Ellen Harlizius-Klück, it is time we recognize weaving as an important part of intellectual history, specifically as a foundational precursor for the formulation of scientific and mathematical concepts. Harlizius-Klück is the principal investigator of the PENELOPE project at the Research Institute for the History of Technology and Science at Deutsches Museum, in Munich, Germany. The mission of the PENELOPE project is to explore the historical contributions of weaving to science and technology. She grounds her research in the hypothesis that "there was significant but tacit contribution of textile technology involved in the advent of science in ancient Greece."[39] Specifically, she argues that certain number properties and algorithms, such as the theories of arithmetic expressed in Euclid's *Elements* dating back to around 300 BCE, developed from weaving. While the weavers themselves were finding forms for thought by translating their ideas into woven cloth, the development of mathematical ideas from weaving is a reversal of this concept and expresses an effort to find thought from form—to discover the underlying mathematical principles that weavers enacted tacitly in their daily practice.

The warp-weighted loom that was used in ancient Greece is an upright frame with warp threads that hang down and are attached to weights at the bottom to provide tension for weaving in the weft threads. The weaving process begins with a prewoven band likely produced by tablet weaving, another ancient form of weaving in which small cards or tablets separate the warp threads and which produces only narrow bands. The band was then turned on its side so that the long former weft threads became the warp threads on the warp-weighted loom.[40] Because of this process, the correct number of warp threads must be determined from the beginning to ensure that it fits the pattern repeats intended for the design. To translate a pattern or image into weaving, "you have to think in thread counts" because patterns are built up thread by thread and row by row to create pictures just like the pixels that make up Pierson-Cox's cross-stitch.[41] Understanding odd, even, and prime numbers and being able to find factors and multiples are all critical for determining which patterns will fit evenly across the cloth and had to be decided when the initial band was created. For instance, no pattern will repeat evenly across a warp that is prime in number.[42]

The mathematical operations that occur in the weaver's mind are often not visible to an observer's eye, but they become explicit in automated punch card looms, a system in which complex weaving patterns are broken down into binary codes to automate the patterning. One punch card corresponds to each row of weaving and indicates which warp threads to lift to pass the weft threads over and under. The most famous loom (although not the first and perhaps not the best, according to Harlizius-Klück) is Jacquard's 1804 loom, which Ada Lovelace and Charles Babbage credit in their creation of the Analytical Engine in the 1830s, a precursor to the modern computer.[43] Lovelace famously said, "We may say most aptly that the Analytical Engine *weaves algebraic patterns* just as the Jacquard-loom weaves flowers and leaves."[44]

But in fact, it is the underlying binary coding of weaving that the punch cards capture that links looms with the modern computer. "This means that it is the invention of coding algebra that really matters," says Harlizius-Klück. And what is algebra but "doing arithmetic in an algorithmic way?"[45] Harlizius-Klück describes an earlier invention known as the crumb-machine, made in southern Germany sometime around 1680–1690, which consisted of wooden bars glued on a loop of linen fabric that transmitted design information to the loom. The crumb-machine worked on groups of threads rather than the individual threads of Jacquard's looms, making it better for weaving pattern repeats and reversals and therefore more algebraically advanced in operation.[46] Lovelace wrote that a necessary adaptation of Jacquard's punch card system was needed for the Analytical Engine, which involved "backing the cards in certain groups according to certain laws" in order to bring "any particular card or set of cards into use any number of times."[47] Unaware of the crumb-machine invented two hundred years earlier and its ability to do just what she outlined, Lovelace proposed advances in weaving technology based on their modification to Jacquard's system.

Before automated looms existed, cloth itself was a tangible manifestation of complex mathematical thought. For thousands of years, weavers managed this complexity in their minds before there were punch cards or computers or even the ability to write anything down and without a formal discipline of mathematics. As journalist Virginia Postrel writes regarding the genius of ancient weavers, "woven cloth represents some of humanity's earliest algorithms. It is embodied code."[48]

In 1997, mathematician Daina Taimiņa learned how to use textiles to express a mathematical idea that hadn't been realized in three dimensions. As she explained in a TEDx talk, she was teaching a course at Cornell University on hyperbolic geometry, a form of non-Euclidean geometry first described by János Bolyai in 1823. Hyperbolic geometry violates Euclid's parallel postulate, which states that between a line and a point outside the line, there is only one line you can draw through that point that will never intersect with the original line—a parallel line. Any other line with even the slightest slant would eventually intersect it. While this seems obvious enough, mathematicians struggled over this postulate, unable to prove or disprove it since Euclid proposed it in 300 BCE. But it does not hold true in hyperbolic geometry. In hyperbolic space, an infinite number of lines can be drawn through a point that are all parallel (more on that later). Taimiņa dreaded having to teach this course after struggling through it as a student at the University of Latvia twenty years earlier. She felt that it required too much imagination for her to translate the two-dimensional chalkboard drawing of intersecting lines that her professor taught from into the curved and undulating surface of a hyperbolic plane. She was determined to give her students a better model to illustrate this abstract mathematical concept—one that mathematicians had thought was impossible to create as a real, three-dimensional object.

Knowing that a hyperbolic plane expands exponentially from any given point, Taimiņa drew out a model of exponential growth—from one comes two, from two comes four, from four comes sixteen,

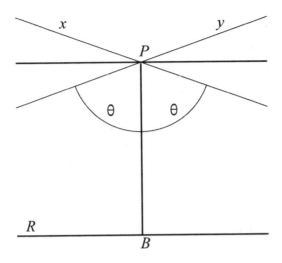

Two-dimensional rendering of a hyperbolic plane.

and so on. She grew up in Latvia making handcrafts and realized that this kind of growth was possible to do in knitting or crochet by increasing stitches—from one stitch you can make two. She first tried to knit a hyperbolic plane, but after a while she had too many stitches on the needles, so she switched to crochet.[49]

The basic crochet equation is: crochet n stitches, increase one and repeat ad infinitum. One can choose any number for n; the smaller the n, the quicker the number of stitches will grow, resulting in a more tightly ruffled shape, while a larger n results in looser curls and twists. For classroom use, Taimiņa found that it was best to use a ratio of 12:13 so that you could increase one in the next row after every twelve single crochet stitches. The piece will grow into a shape with crenulated edges that begin to fold into themselves. She reflected that when you crochet a hyperbolic plane, you get a concrete sense of the piece expanding exponentially. The first rows take no time at all, but the later rows have so many stitches that they can take hours. By making a hyperbolic plane this way, you get a visceral sense of what "hyperbolic" means.

The properties of hyperbolic space can be directly experienced through these woolen models. By embroidering lines across her hyperbolic plane, Taimiṇa was able to represent her professor's chalkboard drawing of straight lines on the crocheted surface. These lines appear curved on the model, but folding the fabric along the line demonstrates that they are in fact straight. Moreover, it's clear to see how Euclid's parallel postulate is violated in hyperbolic space on these models. The straight lines in the geometry of the hyperbolic plane are actually half circles. Therefore, there are an infinite number of these lines that can be drawn through a point and not meet the original line because they curve upward and away from the center point. The crochet models produced by Taimiṇa show that through tangible, accessible materials, people can engage with abstract, theoretical ideas.

Inspired by Taimiṇa's discovery, twin sisters Margaret and Christine Wertheim, a science writer and art professor, respectively, started the *Crochet Coral Reef* project in 2005 to raise awareness of global warming and its impact on coral reefs. It turns out that many organisms in coral reefs have a similarly unique structure: the crenulated forms of corals, kelps, sponges, and sea slugs are manifestations of hyperbolic geometry, which, as Taimiṇa demonstrated, can be represented through crochet. As natives of Queensland, Australia, the devastation of the Great Barrier Reef hit close to home for the Wertheim sisters, who mourned the loss of this vibrant ecosystem just off their coast. Through crochet, they were able to illustrate the beauty and variety of life in coral reefs and show by comparison the bleaching and atrophy of a dying reef. The sisters were soon joined by hundreds of people around the world who crocheted thousands of coral reef organisms, reflecting tens of thousands of hours of human labor, 99 percent of it done by women. Some crafters contributed to Wertheim's installation, which has been exhibited in galleries and museums in Chicago, London, Los Angeles, and New York. Others organized satellite projects to create installations for display in their own communities in more than fifty locations. To date, over twenty thousand people have contributed crochet corals, making it one of the largest community art projects in the world.

As the project has evolved, so have the creatures. Margaret Wertheim explained that they started by crocheting the simple, mathematically perfect models in the coral reef, which she likened to single-celled organisms, but when they later began to deviate from the algorithm—crochet *n* stitches, increase one—the models started to look even more natural: "Now we have this ever-evolving crochet taxonomic tree of life. Just as the morphology and complexity of life on earth is never ending, little embellishments and complexifications in the DNA code lead to new things like giraffes or orchids, so too little embellishments in the crochet code lead to new and wonderous creatures in the evolutionary tree of crochet life."[50] As a reflection of Darwin's theory of evolution, the *Crochet Coral Reef* project has taken on a life and evolutionary process of its own as more people join and add their own creative "DNA" to it, resulting in increasingly complex crochet structures. The art-making process became a tool not just for learning *about* science but for *enacting* methodologies within nature that science uncovers.

Hyperbolic geometry had once stumped Taimiņa, who struggled to visualize it as an actual physical space from its abstract representations. Now it is something that thousands of people around the world, regardless of whether they studied hyperbolic geometry in school, can very easily crochet into a colorful array of forms to make coral reef installations. There are knitting and crochet patterns on Ravelry, an online pattern database and community for knitters and crocheters, for hyperbolic scrunchies, scarves, and socks that anyone with a little yarn and knowledge of knitting or crochet can make and hold in their hands to understand this mathematical concept. "Mathematics is not scary when you can touch it," Taimiņa said.[51] That might be especially true when it is made out of colorful, squishy yarn.

CHAPTER 3

Stitching a Self

In the 1960s, knitwear designer Elizabeth Zimmermann began to revolutionize the home knitting industry in the United States by giving women the tools and encouragement to think for themselves in their knitting rather than being dependent on patterns and experts. While she was an expert knitter and sold many of her own patterns, here's what she wrote in the introduction to her first book, *Knitting Without Tears*:

> I shall have failed in my endeavor if you copy my designs too slavishly; they are intended only as a guide, so be your own designer. No two people knit alike, look alike, think alike; why should their projects be alike? Your sweater should be like your own favorite original recipes—like nobody else's on earth. And a good thing too.[1]

Zimmermann provided instruction on the technical skills needed to achieve whatever effect knitters desired by altering patterns or devising their own. In her hands-on workshops and publications, which included several books and a twice-yearly newsletter called *Wool Gathering*, she offered multiple methods for working various steps in the knitting process and encouraged knitters to experiment to determine what worked best for them. A fan letter from 1971 describes how Zimmermann's methods shifted one woman's experience of knitting:

> Your program opened up a whole new world for me. It showed us how to think and not be afraid of using imagination. Now when I use a pattern, I use it only as a suggestion and not as an absolute. . . . To me, you are the Julia Child of knitting.[2]

In knitting, as in cooking, you can follow someone else's directions exactly or you can figure out what you want to make and how to create it for yourself. While the end result of either approach might yield a sweater or a meal, the two experiences are very different for the creator. Following a pattern or a recipe exactly as written can lead to an increased feeling of dependency on authority, whereas going "off book" can help you learn to trust your own unexpected originality.[3]

A knitter in Edinburgh, Scotland, described her experience modifying patterns as "going through the wardrobe in Narnia into a fantasy land."[4] Approaching knitting creatively opened the door to a world full of possibilities to imagine and create exactly what she wanted. Such experiences can make you wonder where else in life you could make your own decisions, what else you could alter to fit you and better suit your taste. Creative practice is a path to self-discovery. We see ourselves reflected in what we create, in the products of our minds and our hands. In finding a form of self-expression, we inevitably find a self. Psychoanalyst D. W. Winnicott, who wrote extensively on the importance of creative living as a means to self-knowledge and making a meaningful life, presented the challenge and the hope for us all when he said, "Come at the world creatively, create the world. It is only what you create that has meaning for you."[5]

CREATIVITY IN DAILY LIFE

Circumstances have not permitted most women (or men, for that matter) the time to engage in work that was not in service of daily survival or the needs of the community. And even women who had the talent and ability to devote time and creative energy toward writing or art were often barred from doing so by the male guardians of these occupations until the late nineteenth century in much of the Western world. For the most part, genius—and the creativity associated with it—was considered the province of a select group of men. But definitions that connect creativity with genius also neglect the many ways people express creativity in daily life and the richness and meaning that can be gained in doing so. Weaver and scholar Lilly Marsh, who wrote her doctoral dissertation on Zimmermann, said Zimmermann showed women that "a creative life can be lived in an ordinary way or lived in the midst of family and domesticity." It is not "some special rarefied thing that happens somewhere else in a lovely studio. It happens here while the peas are cooking. It happens here when the laundry is happening."[6] Creativity is an innate ability that can be expressed in whatever outlets are available, even the most practical aspects of daily life—how you dress, cook, parent, or make textiles.

Surrealist artist and writer Leonora Carrington demonstrated a particular talent for creative daily living through which she transformed her home into her own highly personal universe. She rebelled against her conservative upper-class British upbringing of the early twentieth century by becoming one of the most prominent female artists in the surrealist movement. She eschewed the role of "muse" relegated to women by the male gatekeepers of the art world, noting later in life, "I didn't have time to be anyone's muse. . . . I was too busy rebelling against my family and learning to be an artist."[7]

She merged the daily work of art with the daily work of care— weaving together the domestic with the fantastical. Her studio was described as "a combined kitchen, nursery, bedroom, kennel, and junk-store."[8] She used whatever materials and techniques she could to express herself and make her world—woodworking, painting, sculpture, writing, and of course various forms of fiber work. Her son Gabriel claimed that his mother's "inner demons would dissolve" when she did embroidery and appliqué. She sewed dolls stuffed with cat hair for her children and painted on bedsheets.[9]

Carrington and her husband, Hungarian photographer Emericko "Chiki" Weisz, lived in Mexico City as refugees from World War II and perhaps also from the conventionality of European life. For several years after her two children were born, she hardly left the house, opting to miss gallery exhibits of her own work and removing herself from the international art scene. Some might have seen her self-imposed restriction to her home as a stifling capitulation to the expectations of traditional motherhood that were pervasive at the time. But to Carrington, her home contained the conditions of her liberation. It was where she could create her own world.

Carrington championed feminism through her paintings, sculptures, novels, and short stories. Her paintings depict scenes of women living together: cooking, sewing, eating, cleaning, in a way that celebrates women's labor and the arts of domestic life. Her 1943 drawing *Kitchen Clock* portrays the kitchen as a magical realm where women could perform alchemical transformations, much like the conversion of raw materials into beautiful cloth. Her 1974 novel *The Hearing Trumpet* portrays three elderly women finding freedom from patriarchal authority through imagination and the art of care and community as they work together to raise goats, forage mushrooms, and make spinning wheels.

Carrington imbued domestic objects and processes with value and power—transforming them from oppressive forces into tools of freedom. Her experimentation with materials suggests that she was not really concerned with the end product of "art"; instead she used these materials to seek some transformative inner freedom that ultimately transcended the materials themselves. The filmmaker Luis Buñuel wrote that her work "liberates us from the miserable reality of our days."[10] Her creative expression, often inspired by or channeled through her daily care for her family and home, appears to have liberated her as well.

While relatively few have had the means and the courage to live as fiercely as Carrington, her life offers a rich example of the ability to use the tools of domesticity to overthrow the social constraints placed on women. In less radical ways, many women similarly found creative outlets in their daily activities, and textile work may have offered more opportunities for creativity than other household tasks.

Nestled in a cozy alcove of Retrosaria, a wool shop in Lisbon with dark wooden shelves and drawers brimming with yarn, I spoke to Rosa Pomar, a textile designer, yarn producer, and historian who studies and records traditional Portuguese textile practices. She recounted a story that, in its simplicity, highlights the creative process of designing a garment in places and times when there were no pattern books, online tutorials, or even a shared lexicon of knitting terms:

> I remember talking to this very old lady in a small village—she was a knitter—and she was telling me about these sweaters that she had made for her kids. She was telling me 'ah, sometimes I wanted to do this specific shape but I didn't know how to do it, and I went to bed and all night I couldn't sleep because I was trying to figure out how to construct it, and then I'd figure it out and go right to my needles.' It's a challenge in abstract thinking, and she was struggling to know the exact construction that she needed to use, but she didn't have the terms to verbalize what she was thinking about it.[11]

This woman had a vision in her mind of a certain shape of sweater, but she did not know if it was called, for instance, a "raglan" or "drop shoulder" sweater. Even if she did, she might not have had any way to look up a pattern if no one in her village knew that form of construction. She had to essentially invent the pattern and do all of the problem-solving in her head in order to bring it to life on her needles. She had an idea for a particular shape, and it captivated her mind until she figured out how to make it.

This type of absorption in creative work is related to Mihaly Csikszentmihalyi's concept of flow—being so involved in an activity that nothing else seems to matter and time passes without notice. The mind is consumed by the task at hand, so there is no room to worry about other problems or experience boredom. Flow typically occurs when you are working at the upper end of your skill level or challenging yourself to do something that is just out of reach. The experience is so enjoyable that people will continue to do it even at a cost, like losing a night's sleep, for the sheer sake of doing it. Csikszentmihalyi said, "The best moments in our lives are not the passive, receptive, relaxing times. . . . The best moments usually occur if a person's body or mind is stretched to its limits in a voluntary effort to accomplish something difficult and worthwhile."[12]

Experimenting with materials, mastering new skills, engaging in processes of discovery, and realizing your vision is fulfilling, captivating, and enlivening. For flow to occur, we must thread the needle between taking on something too challenging that creates anxiety and something too easy that can result in boredom. Csikszentmihalyi wrote that being able to effectively work that edge creates a sense of purposeful action and control over one's materials that extends beyond the activity itself into a sense that "I am alive, that I am somebody, that I matter."[13]

The capacity for flow states comes with practice and making the shift from conscious involvement in complicated steps to automatic movements, like the shift from explicit to implicit processing.[14] In a sense, to be creative you may need your mind to get out of the way, at least some of the time. When the mechanical aspects of a craft are relatively automatic, there is more room for inspiration and improvisation.

In an autobiography from sixteenth-century Britain, one of the earliest known firsthand accounts of an English woman's life, a noblewoman and medical practitioner named Grace Sherrington described what sounds like flow when recounting how she spent her days as a young girl. Following descriptions of more tedious chores and traditional educational activities she added:

Also every day I spent some tyme in works of myne own invention, without sample or patterns before me for carpet or cushion worke, and to drawe flowers and fruit to their lyfe with my pulmett upon paper. All which varietie did greatly recreate my mynde; for I thought of nothing else but that I was doing in every particular one of these exercises.[15]

Sherrington enjoyed the freedom to create, to artfully copy nature with her needle and thread, her mind fully absorbed in her creative endeavor. Textile work is rife with opportunity for flow experiences, particularly for those able to exercise some autonomy over the direction of their projects. Design and technical challenges are balanced with repetitive motions and punctuated by moments of satisfaction as you see your project come to life. Often both the process of making or embellishing cloth and the end product offer rewards. The pleasure in seeing a project grow and take shape fosters absorption in the work.

Of course, many women have not had the privilege that Sherrington did to make textiles that were inspired by their surroundings or sprung from their own minds. Even when they did, this work was often interrupted to care for children or tend to other household or community responsibilities. It had to be picked up and put down, filling the space between other essential tasks. Flow, as the pinnacle of creative experience, was likely a rare and special occurrence for women who made cloth amid their daily lives. Still, women were able to stitch together whatever scraps of time and liberty they had into a creative enterprise.

There was a marked shift in the amount of creative freedom given to women in their practice of embroidery in Europe from the medieval to the Renaissance period. During Sherrington's time and for centuries earlier, professional embroiderers, as well as amateur ones, were often given creative control over their designs. In the thirteenth century, King Henry III of England commissioned a prominent needlewoman, Mabel of Bury St. Edmunds, to create an embroidered banner to be hung near the altar in Westminster Abbey. He supplied the subject—the Virgin Mary and St. John—but left Mabel to determine the rest of the composition, as she "would best know how to see them."[16] Embroidery was valued as an art form, and the embroiderers were given some measure of artistic freedom.

During the Renaissance, arts and crafts became more rigidly divided by gender. Painting began to supplant embroidery as the artistic medium desired by the nobility and clergy, and embroidery became more commonly an amateur domestic craft for women. Women were barred from professional embroidery guilds, and embroidery education at home became very strict, with an emphasis on technical skill rather than creative expression. Girls were taught to make increasingly challenging samplers that provided evidence of their technical proficiency as a measure of their progress toward womanhood. Compared with the medieval period, women were much more constrained in their choice of subject matter and the creative license they could take. Rather than creating their own interpretations of biblical stories or still-life compositions, they were expected to copy existing designs, often based on well-known paintings or pattern books that were typically written by men.[17]

However, creativity, as a relatively modern concept, was not always visible to the world in the moment or recorded in textile history. Even when it was recognized culturally in certain artistic and intellectual pursuits, creativity in women's work was often overlooked. At times, women's creativity was even considered dangerous, a threat to the patriarchal order, so it was kept hidden from sight so much so that women themselves often did not see their own work as creative. It was just something they did either for necessity, as a hobby, or because it was "what women do." The textiles themselves could also obscure the creative process; even to the trained eye, it may have been impossible to discern technical challenges that were inventively overcome or decisions that were made along the way. And while making the actual textile was not always a particularly creative experience in itself, the work allowed women to maintain something personal, perhaps in secret, that was essential to themselves—the ability to let their imaginations roam or generate creative solutions to other problems while they worked.

In *Earthly Paradise*, French writer Colette's autobiography, Colette observes her daughter sewing: "[She] is silent when she sews, silent for hours on end. . . . She is silent, and she—why not write down the word that frightens me—she is thinking."[18] Her daughter's separateness, her will, feels dangerous—she is her own person, absorbed in her work, her thoughts free to wander even when her actions are directed by her mother. In this passage, Colette recognizes the limits of maternal authority—her daughter is a separate being with her own internal life that Colette cannot control. Similarly, society's efforts to control women's actions could only go so far because they could not reach the internal workings of women's minds. Italian American writer Christine Zinni used an early form of Italian needle lace as a metaphor to illustrate this point, saying, "like *punto in aria*, the spaces in between women's 'stitches in the air' also freed us to dream."[19]

Many of the steps of creating textiles are quite monotonous—combing cotton, spinning, preparing a loom, weaving plain cloth. But even for a woman compelled to do repetitive or tedious work for practical necessity or under oppressive force, no one could control what she was thinking as she worked. Her hands may have been bound by thread, but her mind was free.

WORKING WITHIN CONSTRAINTS AND CREATIVE PROBLEM-SOLVING

Weaving demonstrates the diversity of design opportunities within a binary system. Within the space between the warp and weft, there are nearly infinite possibilities to design a textile. Even on the simplest looms, complex patterns can be created through an adroit and time-consuming manual pickup of warp threads by the weaver. Andean weavers in Peru use traditional backstrap looms that look like nothing more than a pile of shaped sticks that hold the warp and use the weaver's body weight to tension the threads. Yet these women create intricate pattern bands by alternating the colors of the warp threads and meticulously counting them to make the pattern by hand with each passing of the weft threads. The resulting woven textiles are among the most complex handmade fabrics in the world, and the patterns are held entirely in the minds of the weavers.

Creative activity not only explores but exceeds simple binary thinking. It involves wrestling with paradoxes—contending with what *is* and exploring what *could be*. In daily life, women have also had to negotiate the conflict between what their value in society *is* and what it *could be* if their many contributions were recognized and valued and if they had the freedom to contribute to society in all the ways they wished. The creative potential that comes from contending with the tension between opposites has been a theme that philosophers, writers, and psychoanalysts have explored throughout history. D. W. Winnicott offered a framework for this space between dichotomies when he coined the term *transitional object* to denote a special material object that an infant becomes attached to during the first year of life. The transitional object, or "lovey," is typically a textile of some sort: a piece of cloth, blanket, or soft toy that may have been made by a mother or grandmother. In fact, Winnicott speaks of infants beginning to "pluck wool and to collect it and to use it for the caressing part of the activity"—a tactile sensation to comfort the child in the absence of the caregiver—and refers to the experience of inhabiting the transitional or intermediate area as "woolgathering."[20] *Woolgathering* was an Old English term for gathering loose tufts of wool that caught on fences or branches as sheep passed by and came to be used colloquially to mean daydreaming. According to Winnicott, becoming attached to this transitional object helps bridge the gap between the infant's early experience of oneness (it is all "me") and the growing awareness that there is a separate external world that the infant cannot control (there is "me" and "not me"). While often a prized possession throughout early childhood, the transitional object eventually loses meaning as the child grows. But the intermediate space that has been created between the inner world of the child and the outside world remains throughout life. It is critical to be able to tolerate and respect the tension between these two positions without trying to resolve it. The paradox itself creates an invaluable space where creativity and play are possible.[21]

Women's textile work creates these transitional spaces both practically, between the desire to create and the limitations of the materials and time, and socially, between individual liberty and societal expectation. Women have often produced textiles alongside other household and community tasks and therefore worked within significant time constraints. Contemporary weaving artist Rilla Marshall shared how her artistic work changed when she became a parent. With these new and substantial limits on her studio time, she had to change the scale of her work and make smaller pieces that she could accomplish in the number of hours she had to weave while also caring for a small child. She began painting her warp threads to add interest and variety to the weaving process and to counter the repetitive aspects of childcare. She drew parallels between the new constraints she felt in her daily life and the parameters of weaving:

> Within what seem to be these very restrictive parameters, there's actually quite a lot of freedom if you take the right approach. And I think the same thing is true for parenthood and continuing some kind of creative pursuit as a parent. The parameters shift dramatically, which in a way forces you to be more focused. What do I want to do, what do I need to get out of these little snippets of time I have in my studio so that it is fulfilling [amid] everything else?[22]

Women have also been tasked with mundane textile-related projects such as mending damaged or worn-out garments, which typically rank low on the creativity scale in terms of textile work. Yet, knitwear designer Flora Collingwood-Norris, who specializes in "visible creative mending," found inspiration in these menial tasks and began to view mending as a creative opportunity. Anyone who has tried repairing knitted items knows that it is nearly impossible to produce a truly invisible mend, especially if you don't have the exact color and weight of yarn as the damaged piece. Rather than mending in a way that leaves an imperfection that people may or may not notice, Collingwood-Norris uses mends to make her own creative statement and change the look of a garment. She described a heightened experience of creativity when working within constraints by contrasting her mending process with her garment design process:

> With mending there are always restraints. You've always got some restrictions, and in a way I think that makes it much easier to be creative, because you can't just do anything so you don't get overwhelmed with having too many ideas or that pressure of thinking that you have to make the most amazing thing ever and you're not quite sure what that is yet. . . . Often the piece you're repairing will give you ideas of how to repair it, so you've already got a starting point. I really enjoy that.[23]

She has found some beautiful solutions to the problems that damaged knitwear present. In one project, she covered a large stain in the center of a sweater with a climbing vine of embroidered flowers. In another, she duplicate-stitched over a threadbare section of a colorwork sweater in a bright contrasting color scheme so the repair would pop. Mending items this way imbues even the most mundane daily chores with creativity and playfulness. It also serves as a reminder that mistakes and imperfections are not permanent and can be transformed into something beautiful.

Like working on mends, working with scraps can also add a layer of constraint to a project. Because of the tremendous amount of time it took to make cloth, in many cultures every usable scrap was precious and worth incorporating into other projects. Out of the salvageable remnants of clothing and bedding that had been worn or outgrown, people from ancient Egypt to medieval Europe to the Depression era in the United States made beautiful and intricate patchwork quilts, garments, and appliqué designs. With only certain scraps in certain colors, textures, and amounts, how do you use what you have on hand to make a quilt that is pleasing to the eye or that tells a story you want to tell? Women spent time and creative energy to make the most meaningful quilts they could from whatever materials they had. Mary White, a mid-twentieth-century quilter from Texas said:

> Sometimes you don't have no control over the way things go. Hail ruins the crops, or a fire burns you out. And then you're just given so much to work with in a life and you have to do the best you can with what you got. That's what piecing is. The materials is passed on to you or is all you can afford to buy . . . that just what's given to you. Your fate. But the way you put them together is your business. You can put them in any order you like. Piecing is orderly.[24]

We often don't have control over what happens to us, but we do have some control over how we respond to it. The way we transform it, the meaning we make of it, what we comply with and what we rebel against make the experience our own. It is said of quilting that no two women would make the same design out of a given set of pieces. Each quilter leaves her individual mark through her own inventive variations on the color, order, and intricacy of the piece-work. The limitations force innovative solutions, ones we might never have discovered if given limitless materials and complete creative freedom.

While the availability of time or materials often dictates the constraints to our creative enterprises, at other times the limitations are socially imposed. In *The Subversive Stitch*, Rozsika Parker exposes the duality of embroidery for women as both a source of constraint and a weapon of resistance.[25] Despite embroidery's association with obedience, patience, stillness, and silence, women have also used it as a psychological and practical means to independence. Take, for example, this poem from an anonymous late seventeenth-century embroidered sampler:

> When I was young I little thought
> That wit must be so dearly bought
> But now experience tells me how
> If I would thrive than I must bow
> And bend unto another's will
> That I might learn both art and skill
> To get my living by my hands
> That I might be free from band
> And my owne dame that I may be
> And free from all such slavery.
> Avoid vaine pastime fle youthful pleasure
> Let moderation allways be they measure
> And so prosed unto the heavenly treasure.[26]

This woman turned the tool of her oppression into a way to free herself from the social structure that taught her to "bend unto another's will." Her initial compliance with the gendered mandate to learn to embroider the alphabet as part of girls' sampler work gave her a way to earn a living and express her own mind as an adult. Using the sampler as a medium, she was able to write what she really thought—a proud assertion of her independence—paradoxically slipped in between more traditional platitudes about the renunciation of personal pleasure, almost as though to escape notice.

Regarding the variety of embroidery samplers and lace designs women created, cross-stitch designer Haley Pierson-Cox, who we met in chapter 2, noted, "So much personal choice can be hidden in plain sight and still fit within the bounds of expectation for something being viewed publicly." She elaborated, "I like being able to be playful and also provocative, but I don't necessarily need to shock. I think there's a lot of room to make that happen, especially if you are working within something as constrained as a literal grid."[27] The propriety of needlework as a medium for expression allows room for a bit of impropriety in what is expressed. It gently "needles" in a way that other media cannot—for instance, the word "fuck" reads very differently in cross stitch than it would in spray paint.

In *Undoing Gender*, philosopher and gender studies scholar Judith Butler aptly describes gender as "a practice of improvisation within a scene of constraint."[28] We internalize the general rules and restrictions and then perform gender extemporaneously within that framework. The woman who embroidered the "When I was young" sampler performed her gendered role in society by speaking her mind with thread, but because she had some room to improvise the role, she was able to take creative license with the content of her sampler. Butler advocates for undoing restrictive sexual and gender roles that require conformity to whatever society considers "normal." Conformity runs contrary to the spirit of creativity. Compliance results in a sense of futility, a loss of autonomy and essential personhood, a sort of death—if you have no sense that you exist, it is not possible to be creative. Creativity requires a departure from society's existing norms and values.

Creative people often have complex personalities. They can appear both smart and naive, playful and disciplined, respectful of tradition but also rebellious. They also tend not to conform to traditional gender roles, which restrict the full expression of self and limit complexity.[29] Virginia Woolf articulated her own belief that a mind that was able to reconcile both its masculine and feminine parts was the most creative:

> The normal and comfortable state of being is that when the two [genders] live in harmony together, spiritually co-operating. If one is a man, still the woman part of the brain must have effect; and a woman also must have intercourse with the man in her. . . . It is when this fusion takes place that the mind is fully fertilized and uses all its faculties. Perhaps a mind that is purely masculine cannot create, any more than a mind that is purely feminine.[30]

The intellectual and artistic circle that Woolf belonged to, the Bloomsbury Group, often used textile work in their creative expression, and both men and women knitted and embroidered. It was used as a means of subverting gender norms for men who did not adhere to traditional models of masculinity, many of whom were gay, and for women who also engaged in traditionally masculine intellectual and artistic pursuits as painters, writers, and furniture designers. Woolf herself had a paradoxical relationship with textile work, both eschewing it as a traditionally feminine activity in favor of writing and yet finding it a great source of comfort and creative expression during times of depression when she could not write. She once noted in a letter to her husband that "knitting is the saving of life," adding that her younger brother had taken it up, too.[31]

Research supports the benefits of integrating traditionally masculine and feminine characteristics for mental well-being and creativity. Psychologist (and avid knitter) Sandra Bem created the Bem Sex-Role Inventory, which organized traditionally masculine traits (for example, self-reliance, aggressiveness, ambition, analytical skills) and traditionally feminine traits (for example, loyalty, warmth, sympathy, gullibility) along independent dimensions rather than as binary pairs (for example, forcefulness versus gentleness).[32] She found that people categorized as androgynous, those scoring high in both masculine and feminine dimensions, were higher functioning, more adaptable, and, not surprisingly, more creative. Just like destruction and creation can be part of the same process, traditional traits of masculinity and femininity can, and ideally should, coexist in the same person. Woolf wrote: "It would be a thousand pities if women wrote like men, or lived like men, or looked like men, for if two sexes are quite inadequate, considering the vastness and variety in the world, how should we manage with one only?"[33]

Crafting Identity and Telling Stories

Textiles moved women's ideas, if not women themselves, beyond the domestic sphere, giving them a voice in the world and in history. Metaphors paralleling a needle and pen as instruments of self-expression have been pervasive in women's writing. In the mid-nineteenth century novel *Der Grune Heinrich* (*Green Henry*), Swiss author Gottfried Keller says, "White linen is the paper of [housewives], which must be on hand in great, well-ordered layers, and therein they write their entire philosophy of life, their woes and their joys." A needle was considered a subordinate tool to a pen by many, particularly in the Western tradition. Seventeenth-century American poet Ann Bradstreet wrote:

> I am obnoxious to each carping tongue
> Who says my hand a needle better fits.[34]

While a pen fits women's hands equally well, if not much better for some, a needle is what most women were given to work with. In some cultures, such as among the the Guna people of Panama, textiles have been considered as valuable a tool of self-expression as language, spoken or written. The Guna continue a long tradition of sacred gatherings, or *congresos*, where prominent men in the community display their eloquent public speaking skills in the center of a gathering house by engaging in discussions about their history, politics, and traditions. Women sit in a circle around the orators, making and embellishing cloth that, like the men's words, reflect the group's cultural values and traditions. Within an established framework for discourse, men are valued for their verbal fluency and flexibility in expressing their ideas. Similarly, within an established framework for textiles, women are valued for their technical expertise and individual creativity in translating these ideas to cloth. Both roles are highly valued by the Guna community and play a critical part in the maintenance and evolution of their culture.[35]

During these gatherings, the women typically work on *molas*, panels of brightly colored cloth that are heavily appliquéd and embroidered and then sewn together to make women's traditional blouses. Some panels are characterized by geometric designs and inspired by nature. These are called *las molas naga* and are believed to have protective powers. Other panels, called *las molas goaniggadi*, depict human figures and scenes from daily life. The imagery used reflects the richness of the world around them, inspired by the wildlife and foliage of the Guna territory, but it also establishes a visual language that is understood by the community and can be used to recount important narratives. A bird in a tree symbolizes a baby in its mother's womb; appliquéd triangles reflect the shape of the Guna's bamboo huts and symbolize protection by the family; zigzag lines represent teeth biting away evil spirits. While beautiful, these symbols are not just aesthetic—they also tell a story.

Similarly, the Miao people in southern China are renowned for their elaborately embroidered "story cloths." The Miao do not have their own written language, and embroidery is referred to as *nu shu*, translating to "women's script." Miao women use weaving and embroidery to tell stories, pass down histories, celebrate their religion, and express their longings. They mix traditional mythology with their own creativity to produce gloriously vivid, shimmering, and fantastical designs. Continuing the parallels between textiles and text, each Miao woman has her own "book of threads" where she stores her embroidery thread between the pages. Christian missionaries in the early twentieth century brought Bibles to the Miao, which the women happily accepted, to the missionaries' great pleasure. However, instead of reading them, Miao women used their Bibles to organize their threads—what a wonderful number of dividers it provided!

According to Miao legend, a heroine named Lan Juan recorded the path of her escape from advancing enemies by embroidering the different landmarks she passed onto her dress as she traveled. At the end of the journey, her dress was covered in her intricately embroidered tale. Miao women honor Lan Juan and their cultural heritage through their embroidery work by stitching the stories of the Miao people into their clothing. Around age sixteen, Miao girls begin to embroider their own wedding dress using the complex language of woven symbols to represent their future dreams. As they embroider their dress, using the tools of their cultural heritage and contemplating their hopes for their adult life, they learn who they are and what they want, stitch by stitch.

Psychologist Lev Vygotsky said: "Speech does not merely serve as the expression of developed thought. Thought is restructured as it is transformed into speech. It is not expressed but completed in the word."[36] Using textiles as a stand-in for speech, we could also say: Textile work does not merely serve as the expression of developed thought. Thought is restructured as it is transformed into cloth. It is not expressed but completed in the stitch.

The process of creating textiles both expresses who we are and creates who we are. We have an idea that arises from within our mind, and realizing it with our hands transforms the idea and ourselves in the process. We see something of our mind reflected back to us in our finished product. This cycle of output and input develops our identity. Rozsika Parker writes:

> The process of creativity—the finding of form for thought—has a transformative impact on the sense of self. The embroiderer holds in her hand a coherent object which exists both outside in the world and inside her head. . . . The embroiderer sees a positive reflection of herself in her work and, importantly, in the reception of her work by others.[37]

Parker parallels this process with Winnicott's theory of mirroring in child development. Within the gaze between baby and caregiver, the child ideally sees something of herself reflected in the response of the caregiver, who may smile if the baby smiles or make a sad face if the baby looks distressed. Here the baby discovers who she is and that she has an impact on the world. Winnicott grounded the capacity for creativity within this cyclical process of mirroring—feeling seen helps develop the baby's sense of her own existence, which allows the baby to be present in her own experience rather than only aware of the other. This awareness of self creates room for play and spontaneity, which are essential to the development of the child's identity.[38] Spontaneity is integral to creativity and requires being aware of our inclinations and trusting ourselves to act on them with minimal deliberation. In this way, spontaneous action reflects a sort of wisdom that goes beyond what the creator is consciously aware of and often surprises the creator herself.

Mayan women improvise a lot of their patterns. The decorations they add to their huipiles (blouses) rely on existing symbols and designs, but they also continuously draw inspiration from the world around them, resulting in the great variety of colors, styles, and images used within a particular region. Field studies show that many of the design decisions a Mayan weaver makes in producing a garment are spontaneous. Often the only conscious decision made prior to beginning the weaving process is the selection of colors for the warp threads. The weaver makes sure that her thread basket includes a variety of colors that, in her opinion, coordinate with those chosen for the warp, so she can choose which ones to add as she decides on the design motifs. She may draw inspiration from her surroundings as she weaves, incorporating things that she sees around her, or from ideas that strike her mind as it wanders while she weaves.[39] The spontaneity present in Mayan weaving underscores the role of textile design as a reflection of personal attitudes, taste, and judgment in Mayan culture. The spontaneous choices we make reflect our will and confirm our existence and individuality. It is in these seemingly small, everyday decisions that we discover who we are.

FINDING A VOICE

In the early 1880s, a new fad spread among women in America: making "crazy quilts"—quilts that defied traditional forms and patterns, combining irregularly sized fabric scraps from cotton to silk to velvet in haphazard arrangements. Crazy quilts often integrated embroidery through visibly top-stitching seams and adding words and images onto the fragments of fabric. They were further embellished with ribbon, lace, beads, and buttons. Women typically traded these materials with each other to increase the variety of textures and colors in a quilt.

Ruth McEnery Stuart was one of the many women who joined in on the fad. She was born into the wealth of antebellum plantation life in Louisiana, and her family was one of the largest slaveholders in the state. After the Civil War, the family's prosperity rapidly declined, and McEnery Stuart worked as a teacher to support herself. In 1879, she married a plantation owner in Arkansas, a widower with eleven children at the time of their marriage. They had one child together before he died in 1883, leaving no will and much debt. It is likely that she made her crazy quilt during or in the initial aftermath of her marriage. Looking back many years later, in 1900 she wrote a letter to her quilt, expressing both her ambivalence toward it and a sense of personal transformation through making it:

Yes, I suppose you continue to be beautiful, my quilt, even after the day of the ordinary crazy-quilt is past. The truth is I put my best self into you. You were to me—before I waked from the delusion—my one poem, the first form in which something within me seemed to find full expression.[40]

Jane Przybysz, director of the McKissick Museum at the University of South Carolina, studied the letter and suggests that for the Victorian middle- to upper-class white woman, "the crazy quilt may have been the 'private theatre' in which she first heard herself speak aloud that which had been unspeakable."[41] It reflected a coming to consciousness—a space for self-expression free from the orderly piecing and patterning she had known.

McEnery Stuart's life changed considerably in the years following her husband's death. In 1888, she embarked on a writing career, and in the early 1890s, she moved to New York City, where she traveled in artistic and literary circles. She was a regular contributor to *Harper's Magazine* and the author of local-color stories that described mostly Black and poor white people who worked on her husband's plantation, Italian immigrants in New Orleans, and the impoverished postbellum "aristocracy."[42] As with Mark Twain, her authorship of such stories is problematic from the current vantage point of racism and cultural appropriation, though they reflected the complex attitudes of wealthy white people toward Black people in the aftermath of slavery.[43]

Though she once found full expression of self in this quilt, by the time she wrote the unpublished letter, which she titled "To Her Crazy-quilt . . . A Study of Values," she had since found it in writing and in her new life as an independent woman (she never remarried). She speaks of a "new consciousness" and expresses her view of the quilt after this awakening:

> But why have you thus ceased to charm me, my pretty quilt? I look and see that you are, as I meant you should be, your own best expression of art, and yet you are no longer a pleasure. No longer are you to my fond eyes a kaleidoscopic color-marvel—a symphony in haphazards—a poem of complements. . . . Each brilliant patch in you, my poor color-study, has become a province in the great map of my state of ignorance. . . . They are German lessons unstudied—Italian poems unlearned, history forgot. The golden thread that connects while it defines them is the whole year—the golden stream of time. . . . It is a gleaming boundary of untilled lands.[44]

McEnery Stuart's self-criticism for her time spent making a crazy quilt rather than engaging in more "serious" scholarship is echoed in an editorial called "Crazy Work and Sane Work," published in *Harper's Bazaar* in 1884, which states that the crazy quilt mania "stood for a misdirected energy and perseverance too common among women" and that their time would be better spent learning to paint, speak a foreign language, or learning "the important science of housekeeping and kitchen chemistry."[45] In a particular blow that laid women's powerlessness in society at their own doorstep, the (male) writer claims: "It is the chief misfortunate and limitation of women that their aims are petty. . . . And most women need to be reminded that the time they daily industriously waste would do for them what it does for men—conquer new worlds."[46] There is no mention of the inculcation of "fancywork" in women's education, often to the exclusion of other subjects, or the social and moral pressures to create an elegantly decorated home. Other critics simultaneously charged crazy quilts with making women too masculine, endangering women's selfless devotion to their families, and engendering moral impropriety and illicit female sexuality.[47] The "crazy" in crazy quilts had two implications—one is chaos or madness in its cacophonous disorder, the other is extreme enthusiasm or a sense of wildness that cannot be constrained by an orderly pattern. Both possibilities would have felt threatening within the repressive Victorian social landscape, and crazy quilts set off a moral panic about the loss of societal control over women.

But despite her own self-reproaches, McEnery Stuart adds in her letter, "And yet—and yet I would not part with you, my crazy, crazy quilt, for in your very irresponsibilities I have been able to see my way to better things."[48] Though she does not specify what the "better things" are, her literary career and her move to New York followed the making of her quilt—and she appears to have found a voice and the courage to express it in media beyond needlework and the walls of the home. She writes, "The thing you seemed to express, as you grew beneath my fingers, were beauty and harmony and a sort of perfection, to attain which is always a delight to the composer, be he architect, musician or simply a sewer of patches, as was I."[49]

In the preface to the 1911 book *Educational Needlecraft*, Margaret McMillan, an advocate for providing education and healthcare to the children of England's working class, encourages the transfer of creativity beyond needlework:

> In becoming good craftswomen girls may become something more. Their work itself leads them to look at last

beyond their homes, and if they look to-day, what do they see? Much beauty and happiness, work and pleasure, but also . . . widespread misery and darkness—a chaos which waits for creators to make of it a new world. That winged power in them, the unresting creative energy, must find a new field for its labour. It cannot be *confined* to the home. What the educated woman of to-morrow will do we cannot foretell, for she will no longer be the slave of routine and tradition.[50]

While finding her voice took McEnery Stuart away from needlework, other artists found that needlework was the best way to express their voices. In the 1980s, multimedia artist Ghada Amer attended art school in Nice, France. There, a professor told her that she could not paint because she was a woman and excluded her from a painting class. Feeling that gender equality was going in the wrong direction in her home country of Egypt with the rise of head and face coverings and modest dress, Amer had moved to France seeking freedom and imagining a place where she could be an artist in the style of Picasso or Matisse. Instead, she found gender inequity to be a universal problem. Being told she could not paint forced her to reconcile her identities as a woman and an artist. There were few women in art books to provide her with a model, since painting was historically the domain of men. Amer expressed not knowing "what to do with my being as a woman," which she decided to address through her artwork.[51]

Over tea and Egyptian sweets in her Harlem studio, Amer shared with me how she came to embroidery. Amer grew up around sewing. Her mother and grandmother sewed, and she and her sisters were tasked with drawing and cutting out the patterns for all of their clothes. Though she was never particularly interested in sewing, she recalled this as a time when the women could gather together and talk freely, escaping the notice of men. Because of its seeming banality, needlework provided cover for women raising questions on what women could do in a space removed from men's sight. Amer decided to take up embroidery as a medium, wanting to paint with thread.

Her first embroidery work, called *Cinq Femmes au Travail* (*Five Women at Work*), shows four women engaged in household tasks, the kinds you would see in advertisements or stock photos. Amer is the invisible fifth woman, whose hands embroidered the canvas. Reflecting on this piece, she said, "This was my statement work—women because I'm a woman and work because I'm going to prove [to] you that I can work. . . . But it was not painting, it was still drawing." To make the thread function more like paint, she began knotting it and letting it hang down to mimic drips of paint. To fill in the spaces of the canvas, she decided to repeat and overlay images—the visual repetition paralleled the repetitive hand motions of stitching. Using gel medium to hold the "drips" of thread in place on the canvas, Amer developed her own form of painting.[52] Simultaneously, she developed her subject matter. She thought, "I need to find a subject that is subversive that would be contrary to the medium so people would look at this and say 'why?' and feel uncomfortable. . . . The way that I think about it is actually like it was a strategy of war. So I took from a porn magazine and I drew her, the woman."[53] Like the women in *Cinq Femmes au Travail*, pornographic images of women are like stock photos—in this case as predictable portrayals of women as sexual objects. Amer said, "You see one, you see one thousand and one . . . so [I] take one woman . . . and then I repeat."[54] The result is a canvas full of images of the same woman (or women) engaging in acts of sexual pleasure alone or with each other.

The war Amer spoke of is a war on men's ideas about women—who women exist for, how they make their voices heard, and whether or not they can paint. Embroidering erotic images of women that were meant for male consumption shifts the meaning of these images, making them about the women's experience of pleasure as subjects rather than as objects of pleasure for men. Unlike her experience sewing as a child, Amer's needlework does not cause her voice to escape notice but rather calls attention to women's invisibility and objectification. It claims a space for women to speak for themselves rather than be spoken for, as expressed in her aptly titled 2022 exhibit *A Woman's Voice Is Revolution*.

Amer speaks in many languages in her work—French, English, and Arabic—though she avoided Arabic for a long time and even refused to do a calligraphy assignment in art school because of the connection to Arabic writing. She was unsure of what to say to Egyptian women, who she felt were so different from her, and wondered if she could really communicate with them at all. Then the Arab Spring happened in the early 2010s, and she became aware of the powerful political and women's rights movements that had been quietly brewing. She realized, "Just because you don't talk, doesn't mean you don't think." Egyptian women had not had a voice, but now Amer heard them speak, which motivated her to speak back by creating work in Arabic, sensing that "if I write it, they will read it. It's an acknowledgment of having someone on the other side that I can talk to."[55]

She noted that for a long time she did not think that her Egyptian heritage influenced her work but has come to realize that the idea of using textiles came naturally to her because of their cultural importance in Egypt. "Your culture comes to you anyway. You don't think about it," she said. The works in Amer's 2023 exhibit, *QR Codes Revisited*, use the Egyptian appliqué technique *khayamiya*, which has adorned the interiors of tents since ancient Egypt. The tentmakers are traditionally men, many of whom work in the Street of the Tentmakers in Cairo. Amer commissioned this work, depicting feminist statements in English and Arabic, to be stitched by male tentmakers. One piece in Arabic is a quote by Egyptian feminist and writer Nawal El Saadawi that translates to: "Oh Woman: Challenge the East, the West, challenge the North, the South, challenge the primacy of the body and be the brain of this world." While stitching erotic images of women with her own hand reflects an effort to reclaim woman's subjectivity in these images, having men stitch feminist statements in this work is an expression of empowerment and a reflection of her achievements as an artist. It also reflects the joint effort of men and women needed to create gender equality.

Amer's work has developed over the last two decades to include traditional forms of painting as well as sculpture in metal, clay, and plants. She often delegates the execution of the embroidery work now because she feels angry at the injustice of being excluded from painting as she stitches. Yet because of this restriction, Amer found a way to express herself artistically as she grappled with the question of how to be a woman and an artist. Had she been allowed to paint, she would have expressed herself differently. But her anger is not destructive; rather, as the needle pierces the fabric, it forces creation onto the threads.[56] From her anger comes art. Like Amer discovered during the Arab Spring, under the cloak of invisibility and silence, a surprising new voice can emerge.

Embroidery artist Michelle Kingdom also attended art school

during the late 1980s. She majored in painting at the University of California, Los Angeles, and graduated into the same male-dominated art world as Amer. After she graduated, Kingdom experimented with "drawing with thread."[57] The raised surface of the work gave her a different feeling than drawing and painting. Having grown up in a family of Russian Jews where everyone sewed, embroidery was "part of the ecosystem . . . another language almost. We didn't really talk about it with each other but it permeated everything."

Because she didn't expect anyone to be interested in her embroidery artistically or commercially, it could be just what she wanted it to be—a place to explore and develop her ideas. As a result, her embroidery work became an increasingly personal and authentic reflection of the inner workings of her mind. She said, "I wanted it to be a really pure vision . . . [I was] trying to evoke some kind of truth and feeling and expression to explain the human condition and get through life."

When her daughter was born in 2002, embroidery felt more relevant to her than ever, being so tied to her own experiences of family from childhood, and she often stitched in the quiet moments of her daughter's naps. Far from being a relaxing pastime though, Kingdom described the process of embroidery as "fighting your way out of this war zone with tiny needles." Her creative process is one of discovery that unfolds as she works. While she starts with an initial plan, she doesn't want to know everything she's going to do before she begins embroidering, so she has some mystery to keep it interesting as she goes. There's a sense of hope gained in moving from the unknown to a place of greater knowing—from darkness to light.

She avoids using traditional stitches or getting tied up in the technical aspects of embroidery. "You're basically drawing in slow motion in tiny increments of straight lines, trying to make them seem as if they have motion and some kind of life. Sometimes I'll rip out satin stitches—it's a beautiful stitch and there's a time and a place when I do want to use that but other times, I want it to look a little bit awkward." Some embroiderers take care that the back of the work is neat, but that does not matter to her. However, she enjoys the metaphorical connotations of the side that is presented and the hidden underside, noting, "The back side of the work is definitely the honest side. The front side is full-on 'we are hiding everything.' Take a peek at the back and it's like the inner workings of the brain," the path of decisions made along the way. The front is product, the back is process. You can't have one without the other, and there is beauty in both.

Kingdom also stated that she is not trying to paint with thread. She appreciates working within the parameters of embroidery materials and is not looking to transform or transcend them. The constraints reflect the history of this practice as women's work: "I want to carry on some of those limitations. I'm not trying to escape from that. I want to make sure we're still remembering the history but [to] hopefully open up new doors about it and have new conversations." She added that embroidery helps "give voice to complicated ideas, to sticky ideas," because it is entwined with these historical connotations. The beauty of her work is undeniable, yet there is always something dark, mysterious, and a bit uncomfortable. She said, "In my mind every piece is a bit of a poison pill disguised as a treat." Her 2018 work *The Height of Folly* depicts chorus girls on stage in a pyramid formation with others suspended in the air on wires, evoking an extravagant vaudeville-style revue. The small scale means you have to look closely to see that the women have animal masks and gas masks on their heads, hold guns, and are wearing bandoliers like pageant sashes. Not all is as it seems, and like the embroidered cloth itself, there is a messy underside to the work that must be taken together with the image presented on the front to understand the whole picture.

Ultimately, she is interested in embroidery as a vehicle for symbolism, a way to express her ideas rendered as coherently as possible with a needle and thread: "I get more savvy as an artist as I go. [It] looks prettier on the outside, more deft needlework, but at the end of the day a good story is a good story. That has to override everything." While Amer's embroidery is painterly, Kingdom's is literary.

Kingdom's work has emerged from her private incubator and is now internationally recognized and exhibited in galleries, but her style has remained an intimate view into her reflections on the world and her place in it. She uses a highly personal, symbolic system of references that makes her works emotionally evocative and allegorical—a collection of codes for the viewer to decipher. "This is our language and I know it's not everyone's language. . . . A lot of people don't sew any more, but for those who did, there is just something about it that is just like your handwriting. It just comes out. It feels natural to hold a needle." For Kingdom, the language of embroidery gives voice to something deep inside of her that has often felt inaccessible to share with others: "The strangeness, beauty, and poignancy of the tactile medium feels like a glimmer into that dreamworld."

As Kingdom's and Amer's work shows, there is a greater freedom to play and experiment when you can operate outside of the canonical system of art. Kingdom said: "The history of it not being taken as seriously as other mediums also allows for more freedom to explore. Less eyes that care to judge, and less rules to fret over breaking. Part of the joy of stitching is intentionally breaking some of those rules, reminding the viewer this is not an attempt to capture photographic reality or illusionary painting. . . . Part of it is the visible hand, but maybe more importantly the exposed heart."

CHAPTER 4

Unraveling Emotions

In the early 1990s, art historian Janet Catherine Berlo, whose research on Native American and Mesoamerican women's art is referenced throughout this book, went through a long depression that left her completely unable to focus on her academic work for a year and a half. She turned to quilting to help her through it. She later detailed her experience in her book *Quilting Lessons*, writing, "When I wasn't quilting, I wasn't alive. On most days, I felt that I literally needed those vibrant hues in order to breathe. Some days my brain craved blue. . . . My body craved the colors and the kinetic act of cutting and piecing, cutting and piecing."[1] The bright colors of fabric and the sense of possibility in arranging them gave her energy and hope. The act of cutting and sewing provided a sense of security and manageability as she "pieced for cover"—the quilting created a protected space to work through her depression.

Berlo preferred improvisational and freewheeling designs to traditional patterns and came to call the output of her sewing efforts "Serendipity Quilts" because they helped her to make "fortunate discoveries accidentally."[2] She let her quilts develop organically without too much rationality or order. She realized, "I have been acting out with fabric what I need to do in my life."[3] She wrote of the parallels between this improvisational way of quilting and the therapy work she had also begun during this time: "Rationality, planning, order, and control are *not* successful strategies in therapy. Opening yourself to experiencing what's on your mind is. In Serendipity Quilts, as well as in therapy, surprising connections are made. Extraordinary patterns emerge. . . . It takes a while to see it."[4] The process of piecing her quilts together helped her listen to herself and trust her intuition to guide her. It allowed her to accept the messiness of her emotional life and her creative process and ultimately pick up her pen again, recognizing that her academic work might also be "enriched by allowing the messiness in."[5] Rather than returning to the book about Native American women's art that she had been working on prior to her depression, instead she wrote *Quilting Lessons*.

Many years later, in the midst of a sudden and difficult divorce, Berlo was struggling to process her anger at her partner of twenty-five years for his abrupt departure. She again turned to quilting. She cut fabric into hands the shape and size of her husband's, burned holes in them, set the tips on fire, and then sewed them onto a quilt to work out her anger in cloth in a way that felt safer than expressing it directly. Mourning the loss of her husband through quilting helped her realize that you can "heal your own heart," words she embroidered onto a piano bench cushion in her living room—"all it takes is a needle and thread, and infinite, infinite patience."[6]

A SECURITY BLANKET

In the 1960s, American psychologist Harry Harlow conducted a series of experiments with rhesus monkey infants that profoundly impacted our understanding of human attachment and the importance of physical affection and emotional bonding. He created monkey "mothers" for these babies, one made of wood and wire with a bottle that dispensed milk and another that was covered in soft terry cloth meant to resemble fur, but that did not provide any food. The rhesus infants overwhelmingly preferred the cloth mothers, cuddling with them often and visiting the wire mothers only for sustenance. The young monkeys would also turn to their cloth surrogate for comfort and security after a period of exploration. If the cloth mother was removed from the room, they experienced visible distress: freezing, rocking, screaming, or crying. While these experiments would now be considered unethical due to the distress induced in the monkeys, it showed us, as Harlow concluded, that "contact comfort" is essential to the psychological development and health of children, monkey or human.[7]

Textiles evoke early memories of touch, connection, and comfort. Babies are swaddled in cloth. As mentioned in chapter 3, stuffed animals and blankets often become items that give children a sense of security, like Winnicott's transitional object. Children snuggle under the covers with caregivers or siblings and get "tucked in" at bedtime, enveloped in the sheets. At any age, curling up under a quilt provides a sense of warmth and containment. When we're having a bad day, we say things like, "I just want to get in bed and pull the covers over my head." Many of us have items of clothing—an oversized sweatshirt or a pilled cardigan—that we would never wear in public but provide a sense of comfort at home.

The emotional experience of textile work is about both process and product. People often choose yarn or fabric based on how it feels against their skin or how they respond to the color, like the way Berlo craved blues. We may take on a small project when we need to feel a sense of gratification and achievement, a more intricate project to distract our attention or remind ourselves how much we're capable of, or a long, repetitive project when we need to come home to something familiar and rest our mind. We engage with materials that evoke feelings of comfort and warmth as the product is evolving. An in-progress sweater rests in our lap and a crocheted blanket covers our body as we work. We touch every bit of yarn as we warp a loom and weave fabric. The process of creating textiles facilitates mindful attention to the present moment and bodily sensation—the feel of the materials and the motion of our bodies. Its outward focus can move us beyond internal preoccupations. Counting stitches or holding a complex pattern in mind may distract a knitter, crocheter, or weaver from worries. We lose self-consciousness through absorption in the activity. The repetition involved can lead to a hypnotic, calm state, a kind of meditation through motion.[8] Textile work confers a sense of control and mastery that can counterbalance the lack of control we may experience over what is happening in our larger world. When we make, repair, or create things, we feel vital and effective. A forty-two-year-old woman in Finland expressed the emotional impact of textile crafting saying, "All these years I have been crafting, this has not been for my own pleasure, but it has had another meaning. I have come to the conclusion that I have fled the present moment. I have covered myself from self-destruction, I have calmed down, I have been able to stand up."[9]

Research has shown that skilled hand activities such as knitting, woodworking, and gardening can reduce stress and relieve anxiety and depression. Depression symptoms are related to lower levels of serotonin, known as the "feel good" chemical in the brain, which is the target of pharmacological treatments such as selective serotonin reuptake inhibitors (SSRIs). Repetitive, rhythmic tasks, such as knitting and weaving, are known to activate the release of serotonin.[10] Depression is also related to increased levels of the stress hormone cortisol and low levels of dopamine, a neurochemical involved in movement, pleasure, and anticipated rewards. What we do impacts these neurochemicals, so we can change our brain chemistry through our actions. The idea that action precedes emotion is the basis for cognitive behavioral treatments such as behavioral activation, which encourages people who are depressed to do things like go for a walk, visit a friend, or tidy their home, even when they don't feel like it. These activities can enhance mood and provide a sense of accomplishment to combat the feelings of hopelessness and helplessness associated with depression.

A survey of 3,545 female knitters worldwide found a positive association between knitting frequency and feelings of happiness and calm.[11] Those who knitted daily experienced the most benefit. Of respondents with depression, 81 percent reported feeling "happy" after knitting, and 54 percent reported feeling "very happy." Among respondents who reported that they suffered chronic pain, 88 percent felt that knitting gave them a sense of accomplishment and a means of coping with their pain. Serotonin is an analgesic, so the intensity of perceived pain may be lessened as a result of the repetitive movements of knitting. The notion that crafting can facilitate emotional well-being is not new. During the nineteenth century, doctors prescribed knitting for women to counteract nervousness and "hysteria."[12] Of course, it may not supplant all the benefits of more modern pharmacological treatment and psychotherapy, but it can be a helpful addition for some.

Neuroscientist Kelly Lambert suggests that the movement away from manual labor in many parts of the world has had a negative impact on our brains and contributes to mental health issues such as depression and anxiety. When we don't interact with our material world in ways that produce positive tangible results, we can experience a sense of passivity and learned helplessness characteristic of depression.[13] In her research, she found that rats that had to dig for treats over several weeks exhibited lower stress and greater emotional resilience during a difficult problem-solving task compared with rats who had just been given their treats. These "effort-based rewards," positive outcomes that come from invested effort, develop learned persistence—as opposed to learned helplessness—which enhances emotional resilience.[14] The effort-based rewards in textile work are apparent. You can see your progress as you work—a knitted scarf hangs down farther from your needles, a woven blanket inches up the loom, a ball of spun yarn gets bigger as the pile of unspun roving gets smaller. Anticipating the final product and the accompanying sense of accomplishment increases the release of dopamine. We are rewarded for our effort in real time.

In a research study, art therapist Ann Futterman Collier surveyed an international sample of 891 participants (the majority of whom were white, middle-aged to older women from the United States) who engaged in textile-related crafts, mostly as hobbies rather than for economic need.[15] About half of these women reported using textile-making techniques (knitting, crocheting, weaving, needle-work, spinning) and related activities (project planning, shopping for yarn, sorting supplies) for mood regulation; she termed this group "textile-copers." The other half reported using non-textile-related activities for mood regulation, such as taking a walk, reading, venting, engaging in religious activity, or relaxing; these were the "non-textile-copers." Textile-copers reported significantly greater success in transforming their negative moods compared with the non-textile-copers using their preferred coping method. Textile-copers also noted that they became more absorbed in their crafting activity and reported feeling more rejuvenated afterward than non-textile-copers did when engaging in their coping activities.

Notably, the textile-copers reported that they had tried more textile techniques, engaged in textile work more frequently, and had higher skill levels in their craft than non-textile-copers. Many non-textile-copers said that they did not want to do their textile crafts when upset for fear that it would "put negative energy" into the project or they would make too many mistakes. In contrast, textile-copers had so mastered their textile-making skills that they knew how to put aside or transform anxiety or sadness while engaged in their craft. Often, textile making offered them a creative outlet for their concerns. The higher skill level of the textile-copers may have facilitated flow experiences when crafting, which helped them trans-form their mood through the positive experience of energized focus and seeing the rewards of their efforts. During flow, there is very little attention left over to worry about problems.[16]

Making textiles can offer a slightly altered version of experiences we have in other aspects of life—a version where things can be undone and redone, mistakes can be fixed, and where we can experience visible, tangible progress or, in a circumscribed way, mourn a loss, as when a piece doesn't turn out as we'd hoped or gets damaged. Textile work is forgiving. We can unravel or unpick stitches, mend holes and tears, reuse materials, and rework pieces. If a sweater turns out a bit too small, then we can block it out larger; a little too big and we can shrink it slightly in the dryer, as long as it's not superwash wool. If it's way off, we can gift it to a friend who it will fit better or, at worst, we can unravel and reknit the sweater. The stakes are generally lower than in many areas of life, but the rewards can be great.

In a personal essay, author and knitter Ann Hood writes about how she relied on knitting as a coping mechanism after the death of her five-year-old daughter. She recalls her first interaction with the local yarn store owner who taught her to knit:

> "In knitting," she said as she began to cast on again, "you can fix everything." Ah, the words I needed to hear most. At last, here was something I couldn't ruin. Something I could do over, and over, and over. In life, I know now, we can take that lover back or scream louder than anyone has ever screamed, but we can't rearrange the pieces. Not so in knitting. Which is why when I find myself trying to change the ending, I pick up my needles and yarn instead."[17]

Hood took up knitting in the throes of a tragedy she could not change in order to connect with her own sense of agency. The ability to visibly exert control and see material progress can be a powerful way of meeting these psychological needs that are not so easily met in other areas of life.

Sarah Mosteller, an artist and art therapist, learned to knit following a serious rafting accident at age twenty that required years of physical rehabilitation to get her body working again. She recalled that while she couldn't walk or bathe herself, "in knitting I could control everything. I could create a garment and feel really in control and autonomous and see that my hands had these abilities even though the rest of my body felt really stagnant and stuck."[18] She started knitting with wire one year after her accident, which, in hindsight, she believes was a way to test her window for tolerating discomfort. Working with wire was much harder and often caused pain in her hands. It replicated the discomfort she experienced in her body, but in a way that she could control. She could decide when to pick it up and put it down, and the pain was in service of something productive. Even though she didn't consciously choose to knit with wire to meet a psychological need, there was an intuitive pull to create this therapeutic experience in her knitting. "Bodily autonomy has been part of my own therapy journey; coming back to my body, coming back to myself. Knitting has really helped with that." She added that knitting integrated things for her—just like the loops hooking together to form a fabric, it linked her body and mind in the aftermath of her accident, when she felt pulled to detach from her body to cope with the pain and loss of control. Betsan Corkhill, a physiotherapist and advocate for the therapeutic benefit of textile work to improve mental and physical well-being, has this to say: "Knitting creates a strong, resilient, flexible fabric. Therapeutic knitting seeks to create strong, resilient, flexible minds in the process."[19]

FALLING TO PIECES
AND UNRAVELING

Tearing cloth is cited numerous times in the Old Testament as a ritualized act of mourning, "exposing the frayed edges of grief and the tattered space of loss," as artist Deborah Valoma wrote.[20] Textiles have long been included as a part of burial rituals and used as a means of processing grief. Through grieving, we experience the physical loss of a person and the changes to life that their death brings. We must figure out how to live without them. This requires an unraveling or dismantling of what was in order to create what is possible going forward.

Christy Thompson, a textile artist and art therapist in Canada, unraveled the knitted clothes of her brother, Kelly, to make a burial shroud after he was lost in a landslide while hiking the Annapurna Circuit in Nepal. His body was never recovered, and the shroud was a symbolic means of reconstructing his physical remains. She explained, "I methodically unraveled Kelly's clothes, a process that reminded me that grief is the undoing of a life once known. Every inch of the fibre passed through my hands as I loosely wound the yarn into balls and wondered, 'Are there traces of your DNA in the fibres?' "[21] The process of weaving the shroud became a metaphor for maintaining her connection to her brother, and the finished object became a tangible way of keeping his presence alive in their family.

Judith Butler writes, "Let's face it. We're undone by each other. And if we're not, we're missing something. If this seems so clearly the case with grief, it is only because it was already the case with desire. One does not always stay intact. It may be that one wants to, or does, but it may also be that despite one's best efforts, one is undone, in the face of the other, by the touch, by the scent, by the feel, by the prospect of the touch, by the memory of the feel."[22] Creating textiles from the clothing of lost loved ones can re-create something of the sensory experience of that person. The feel of their clothing when you hugged them, the smell, the memories attached to certain garments, even their sweat, blood, and skin are all embedded in the cloth. Textiles are an archive showing the traces of daily life. They store memory in the form of stains, holes, patches, stretching, pilling, and other signs of wear.[23]

So much of textile work is in a constant state of transition between integration and disintegration. Fabric is woven and made into an object that might, in some cases, be cut apart and made into something else, smaller and smaller pieces salvaged for reuse, until the fabric is ultimately discarded and turns to dust. This process can provide a framework that helps us go to pieces without feeling as though we are falling apart.[24] If we don't fear the experience of coming undone, we can embrace the creative potential of deconstruction and disintegration. Psychoanalyst Philip Bromberg writes: "A human being's ability to live a life with both authenticity and self-awareness depends on the presence of an ongoing dialectic between separateness and unity of one's self-states. . . . Health is the ability to stand in the spaces between realities without losing any of them—the capacity to feel like one self while being many."[25] The fragmentation of identity into different ways of being, or aspects of self, can be a form of self-protection in the aftermath of trauma, known as dissociation. We are broken apart into shards that no longer seem to fit together; the aim of therapy, then, is to help regain the capacity for unity. But Bromberg also highlights the benefits of allowing ourselves to move away from unity and "stand in the spaces" to observe our multiple versions of self. Ideally, we can allow ourselves a breaking apart, reorganization, and reinterpretation of these aspects of self. New opportunities emerge when we attempt to reconcile and make meaning of these, possibly contradictory, selves. We discover who we are by how we put the pieces back together. For Bromberg, standing in the spaces is the basis of creativity, play, and personal growth.

Textile techniques can serve as rich and useful metaphors for psychological processes and can be used in art therapy to facilitate identity integration and disintegration. For one woman, a twenty-four-year-old white female struggling with anorexia nervosa who we'll call Emory, unraveling her knitting served as a pathway to integration—a way to put herself back together.[26] During her treatment in an intensive outpatient eating disorder program, Emory was referred for individual and group art therapy with art therapist and wire-knitting artist Sarah Mosteller. Prior to treatment, Emory knit entire garments and then immediately unraveled them in a methodical manner, winding the yarn into a tight, neat ball. She reported that unraveling provided a sensation of "release." This ritual had begun when she made a mistake in a pattern and unraveled a bit to fix it. She enjoyed the sensation so much that she ended up unraveling the entire cardigan. She noted that since she enjoys knitting, she doesn't mind undoing her work.

During an individual session early in treatment, Emory expressed a desire to unravel the piece she had been knitting. The therapist asked Emory to verbally walk her through what the unraveling process looks like for her. "Usually, I would unravel slowly and methodically roll up the yarn into a consolidated ball," she said. The therapist inquired what she imagined the process would be like if the yarn was unraveled and not immediately put into a ball. Emory replied that it would be "uncomfortable and messy" and would require her to "take up space" but she wanted to try. As Emory began letting the unraveling yarn spread across the table, she expressed concern about "tangling the string." The therapist encouraged her to take her time and asked what it might be like if the string became tangled. "It would be okay if the string got tangled. . . . It is actually freeing to take up space. The green yarn is sort of beautiful. I am not worried about where it goes," Emory replied. After unraveling, she remarked that "the messiness of the yarn is like letting go and leaving it all out on the table. The ball is holding it all in."[27]

The feeling of "letting go" that Emory experienced unraveling the yarn in this way requires trust—an ability to surrender to the process. Psychoanalyst Emmanuel Ghent wrote about the longing to surrender, not in the sense of defeat but rather with a quality of liberating or letting go of the false self in the hopes of finding a truer version of self.[28] It is a desire to free ourselves of our defenses and deceptions—protections against anxiety, shame, guilt, anger—and "come clean" so we can be known and recognized. Leaving the yarn out on the table rather than winding it into a tight ball where so much is controlled and hidden reflected Emory's efforts to let go of these defenses and let herself be known to the therapist and to herself.

Emory's unraveling involved notions of doing and undoing through which she attempted to relieve herself of being responsible for things she may not be able to tolerate, such as imperfections or "taking up space." She destroyed what she created and therefore never had to experience the sense of loss that would come from completing a project or the judgment that might come from presenting a finished object to the world. Her unraveling put her in a perpetual state of transition that did not permit her to move forward, but unraveling the yarn in session and letting it spill out on the table allowed her to experience a sense of surrender—what it would be like to be free from the defensive structure she had built around herself that was both protecting her and hurting her. Experiencing this feeling of being undone and out of control in the safety of a therapeutic environment allowed her the space to wander into new realms of learning, bolstering curiosity and compassion between the different parts of herself.

In a later group therapy session, Emory shared a wish with the group to unravel a work in progress, citing an unevenness in the stitching that was bothering her. The group encouraged her to keep knitting and provided positive feedback about her work. Acknowledging that "it would be okay if I unraveled it, and it would be okay if I kept knitting," she chose to continue knitting. In an individual session at the end of treatment, Emory arrived wearing a large, chunky sweater that spanned all the way down to her knees. It seemed to envelop her as she sat down wrapping it around the front of her body. The therapist asked if she had knitted the sweater. Emory replied with a soft smile saying, "Yes. I finally knit my cocoon."[29] The sweater was a new means of protection during her transformation, one that did not reflect a need for control but rather a way to comfort and soothe herself during this time of change and growth. Reflecting on her treatment, she said she "was given a space and allowed to unravel and be put back together." She allowed herself to let go, take up space, and tolerate the mess and potential tangles of integration and connection.

TRAUMA AND TRANSITION

Tales of women using textiles to share unspeakable experiences stretch as far back as Greek mythology. Ovid's *Metamorphoses* recounts the story of Philomela, who was abducted and raped by her sister's husband, King Tereus. When she threatened to expose his crime, he cut out her tongue, raped her again, and hid her in a cottage in the forest. With no way to speak or write, how could she tell of her abuse, warn her sister of Tereus's true character, and have any hope of being found? As the story goes, "she had a loom to work with, and with purple on white background, wove her story in and out." Philomela sent the textile to her sister, Procne, who understood Philomela's message as soon as she unrolled the cloth.[30] Procne found where Philomela had been hidden, rescued her from her captivity, and together they exacted revenge on Tereus.

Moving from ancient myth to more recent history, during the repressive Pinochet government of the 1970s and '80s, Chilean women appliquéd and embroidered images on scraps of fabrics from flour sacks and lost loved ones' clothing to represent their family members' torture, imprisonment, and death. These story cloths, known as *arpilleras*, transferred a story or memory from person to cloth, making it tangible and visible, each stitch helping to process a painful experience. Often, multiple arpilleras made by different women were stitched together like a quilt, uniting the experiences of the community to facilitate collective healing. Like Philomela's woven message, arpilleras were secretly sent across the border to alert the world to what was happening in Chile.

The neurobiology of trauma supports the therapeutic value of creating story cloths. When we face a mortal threat, the verbal/analytical centers of the brain in the cerebral cortex automatically shut down, allowing the autonomic nervous system to activate in the service of survival. Energy shifts to privilege sensorimotor and visual processing as the individual scans the environment for opportunities to escape.[31] As a result, traumatic experiences are held and processed in bodily sensations and visual images, not in words. Because they are essentially nonverbal, it makes sense to employ a nonverbal channel when accessing these experiences. Coordinating hand movements in knitting, weaving, and sewing also create an experience of bilateral stimulation that can help process traumatic memories between the brain's hemispheres and promote brain plasticity, the ability for neural networks to develop and reorganize in response to experience. Studies show that performing a repetitive visual-spatial task during or shortly after a traumatic event significantly reduces the incidence of flashbacks.[32] Psychologists have implemented these same principles in modes of therapy, including eye movement desensitization and reprocessing (EMDR) therapy, which relies on bilateral stimulation. Through side-to-side eye movements, alternating hand taps, or alternating auditory tones, EDMR therapy aims to target memories of the trauma that are stored in a fragmented way in the brain leading to common symptoms of post-traumatic stress like flashbacks and reexperiencing. Sewing and other repetitive handwork while processing these memories may help integrate them into the larger brain network so they can be altered and reintegrated as memories that do not intrude into the present with such intensity.

Today, a community-based therapy program called the Common Threads Project draws upon this research and integrates the creation of story cloths into a trauma recovery program designed for survivors of sexual and gender-based violence, trauma, and displacement in conflict-affected areas. The program has served people,

Andean weaver Marcela Salas Calcina works on her loom on a hilltop above Cusco, Peru.

A Navajo wedding basket showing the "weaver's path," or "spirit line," displayed at the Shaped by the Loom *exhibition at the Bard Graduate Center.*

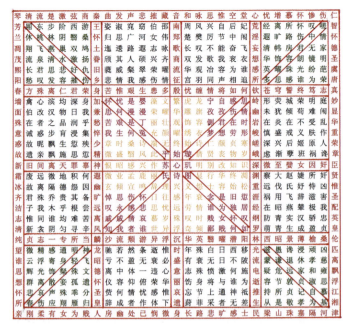

A re-creation of Su Hui's "Star Gauge," a masterful embroidered poem from fourth-century China that can be read horizontally, vertically, and diagonally.

"Pod World: Plastic Fantastic Too," from the Crochet Coral Reef *project by Christine and Margaret Wertheim and the Institute for Figuring, featuring plastic corals by Christine Wertheim and Kathleen Greco. These crocheted hyperbolic structures mimic the natural structure of coral.*

Knitwear designer Flora Collingwood-Norris specializes in visible creative mending, such as this sweater, visibly repaired with floral designs.

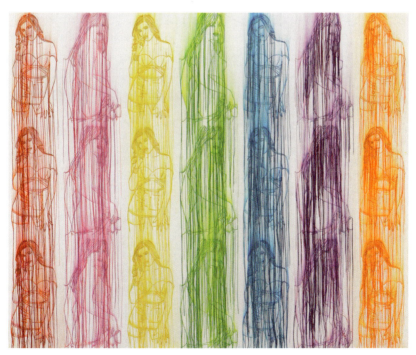

Ghada Amer paints with thread to transform pornographic images of women intended for male consumption into depictions of independent female sexuality, as seen in her work Rainbow Lulu.

Michelle Kingdom's piece The Height of Folly *juxtaposes the delicate work of hand embroidery with themes of political corruption, capitalism, and war.*

This story cloth, titled The Rosebush, *was stitched as part of the trauma recovery program Common Threads Project, in Lago Agrio, Ecuador.*

Holocaust survivor Esther Nisenthal Krinitz began to create embroidered memories later in her life to process her childhood trauma. This piece is titled We Fled Across the Fields.

In 10,000 Stitches with No Goal *(2022), artist Deborah Valoma repeats an Armenian needle lace stitch as a way to connect to generations of Armenian women before her.*

Navajo Germantown Eye-Dazzler blanket circa 1900, from the Shaped by the Loom *exhibition at Bard Graduate Center.*

Artist Mia Hansson is pictured here with her Bayeux Tapestry re-creation.

Three generations of Gee's Bend quilters pictured alongside some of their quilts: (from left) Claudia Pettway Charley, Tinnie Pettway, and Francesca Charley.

A suffrage banner created in 1908 by Mary Lowndes, founder of Artists' Suffrage League, honoring female graduates of Cambridge (who weren't officially awarded degrees until 1948).

Su Richardson, a participant in the Postal Art Event, created this fabric sculpture, Bear It in Mind, *in 1976 to reflect the many roles a mother was expected to fulfill in the home.*

Switch-Over, a graphic embroidery installation by Aheneah on a street in Vila Franca de Xira, Portugal, blends digital and analog elements by using cross stitch to mimic pixels.

Olutosin Oladosu Adebowale's fabric paintings use scraps of Ankara fabrics as part of her ethos of transforming trash into objects of beauty. This painting is a self-portrait.

primarily women either by birth or identification, in Bosnia, Nigeria, the Democratic Republic of Congo, Ecuador, Nepal, as well as refugees at several sites in the United States. Participants in the sewing circle learn and practice a variety of simple embroidery stitches as a self-soothing activity, which regulates the autonomic nervous system—each stitch, a breath as they pull the thread through the fabric. The repetitive rhythmic action of sewing is meditative and calming to the nervous system of a trauma survivor, which is typically on high alert as a survival strategy. Hand sewing serves as a form of self-regulation, grounding participants when they recall painful and overwhelming memories.[33]

Group members are given prompts to help them depict their experiences and memories in the story cloths: "This is what I cannot put into words," "This is a moment I will never forget," "This is what I need you to know." Women begin with images and over time begin to put these experiences into words so that the stories can be processed and reinterpreted.[34] When hands are busy and eye contact is not expected, participants may feel freer to share experiences that evoke feelings of shame. In a way, it replicates the experience of being on a therapy couch with your back to the therapist, as is common in psychoanalytic treatment.

Participants stitch the border of the story cloth first, using this as a metaphor for the containment that is needed for the gradual exploration of such personal stories. Like trauma work, the story cloth happens at a slow pace. It takes time and patience. Each stitch brings the participants a little closer to wholeness. Some feel they can finally cry because the cloth can absorb the tears. As the participants work on sewing their story cloths, they may disclose different elements of their stories, as they are ready, with a partner, a small group, or a facilitator. Making their experience visible and tangible allows others to bear witness as part of the healing process—hearing their stories, acknowledging their pain, and affirming their hopes. Often the experience of one individual resonates with others in the group, reducing the isolation of the trauma and bonding them together.[35] As trauma expert Judith Herman declared, collective trauma merits a collective healing process, where "the solidarity of a group provides the strongest protection against terror and despair, and the strongest antidote to traumatic experience."[36]

As part of the program, a young woman in eastern Democratic Republic of Congo, who we'll call Sylvie, created a story cloth that allowed her to tell her story for the first time. Sylvie was brutally raped and held captive for over a year, during which time she became pregnant and had a child. Sylvie's family and the perpetrator's family tried to force her to marry this man to preserve the family's honor. With amazing courage, she defied them and escaped. In the cloth, you can see the perpetrator and his father chasing Sylvie in their vehicle while her family members stand by on one side of the cloth. Some members of the sewing circle assumed that her figure was sewn in white because she is wearing a wedding dress. Sylvie explained, "I made myself invisible because no one really sees me." The facilitators took the opportunity to explore this feeling with the whole circle, inviting others to share their experiences of feeling invisible. Someone in the group pointed out that Sylvie's mother is stitched without hands or feet, which Sylvie had not realized. Sylvie had felt particularly angry and betrayed by her mother for failing to protect her and pressuring her to marry her rapist. By reflecting on this detail, Sylvie realized that her mother was deprived of agency and held captive, much like she had been. The group said, "Look, you have hands and feet. You ran here with your feet. You used your hands to make this story cloth. You're not going to be like your mother." Sylvie's anger at her mother shifted toward empathy and sadness for her mother's own helplessness and life circumstances. She resolved to chart a different course for herself.[37]

The space a story cloth creates for memories and ideas to be expressed in images rather than words can be especially important for people who have suffered political silencing or have been prevented from speaking the truth due to the shame of social stigma. The intensity of the trauma itself can render one speechless. A Colombian woman in a Common Threads group was trying to process and grieve the rape and murder of her teenage daughter by members of the paramilitary. Fearing for her own life, the mother had fled to Ecuador, where she continued to lack the safety needed to process her trauma and continued to be unable to speak about what had happened to her daughter. When she first entered the sewing circle, she was silent and did not make eye contact. But she did manage to stitch the memory into her story cloth—her daughter's lifeless body lying on the ground surrounded by four men in military dress. She sewed a few dark trees and a starry night sky into the scene. By the end of a few months, she added two bright elements to it. When asked about them by members of the group, she said, "That rosebush is my daughter's soul that goes on blooming. The yellow bird is her voice; I can hear it again." She was finally able to grieve and begin the healing process.[38]

Some women have long felt trapped by the impact of their traumatic experiences, which often remain frozen in time and perpetually reexperienced as a painful traumatic present.[39] By making a story cloth, some feel they have released the story. They can experience freedom in the process of creation, which can be particularly liberating for women whose agency has been denied through interpersonal trauma or severely restricted by cultural norms. A circle member in Bosnia shared, "Even if I was sad and upset, I also felt relief when I finished sewing of some parts. . . . I don't know, like I left it on the canvas. . . . It is still inside of me, but it doesn't control me so much."[40]

The purpose of making a story cloth is not simply to get it "out" but rather to experience and integrate the story in a new way. Making something beautiful out of a horrific event can help transform the pain and create a sense of satisfaction and pride to combat the feelings of helplessness and shame that result from trauma.[41] Symbolizing events and feelings in visual images creates psychological distance from the actual experience—space to think about what happened, make meaning of the traumatic experience, and externalize overwhelming emotions in a less threatening way. Once shameful internal fears and conflicts are made external, they can be shared with others who can connect to them from their own experience and support the emotional processing. By sharing their struggles through these story cloths, the women are no longer alone with the trauma. It can be taken from inside them, through their hand, and into the world.[42]

Similarly, many immigrants to the United States experience trauma during their journey. Textile artist and activist Margarita Cabrera created a community art initiative called Space in Between, in which she holds workshops for female immigrants to the United States from Mexico and Central America. The title is inspired by the Nahuatl Aztec word *nepantla*, which means "the space in the middle." In Cabrera's work, the title references marginalized cultures and their strategies for survival. In these workshops, women embroider their harrowing experiences crossing the US border on fabric from US Border Patrol uniforms. They use the traditional sewing and embroidery techniques from the town of Los Tenangos in Hidalgo, Mexico—colorful narratives reflecting popular culture, traditional rituals, and myths of the Otomi Indigenous communities. Through this process, women tell their stories and share the emotional experiences of their border crossing—the heartbreak of leaving their homes, the struggles along the way, and their hopes for a better future. Their embroidered stories are stitched together to create sculptures of desert plants, reflective of the landscapes they traversed, and symbolizing their fortitude and survival under difficult circumstances. The "plants" are then exhibited in groups, reflecting the shared experience of these female immigrants—a symbol of solidarity for these "desert warriors."

There is a human need to find a home in the world. The Space in Between project allows women to stitch a bridge between worlds—the home they left behind and the new home they are creating. Making and exhibiting this work in a group setting allows the women to engage in genuine dialogue, to see one another with respect, and to acknowledge their experiences, humanity, and dignity. It allows others to bear witness to their immigration experience and personal transformation. Trauma often radically challenges and changes our worldview, which can make us feel like strangers in a strange land, even if we are not immigrants. As Judith Herman writes, "Sharing the traumatic experience with others is a precondition for the restitution of a meaningful world."[43]

Repair and Remembrance

Louise Bourgeois, the iconic multimedia installation artist, spoke of the act of sewing as a process of emotional repair. Her mother enjoyed repairing eighteenth- and nineteenth-century tapestries, and watching her mother work instilled a deep appreciation for the possibility of repair within Bourgeois: "When I was growing up, all the women in my house were using needles. I've always had a fascination with the needle, the magic power of the needle. The needle is used to repair the damage. It's a claim to forgiveness. It is never aggressive, it's not a pin."[44] To repair is to acknowledge and respond to the fragility of our world in a productive way, not by simply throwing our hands up in despair after the damage, but by employing the skills of the mind, hand, and heart to mend an earlier moment in history.[45]

Textile memorials reflect an effort to mend what has been damaged—often an entire community or group of people. Memorial quilts have been made to preserve the memory of lost loved ones, to gift to a friend or family member who is moving away, or to commemorate a mass atrocity.

Like story cloths, they can also be a way of reclaiming narratives and breaking silence. The AIDS quilt is one of the largest textile memorials, spanning 1.3 million square feet and weighing fifty-four tons. Begun in 1987 in San Francisco to commemorate the lost lives of thousands of gay men in the local community, the quilt became a national project that now comprises fifty thousand panels honoring the lives of more than a hundred thousand of the over seven hundred thousand people who have died of AIDS in the United States. It has served as a source of comfort for those who have lost loved ones, a way to grieve the loss of a generation, a tool for raising awareness of HIV and AIDS, and a means of protesting the lack of government action.

Carla Hemlock's sewing commemorated a different social issue. Her powerful memorial quilt *Holding You Tight Until You Are Found* honors the lives of thousands of Kahnawake Mohawk children who were killed in church-operated residential boarding schools in Canada between 1831 and 1997. She includes the line, "The final solution to our Indian problem," an appalling quote from Duncan Campbell Scott, who was the deputy superintendent of the Canadian Department of Indian Affairs from 1913 to 1932. His words expose these deaths as part of the government's effort to eradicate the Indigenous population. Textile works like Hemlock's and the community AIDS quilt break the silence and tell stories that need to be heard, making them visible and tangible so they can be reckoned with personally and collectively.

Memory is a critical aspect of one's self.[46] To retain memory is to retain one's identity—both individually and collectively. At age fifty, Esther Nisenthal Krinitz, who was a child in Poland during World War II, began to memorialize through embroidery her experience surviving the Holocaust.[47] Women's Holocaust survival narratives were less likely to be written after the war than men's and often remain shrouded in silence or told through the lens of a male author.[48] Using textile work in later life to work through childhood trauma was Krinitz's way of telling her story and affirming her identity.

At age fifteen, Krinitz and her thirteen-year-old sister, Mania, stayed behind while the rest of their family and nearly all of the Jews in her village of Mniszek boarded wagons headed for Kraśnik Station, where they were shot upon arrival. As an adult, Krinitz told her two daughters the stories of her childhood and her survival, the good memories and the bad: how she loved Passover and was proud that her mother made the best matzo dough. How her family ran through a field of wildflowers to hide in the woods during a raid of their home by the Gestapo. How, after their family left for Kraśnik Station, she and Mania pretended to be Catholic, changing their names to Juszia and Marisha and speaking only Polish instead of the Yiddish they had spoken in their home.

Though she had already *told* her daughters much about her childhood as they were growing up, Krinitz decided she wanted to *show* them what it was like for her. She didn't know how to draw or paint, but she was very skilled at sewing and embroidery. She remembered exactly what the roof of her childhood home looked like. Taking a piece of thread and a ruler, she drew it out on fabric and then embroidered it, pleased to find that it looked just like the roof she held in her mind. From there she couldn't stop. She captured thirty-six of her memories in embroidery. Each stitch was a kind of remembering, of knowing a moment.

Krinitz's embroidered memories were meant not only to show her daughters what her childhood was like but also to show them who she was. Now, exhibited across the world and published in books, they have become a way for many generations to understand and bear witness to the horrific events of the Holocaust. Her work makes clear psychoanalyst Hans Loewald's idea that an "individual not only has a history which an observer may unravel and describe, but [s]he is history and makes [her] history by virtue of [her] memorial activity in which past-present-future are created as mutually interacting modes of time."[49] Stitching her stories allowed Krinitz to reexperience the past in the present, from the safe distance of her home in Maryland, surrounded by the love and support of her children and grandchildren. By documenting her history, she made a new history for herself, one that lives on in the memories of all who see her work.

Often a single lifespan is not nearly long enough to process our traumas, and they are left to subsequent generations to grapple with. Many who study intergenerational trauma, particularly ones stemming from genocides such as the Holocaust, note that it often takes three generations to stop the transmission of trauma's aftershock. That is the generation when the inherited trauma has become digestible enough to creatively transform it into something new that can be passed down without traumatic reverberations. This is what artist and scholar Deborah Valoma, whose great-grandparents fled Armenia during the Armenian genocide in the early twentieth century, aims to do with her textile project, which focuses on maintaining her family's textile collection and the knowledge of a traditional Armenian lace stitch.

During World War I, 1.5 million Armenians were systematically killed. Survival depended on one's ability to flee. Valoma's great-grandparents escaped and immigrated to the United States. They rarely spoke of their lives in Armenia to their children and grandchildren. Valoma lamented how little is known about their experiences but expressed an understanding of the intensity of the traumas that they must have faced and the difficulty of putting them into words:

> One of the things that apparently happened in the Armenian Death March is that women couldn't manage carrying two or three children and they would make decisions about who to leave on the road. Sometimes grandmothers would stay with the child that was left. So, the trauma gets laced with this possibility or insinuation of culpability that makes it all the more difficult. For me it's been important to acknowledge that the trauma has been more than just loss.[50]

Valoma tried to get as much information as she could about her family history. As her mother began to lose her memory due to cognitive decline, Valoma took out all the family photos, dating back to 1865, and went through them one by one with her mother, writing down everything she said, but there was little to record—her mother had not been told much either. Looking for other sources of information, Valoma found that almost all the official records pregenocide were lost because the churches where the records were kept were destroyed in the war. She was able to find some information from the Turkish census with the help of Armenian genealogists, but the government didn't record women's lives, not even to write their names down. So, she turned to a different source: a collection of one hundred textiles that came from seven different family members who fled Armenia and Turkey during the genocide. Valoma's grandmother had become the repository for the collection, and Valoma inherited that role, which she viewed as both "a burden and a blessing." While the women of her family are invisible in the census, they are ever present in this precious ancestral textile collection:

> When I unpacked this collection it sank me into a history of despair. What touched me so much about it is that they preserved these things. They held onto what they made and the knowledge of how to make it for dear life as a way of holding onto the old country, their heritage, the memories of their family. In my family, they never talked about it. . . . But what I do have is this collection of textiles, so they became documents for me.

The textile collection inspired Valoma to learn Armenian needle lace, a practice that has largely died out over the generations since her great-grandmother learned it as a child in Armenia. Valoma, an expert weaver, knitter, and crocheter, as well as a textile arts professor, noted how difficult this form of lacemaking is—much harder than crochet and knitting. She recalled her grandmother showing her how to do the stitch in her grandparents' kitchen in Fresno, California, when Valoma was eleven years old. Her grandfather, who was a mechanical engineer and a graduate of MIT, walked behind them and very casually said, "I could make a machine to do that faster and better." Valoma was stopped in her tracks by his comment and recalled, "I had a huge surge of rage at the incredible disregard for what my grandmother did and the disregard for the history of women's work and for his own mother and grandmother and the lineage that they brought from Armenia to the diaspora. That flamed me in a kind of way that created a sense of mission to challenge the hierarchies of value that exist in academia and the contemporary art world."

Valoma embarked on a long-term project using this Armenian lace stitch, which she has relearned with the help of two older Armenian women, one in California and one in Massachusetts, who still practice this unique form of needle lace. The project is simply doing the stitch over and over again. There is no stopping point or finished object in mind, just the repetitive motion of the stitch. While the project appears simple, her personal experience of the work is profound:

> Each stitch has almost become like notes in a song, and it's a song I was never taught. . . . The heritage was so diffused by the time it came to me that what I feel like I'm carrying is the language that they spoke, the songs that they sang, the food that they made, and it feels like if I do

a million of these stitches or ten million of these stitches, I will be able to not just hear the song but to sing the song. [The project] is just the process and I can watch my hands and see my grandmother's hands as she made certain movements to make the same stitch, and that's what I'm looking for, just that feeling that I am resurrecting and healing.

Generations are bound by this thread that moves through her hands. The seeming endlessness of the repetition is on the scale of the trauma itself.

Valoma highlighted how appropriate it is that textiles hold this family history for her: "Textiles are inherently about loss. They are the embodiment of loss and so to investigate intergenerational trauma based on loss, textiles are the natural language for that. The very notion of textiles as ephemeral makes it all the more poignant and all the more poetically nuanced to unravel the histories through this ephemeral form." It is often the knowledge of the process, rather than the textiles themselves, that withstands the test of time, handed down intergenerationally. The movements between the threads are temporary but exist in the embodied experience of the maker rather than any finished product. Similarly, the effects of trauma are passed down through interactions between generations and impact us psychologically and even epigenetically. But just as trauma alters us, we can alter it. Textile work can provide both a means and a metaphor for that alteration. We can mend garments that have been passed down by our ancestors to give a repaired piece to the next generation—a new intergenerational narrative that includes the memory of the repair.

CHAPTER 5

The Social Fabric

The people of the Native American Crow Tribe have a myth about a woman's ability to perform a seemingly impossible task. According to legend, a husband demanded that his wife tan a buffalo hide and embroider it with quills in a single day to make a blanket for him. The woman took the buffalo skin to the woods, laid it out, and began to cry because she knew that she could not complete the task in so short a time. Tanning a hide alone takes days or even weeks. A badger came to her and asked why she was crying. Through her tears, she explained the insurmountable challenge. The badger assured her that it could be easily done and ran off to get assistance. She returned with three more female badgers and with four female beavers. These eight spread out the hide and staked it tight. Then female rats, moles, and mice came, along with female ants, bees, and flies. The flies took the flesh from the hide, the bees dried it before the sun was very high, the ants scraped it, and the mice bit off the rough parts to make it smooth. Then the animals removed the stakes and a skunk worked the hide along with the beavers and badgers until it was soft. A porcupine took out its quills and the ants helped the woman with the embroidery until it was decorated with stripes of quill work. When it was finished, the animals rolled up the blanket and sent the woman home with it along with a warning that her husband meant to kill her. They had already devised a plan to prevent her death and gave her detailed instructions on how to survive—a truly lifesaving team of female helpers.[1]

This tale is a beautiful portrayal of the necessity and rewards of female solidarity. It also highlights the cooperation among Native American women of the Great Plains when faced with a challenging artistic task. The tanning and dressing of hides and their ornamentation with quillwork and beadwork were undertaken as a sacred endeavor within the realm of women's artistic societies.[2] It was a way for women to work together, support each other, and carry on cultural traditions.

WORKING TOGETHER

Textile production created opportunities for women to make new connections, collaborate, and bond over their work. Historically, the sexual division of labor was not a source of isolation, as it later became under capitalism, where the family unit is central. Rather, it brought women together in communal labor. In patriarchal societies that seek to divide women and often remove women from their families of origin through marriage, joining forces gave women a sense of solidarity and a greater voice in their communities. Cooperation in textile production has long been a source of power and protection for women.[3]

In *Women's Work*, archaeologist and textile scholar Elizabeth

Wayland Barber describes the "courtyard and outrider" economy of the Neolithic and Early Bronze ages of at least four thousand years ago, where women gathered in the communal courtyard area to work on craft projects—spinning, weaving, pottery—while the children played. Producing textiles became central to socialization, particularly in the winter months when there was little else to do. Barber notes that Neolithic textiles are remarkably ornate—multiple colors are used to weave patterns, and beads and embroidery are used to adorn the cloth. She surmises that the fun that was had spinning and weaving together may help explain the tendency to embellish fabric and make things that were not purely utilitarian.[4] The extra time spent making something beautiful allowed extra time to be with friends—learning from each other, inspiring each other, and joining their efforts and materials.

In more recent times, women in northern Europe from at least the eighteenth century on gathered for "spinning bees," communal events that allowed women to keep each other company and share materials while they spun yarn.[5] During the dark days of winter, spinning bees also allowed women to share the light and warmth of a fire rather than expending those resources individually to work in their own homes. Quilts were often made in collaboration, with a number of women making blocks that were then sewn together. Quilting bees allowed women to complete the tedious work of stitching the layers together. Because of the communal effort, it was important that every woman who stitched on a quilt was an expert with the needle, so that no one was disappointed that the quilt they had spent months or years piecing was spoiled by poor top stitching. Poorly developed sewing skills meant being left out of important social gatherings.[6] In Shetland, the communal aspect of textile work is an important part of the culture, with women knitting together at social functions. Fair Isle knitter Hazel Tindall recalls her mother saying "tuck your sock," which meant take your knitting, when they would go to a party and the women would knit the whole night.[7] Creating cloth provided a social outlet and shaped the time women spent together while working toward an economically beneficial craft.

A study of over three thousand knitters found that knitting in a group significantly impacted their perceived happiness and improved social contact and communication with others.[8] Making things together, whether collaboratively or just in the company of others, eases social interaction. When the brain is occupied with a background task, conversations become easier, deeper, and more intimate because people are less self-conscious.[9] A shared interest creates a sense of immediate belonging and provides a natural topic of conversation. Knitting groups can help develop people's social skills and increase their confidence, which can then lead to improved interpersonal interactions outside of knitting circles. Writer and knitter Ann Hood learned a lot from her experiences in knitting groups:

> By now I have gone to many, many knitting circles. And I realize that because of them, I actually do better in all kinds of groups. I have learned to listen, even to the person who can't stop talking about her knitting, her vacation, her husband. I have learned to respect people who are really different from me: younger or older; politically; socioeconomically; in every possible way. . . . And I have learned that I don't always have something to say, or something to add to a group. That sometimes, I just want

the company of other people. I just want to sit in a circle and knit. By doing this, maybe I am learning how to be a group person after all.[10]

When you're making something in a group, it is perfectly acceptable to work quietly if you feel shy or are not in the mood to make conversation. Psychoanalyst Jessica Benjamin writes that the ability to disengage is a necessary condition of freely engaging and is the basis of mutuality in relationships.[11] Without another activity to focus on, people often feel compelled to keep a conversation going, which may make the interaction feel forced or keep people from beginning a conversation at all. Many people who attend knitting groups tend to work on simpler or more tedious aspects of projects so they can devote more mental energy to conversing and because the rote aspects of textile work are made more enjoyable by the company of others. In fact, knitting group members cite attending group more for the sense of belonging and social interaction than for the knitting process or technical support.[12]

Collaboration in the creation of textiles enables conversations between women that, like quilts, end up as something greater than the sum of their parts. William S. Burroughs and Brion Gysin, prominent artists of the Beat Generation, wrote about the concept of a "third mind" that represents the added possibility that arises when two minds come together—the "unseen collaborator" that exists only in the meeting of two minds in creative collaboration: "Two subjectivities that metamorphose into a third; it is from this collusion that a new author emerges, an absent third person, invisible and beyond grasp."[13] Likewise, a quilt created by many hands sharing resources is beyond what any individual could create alone.

The act of quilting in a group allows women to share their stories and their fabric pieces, transforming both. What emerges is not only a quilt but a memorable experience. A quilt is also in dialogue with the viewer—another sort of third mind—who creates their own meaning from the object.

Burroughs and Gysin collaborated using what they called "the cut-up technique," which involved taking existing pieces of text, cutting up the pages, and rearranging the pieces to form new narratives. They explain, "The cut-up method brings to writers the collage, which has been used by painters for fifty years. And used by the moving and still camera."[14] The authors mention nothing of quilts, which of course preceded cameras and the collage method in modern visual arts, for which Picasso and Braque tend to be given credit. Yet quilts are undoubtedly a form of this "cut-up" method, and the narratives created by them similarly depend on the arrangement of the pieces. In 1977, Canadian multimedia artist Miriam Schapiro and American painter Melissa Meyer coined the term *femmage* to describe women's long-standing practice of saving and assembling the scraps of daily life in unique and interesting ways, such as in quilting, scrapbooking, paper cutting, and beading—transforming collected materials into something decorative and functional. They stressed its importance as a predominantly female artistic expression that created a "secret language" among women through the symbolism of the materials and their juxtaposition.[15]

At the second annual Gee's Bend Airing of the Quilts Festival in rural Alabama, I met with quilter Marlene Bennett Jones, who sat surrounded by her quilts hanging on clotheslines in the sun, to learn more about how quilting had fostered a sense of community for her. The festival celebrates the heritage of quilting in Gee's Bend, a rural community financially impoverished by a long history of slavery and disenfranchisement that has become renowned for the quilts women made from the little they had available to them. The women of Gee's Bend have quilted for generations, beginning during slavery as a survival strategy as well as a powerful expression of creativity and agency. The festival began at the Freedom Quilting Bee Legacy museum in the Martin Luther King Jr. Memorial Sewing Center, built in 1969 by the Freedom Quilting Bee (more on that in chapter 6). For the next ten miles along County Route 29, colorful quilts lined the road—hung on fences, clotheslines, and front porches—culminating at the fairground with booths brimming with patchwork, old and new.

In my interview with Bennett Jones a few days after the bustle of the festival, she described how she saw the pieces of a quilt like a dialogue between people. The quilt pieces "have to communicate; if they can't communicate that means that they can't go together. This is how I do my quilts now. I look at the pieces to see who can get along with who and make sure there are no bad neighbors or anything. . . . You can't maybe even explain why those pieces go together—you just see it, it feels right together."[16]

She sees similarities between the process of piecing a quilt together and the connections between people that it can foster. Speaking about the festival, where we had met that weekend, she noted: "It's people from all over the world talking, laughing—well, these quilts brought people together. And people travel all over the world chasing quilts and once you meet someone and get to talking . . . you're connecting with them [like] the quilt pieces are connecting and talking to each other, that's what it's all about."

The festival had over two thousand attendees, many of whom traveled from other states and even other countries to see the work of over sixty Gee's Bend quilters. Some quilts were on display as historical documents, and others were up for sale. I overheard attendees at the festival marveling at the designs and use of color as well as noting technical details of the work, such as whether the quilts had mitered corners or were pieced by hand or by machine. Some attendees stitched on the open lawn while church choirs sang on the stage; others took classes from Gee's Bend quilters in tents, learning to piece a block by hand while talking and laughing with strangers who felt like friends in this shared endeavor. Bennett Jones was right—quilting brings people together and demonstrates the potential for what can be created through joining people and materials. Notably, Black and white women sometimes quilted together in the South in the early part of the twentieth century, even when everything else was segregated.[17]

Other forms of textile making also have the potential to bring diverse groups of people together in meaningful ways. Weaver and scholar Lilly Marsh shared how she has created community around weaving by connecting relatively distinct groups in the fiber world to enrich her community through its variety. Marsh is a founding member of the Hudson Valley Textile Project in New York State, which aims to support environmentally responsible and economically sustainable farm-to-fabric supply chains in the region, creating a network of people involved in all aspects of textile production. Working together across a supply chain expands and integrates communities, connecting people from different walks of life. Marsh, like many other members of the project, participates in the full sequence of local textile production. She helps local farmers birth lambs and shear wool and then coordinates with a local fiber mill to spin it into yarn, which she dyes and weaves into items such as blankets, table runners, and scarves for farms to sell.

Her engagement in all of these aspects of making and selling cloth allows her to bring together people who often don't know each other because these jobs have become specialized and siloed. She said: "Weaving suffers from incredible classism—the guild structures embed older, wealthy, white women in socially and culturally powerful positions. By focusing not on the . . . community of weavers but instead on the . . . community that runs from fiber source to finished product, I'm able to be part of the lives of farmers, processors, workers, artisans, designers, shopkeepers, and consumers that are much more diverse." She added that this community "is not immune from the structural racism and classism of the general society, but it is a place in which individual expression, and the individual voice, can still be heard . . . perhaps because it is still a rather invisible community hiding in plain sight of the world."[18] If you're not a fiber person, you may not know about the many sheep and wool festivals, knitting and sewing circles, lace and weaving guilds all around the world, and you may not understand what this work means to the people who do it.

Handcrafters seek community around their craft and connect with other crafters to discuss aspects of their craft that others might not understand. A fellow knitter will notice that you've used three colors in rows of stranded knitting (more difficult than two colors because we only have two hands) or that your lace shawl has a particularly intricate pattern that requires lacework on both the right and wrong side of the knitting (rather than just on the right side and purling back on the wrong side). Someone who doesn't knit may not pick up on those process details even if they marvel at the overall product. Hazel Tindall remembers Shetland women gathering at weddings and other social events to admire the lace knit cardigans and shawls that they wore for more formal occasions. But more than admiring these garments, they were studying them closely to see what lacework patterns had been used.[19] They were aware of both the technical and aesthetic aspects of the work.

While women have historically worked together to make textiles, there were times when they became more isolated. Knitting circles and quilting bees fell out of favor in many Western communities, especially among younger urban women, in the latter half of the twentieth century. Desiring community and wanting to show that knitting can be a powerful act of feminism, Debbie Stoller started a Stitch 'n Bitch group in New York City's East Village in 1999, open to anyone who wanted to knit or learn to knit. The phrase "Stitch and Bitch" dates back to the 1940s in the United States during World War II to describe organized gatherings of women who would knit for the war effort and talk about everything from parenting to politics, often providing support for each other while their husbands were overseas.[20] Stoller's group was not so different—they talked about current events, human rights, and of course their knitting projects—though knitting in a trendy Manhattan coffeehouse seemed anachronistic to many observers who couldn't help but make comments about their grandmas or just appeared confused by their hobby. Stoller says, "I might as well have been churning butter on the crosstown bus."[21] She was intent on normalizing this activity and expanding the associations people had to knitting. In 2000, she wrote about her knitting groups in the feminist publication *BUST* magazine, and Stitch 'n Bitch groups began forming in cities all over the world. It was a means of reclaiming women's domestic and artistic work in feminist circles and building a community of like-minded people— women and men who found satisfaction, pleasure, and connection through this craft.

While there are now thousands of Stitch 'n Bitch groups all over the world, many textile crafters can also find community online. Technology allows what was historically a relatively local practice to be shared in an international community through social platforms like Ravelry, an online knitting community that has nearly nine million members. On the site, you can search an extensive crochet and knitting pattern database, find local knitting groups, connect with people who love the same knitwear designer or yarn dyer, and join knit-a-longs (KALs) to share photos of your progress with others making the same design. Arachne, another social and technical platform, is specifically dedicated to lacemaking. And, of course, Instagram and TikTok are used by artists and crafters of all sorts, facilitating connections between people within subgenres of art forms, exposing people to new media and techniques, and providing quick how-to videos that make the skills accessible.

A more recent online platform, Knit.Club, was started by American knitwear designer Lindsay Degen after she struggled to find community during the COVID pandemic. Geared primarily toward knitters from ages eighteen to thirty-five, Knit.Club seeks to create a safe space for queer and BIPOC knitters and provide the sense of connection that Degen craved. The platform facilitates online and in-person meetups, knit-a-longs, and tutorials. She shared that she recently had a member of Knit.Club pick her up at the airport when she traveled to another city, highlighting the strength of relationships she has formed on the site: "Knit.Club just feels like genuine connections, friendships you might not have had, people to talk to that you didn't have to talk to before. I have really wonderful friendships in real life but most of them don't knit so I can't share a part of myself."[22] What we make reflects and shapes who we are, and being able to share that with others is a meaningful part of our identity as social beings. It is no wonder that woven fabric, webs, and nets are so often metaphors for sociocultural relationships. Cloth is connective tissue.

The Ties That Bind

British textile artist Angela Maddock created a project called Bloodline with her mother, in which they each knit one end of the same twelve-stitch-wide band of blood-red knitting at the same time. She says that the piece documents their continued attachment despite living at a distance—"as we knit, we move further apart and yet remain connected."[23] It was difficult to knit together just after the stitches were cast on because their bodies were so close that it was uncomfortable for a mother and adult daughter. There was relief in the distance that was created as the piece grew, as when a child grows and separates from the parent. Maddock imagined that as the cord grew, they would sit farther apart, but noted that they often ended up near each other with the pile of red knitting coiled between them.

Maddock explains: "The knitting of this wobbly, imperfect red line is a potentiate language, a reflective/reflexive process, a kind of 'thinking through practice,' but it is also the manifestation of a continuing bond between mother and daughter, a knitted thing, a gift from one to the other, and a sign of relatedness."[24] This language of knitting that she shares with her mother is one that, to Maddock, defies symbolic meaning—it is not just a substitute for words but rather a way of communicating that transcends words. She likens this to the preverbal connection between a mother (or any caregiver) and a child. It is a language that is embodied; the unspoken feelings conveyed through the holding of the child, whether gentle or rough, loving or frustrated, are recreated in the process of knitting this connecting tie between her and her mother.

Maddock writes that the enduring feelings of loss and grief over her brother's murder as a teenager are present between her and her mother when they knit: "I am tethered to her whenever we knit, a grown woman tied to her mother . . . this tether exists as an empathic connection, a continuing bond of suffering shared and understood."[25] Implied in Bloodline is also the inevitable loss of their relationship one day—"our knitting is an expression of attachment that contains within it the promise of loss, it will end when one of us is finished."[26] Yet, the long red strand of knitting that they have created will remain as a physical manifestation of their relationship—a relationship that, like the knitted cord, is cocreated through the mutual investment of time and energy.

Bringing threads together into fabric, whether by weaving, crocheting, twisting, or knitting, is a form of bonding. Cloth naturally evokes ideas of connectedness or tying. It unites people in marriage in the Celtic handfasting practice. It has been used to bind agreements between people when exchanged and to legitimize power through its accumulation. At the same time, it suggests the fragility of social and political relationships, such as the untying of spirits from the world of the living after death in the Andean funerary khipu. Cloth is not permanent, nor are relationships or the agreements between people that cloth is used to sanctify.

As these many metaphors for social bonds suggest, the practice of making textiles is often a way of forging relationships and creating a connection between people. In *The Subversive Stitch*, Rozsika Parker explores the role of embroidery in socializing girls into female-gendered traits beginning in early childhood. She writes:

"Embroiderers that I interviewed all admitted that embroidery had provided a means of gaining affirmation and attention from the adult world. . . . To embroider announced to adults that she was good and feminine, not naughty and masculine. This path to adult approval and conformity appealed because it provided a way of gaining needed love and attention."[27] Thus, we will do what is expected of us, to the extent that it is tolerable, for the sense of belonging and attachment to others that is so fundamental to human survival. Demonstrating skill in embroidery, spinning, knitting, or weaving has been a way for girls in many different cultural and historical contexts to gain approval and security in relationships. Because of their utility, economic value, or associations with desired traits, such skills could make caregivers proud, provide status in a community, and even improve marital opportunities, creating bonds that secured a woman's place in the social landscape.

Often, grandmothers and mothers passed down skills in textile craft, creating an intergenerational link through this work. The physical connection when teaching a textile craft reflects the intimacy of sharing these skills: as a teacher puts her hands on the student's hands to guide the movement of the needle or demonstrate how to hold the yarn, her arms wrap around the learner's body in a sort of embrace. Some people I interviewed remembered that the practice of learning a textile craft was a time that they felt closest to an otherwise distant caregiver. Yet some touches are not as gentle— many weavers in Peru recalled having their knuckles rapped by their mother or grandmother when they made a mistake.

In many cases, the learning process is a gift for both the teacher and the student. The teacher can experience a sense of purpose and continuity in transmitting a skill, and the student can acquire knowledge while feeling a personal connection to her family and ancestors through her work. A project in Lisbon, Portugal, called *A Avó Veio Trabalhar*, which translates to "Grandma Came to Work," recognizes the benefits of this intergenerational transmission. Women ages sixty years and over teach fiber crafts such as embroidery and knitting to younger generations interested in learning these crafts. Portuguese knitting designer and historian Rosa Pomar explained that the generational gap in learning how to knit and sew is largely due to a feminist revolt against these practices in her mother's generation. But among young Portuguese women, there has been a resurgence of interest in learning these skills, now that they are further removed from the compulsory gender-based connotations that once were held.[28] Rather than rejecting textile crafts like their mothers did, many young women are eager to learn, and it is their grandmothers' generation that has the skills. The founders of *A Avó Veio Trabalhar* aim to help older people maintain a connection to their community after retiring, which so often removes them from the social networks of the workplace and a sense of purpose in the world. The opportunity to teach younger generations knitting, embroidery, and crochet helps these women recognize their unique talents, engage in generative and creative work, and have a positive impact on their community by contributing something of value to future generations.

As students, we always remember who taught us the skills that we use and value. Juana Huaman Willca, who lives in a remote village at nearly fourteen thousand feet elevation on the Lares Pass in Peru's Sacred Valley, still thinks of her mother and grandmother as she weaves, even though she has not seen them since she married and moved away from home eighteen years ago. She feels their skills, and those of countless generations of Incan women before her, move through her hands across the loom. She smiled as she talked about her love of weaving and how she weaves happiness into each textile to wrap her eight children in her joy. Her sense of connection to her ancestors adds to her happiness. With her children playing around the loom and her other family members in mind as she weaves, everyone is together.[29]

Often, even when we work by ourselves, we are never really alone. Through the process of making textiles, we can be connected with people who are at a great distance or even those who have died. Gee's Bend quilter Marlene Bennett Jones was accustomed to spending Christmas in Alabama with several of her fourteen siblings. The year she turned sixty-five, she opted to stay home. A sister called her on Christmas morning and asked what she was doing. She replied, "I'm sitting in the middle of the floor talking to my mother and father."[30] Bennett Jones laughed recounting this story as she imagined her sister calling their other siblings to tell them, "Marlene done lost her mind." She explained that her mother, who had taught her to quilt, died ten years earlier, and her father had passed the following year. Bennett Jones had cleaned out their house and taken all of their clothes home with her. That Christmas Day, she was sitting on the floor surrounded by fifteen garbage bags of her parents' clothes, cutting pieces and sewing. She made twenty-one quilts out of the clothing and gave one to each of her siblings. She kept the rest so she could feel close to her parents.

Avid knitters Masey Kaplan and Jen Simonic would often be asked by friends to finish knitting projects left undone by deceased loved ones. As the requests increased, they realized that not everyone knows willing and enthusiastic knitters who are able to finish these meaningful pieces. Together, Kaplan and Simonic created a nonprofit organization called Loose Ends based in their respective cities of Portland, Maine, and Seattle, Washington, where they act as matchmakers—or, as they say, they K2Tog (knit two together)—by connecting nearby volunteers who have the necessary needlecraft skills to people with projects in need of completion. The "finisher" is essentially working together with someone who has died or become disabled, tying up the loose ends of their projects. In addition to a finished project, a relationship is created between the finisher and the family of the deceased or the person who started the project and is unable to finish it. "The most fulfilling thing for me, so far, has been watching strangers take care of each other," said Kaplan.[31]

Donna Savastio, of Framingham, Massachusetts, started a rug for her sister and had invested over one hundred hours into the project. As her Alzheimer's progressed, she was unable to keep working on it. Her husband contacted Loose Ends about the rug, and one morning, a volunteer named Jan Rohwetter showed up to collect the project. Rohwetter had recently lost her mom, who had also suffered from dementia. "This is something that I would have loved to be able to do for my mom," she said. "That is why I'm here."[32] Rohwetter finished the rug, marking where Savastio's work ended with loops from the tassels of a scarf that had special meaning to Savastio. "Every loop was with love and thinking of you and my mom," said Rohwetter.[33] Savastio decided to hold onto the rug for just a little while to enjoy it before delivering it to her sister as planned. Simonic said, "What makes our lives worth living is knowing people loved and cared for and appreciated us, and what better use of someone's time than to make something that demonstrates that love? That's what we do."[34]

Within a year of starting Loose Ends, twenty-six thousand people from over sixty different countries have volunteered to be finishers, and twenty-five hundred projects are in progress or have been completed. A Chinese proverb says, "An invisible red thread connects those who are destined to meet, regardless of time, place, or circumstance. The thread may stretch or tangle, but it will never break." Textile crafts bring people together who may not have met otherwise and bind them through the shared process of learning and creating and bringing one another comfort and joy.

A CULTURAL THREAD

Archaeologist Elizabeth Wayland Barber writes, "Human cultures have over time built a sort of language through clothing, allowing us to communicate even with our mouths shut."[35] Cloth as a "social skin" transforms us into social beings and communicates who we are and where we belong.[36] Fabric marks the body with social text in a language that everyone in the society speaks. For the Dogon of Africa, "to be naked is to be speechless."[37] Their *bogolanfini*, or mudcloth, awash with resist-dyed geometric symbols, marks an essential element of their cultural identity. As the creators of cloth, women have participated in the creation of social and cultural identity for millennia. Cultural memory is a form of collective memory embodied in texts, rites, monuments, celebrations, and other objects that serve as reminders of important events and their meanings. Textiles are carriers of cultural memory, so much so that when the Spanish conquered the Incan Empire in the mid-sixteenth century, the Incans offered them gold and silver but hid or even destroyed their textiles so that these precious objects did not fall into the wrong hands.

When ways of life are threatened, textile traditions become especially important as carriers of cultural information. During the reservation period for Native Americans in the Great Plains at the end of the nineteenth century, Indigenous women's beadwork became increasingly extravagant, covering the entire dress and even the soles of moccasins. With many of their freedoms curtailed by the shift away from a nomadic lifestyle, women had more time for artistry, and what they created was even more valuable for maintaining cultural meaning when many other traditional aspects of life were no longer possible.[38]

Textile practices reflect the evolution of culture as new circumstances, such as migration, colonization, and technological advances, interact with traditional practices. Navajo cloth now commonly incorporates blue and red thread, but these colors are cultural adaptations made through contact with Western settlers. The Spanish introduced indigo dyes during their colonization of Mesoamerica in the seventeenth century. Their use traveled along the Santa Fe Trail, running from Mexico City to Santa Fe, New Mexico, and quickly replaced the Navajo dyes of blue clay and sumac, which did not result in the same depth of color and permanence as indigo. In the early nineteenth century, machine-woven red woolen cloth from England and Spain made its way into Navajo communities, perhaps initially from discarded uniforms of Spanish soldiers and later as an imported trade cloth.[39] It was used by the Spanish for garment insulation, but Navajo women took a different approach and unraveled the cloth, sometimes even recarding and spinning the threads, to incorporate this red yarn, called bayeta, into their traditional woven blankets. This creative incorporation of European materials occurred during the displacement and enslavement of the Navajo people. Beginning in the 1820s, Spanish colonizers in Mexico were trying to gain control over Navajo lands. They often captured and enslaved Navajo weavers, selling their textiles for their own economic gain.

In the 1860s, the United States mounted a "scorched-earth campaign" to destroy the Navajo way of life by forcing them onto reservations. As part of the campaign, the military destroyed the Navajo's vast herds of Churro sheep. Beginning in 1868, before new sheep breeds were ultimately reintroduced to the Navajo reservations, mill-spun, aniline-dyed yarns from Germantown, Pennsylvania, were given to the Navajo—over seventy-two thousand pounds during the remaining part of the nineteenth century.[40] Often called the "Eye-Dazzler" period, the color palette of their woven textiles changed drastically during this time and inspired new weaving designs. Navajo women's textiles also began to incorporate new images, like trains and guns, into their usual iconography.[41] It was also during this period that selling blankets to tourists became an important source of income for the Navajo living on reservations. Choctaw/Chickasaw scholar heather ahtone wrote, "Change is part of survival and, for Native women, change has meant a delicate balance between maintaining order and allowing for fluidity through artistic creation. We invigorate our customary practices by introducing new materials, allowing our designs, which often have specific cultural references, to shift and breathe. Change is powerful."[42]

This mixture of cultural, temporal, and creative adaptation is evident in women's textile work all over the world. Art historian Janet Catherine Berlo describes modern Latin American textile traditions as a form of bricolage, a term used to describe the skill of using materials at hand to make something new.[43] Combining local, imported, natural, and synthetic materials and using both traditional and foreign cultural iconography, Latin American women (and women in many other parts of the world) transform odds and ends into useful garments, household items, and works of art. Much more than a passive, defensive response to centuries of colonization, the adaptions and appropriations are deliberate and sometimes subversive, making these women "active agents of culture."[44]

Among the Guna women in Panama, many modern molas, panels used to make women's blouses, merge nontraditional imagery and materials with the styles and techniques that have been used for centuries. Molas are made using a reverse appliqué technique where multiple layers of fabric are sewn together and then cut away in shapes to reveal the colors in the layers of fabric beneath. Embroidered details are added as well. While grounded in traditional textile practices, modern molas ultimately reflect the contemporary culture and personal world of the women making them. One mola blouse, made by a Guna woman in Panama in the mid-twentieth century, depicts the label of a box of Parrot Safety Matches with "Made in Sweden" embroidered as part of the label. Merging a modern commercial design with this otherwise traditional garment and integrating cross-cultural influences is an excellent representation of bricolage.[45] It speaks to the creativity of the woman who had the idea to use this image in her textile work and also reflects the evolution of culture—how new processes, materials, and images are incorporated into traditional forms.

STITCHING HISTORY

In *Weaving the Word*, Kathryn Sullivan Kruger, a professor of English, examines the link between written texts and woven textiles. Kruger asserts that before stories were recorded through written text, cloth preserved and communicated these important social messages. Kruger argues for expanding the idea of literary history to include women's role in transmitting traditions, stories, and myths via fabric. By including textiles in our study of literature and history, we will find many female authors.[46] She also maintains that during times when weaving was analogous to storytelling, "women's endeavors were equal to culture and were not considered beneath culture or marginal to it," as we saw with the Guna *congresos*, where women making molas and men discussing sociopolitical issues were both seen as contributing to the evolution and transmission of ideas and traditions.[47] Cloth tells stories, records histories, and shapes culture in a synergistic interaction that makes it impossible to disentangle the effect of one on the other.

The Bayeux Tapestry, an eleventh-century embroidered account of the Norman conquest of England in 1066 by William the Conqueror, is a clear example of textiles as historical texts. While the events of this epic battle are enshrined in woolen thread on linen, no one knows who stitched it. An eighteenth-century legend has it that Queen Matilda, William the Conqueror's wife, carried out the embroidery with her ladies in waiting. While a romantic notion, this was certainly not the case. Most scholars believe that a group of Anglo-Saxon embroiderers stitched it near Canterbury, England.[48] All the surviving evidence indicates that only women in early medieval England embroidered and that it was a highly regarded female occupation.[49] However, there is no known convention of women embroidering on such a large scale—the tapestry is seventy meters long—or for such an important political purpose (though female embroiderers certainly took commissions from kings, such as Mabel of Bury St. Edmunds, as discussed in chapter 3). This has led some to speculate that perhaps it was not the work of women, and Bayeux Tapestry Museum curator Antoine Verney has suggested that men could have been trained in embroidery to execute this important royal commission, potentially in Normandy, since the tapestry resided in the Bayeux Cathedral for centuries.[50]

Textile archaeologist Alexandra Lester-Makin, an expert in early medieval embroidery and the Bayeux Tapestry, disputes this idea, noting that the needlework on the tapestry is highly skilled. She thinks it unlikely that it was the work of a team who had just recently learned to embroider.[51] There is evidence of female embroidery workshops in England in the eleventh century, indicating the likelihood that the tapestry was created by women.[52] A skilled embroiderer would have organized and overseen the production process to maintain consistency and coordinate the many embroiderers working on the piece at the same time.[53] Many women's hands would have also been involved in spinning and weaving the linen and spinning and dyeing the wool embroidery thread. Notably, the style of embroidery used on the tapestry is meant to conserve thread, likely due to a firsthand awareness of how very labor intensive it is to produce from having spun wool themselves. The thread wraps around the back of the work only in short couching stitches, so the majority of the wool is laid down in long stitches on just the front surface of the work. This style of embroidery is a relatively quick way to fill in large spaces, much like painting, and evokes the brush strokes of illuminated manuscripts.

The women doing the embroidery work may have had some creative license over the messages that were communicated and immortalized in the tapestry. Some experts on the tapestry suggest that while the main story running horizontally across the center was dictated and likely sketched by men to record the details of the conquest, the borders were left to the discretion of the embroiderers, who included animals—often dragons, lions, and griffins—and scenes from Aesop's fables alluding to ideals of medieval morality.[54] Certain fables are embroidered more than once, like "The Fox and the Crow" and "The Wolf and the Crane." They are drawn differently and appear to be embroidered by different hands, suggesting that each embroiderer was likely unaware that another had chosen to stitch the same image or scene.[55] The fables in the borders can be read as commentary on the main action of the tapestry—perhaps a way for the Anglo-Saxons to tell their version of the story in the margins of the Norman tale.

Lester-Makin expressed that as much as she would like to believe this was the case, she is not sure that women would have been given such freedom over the border content.[56] However, that doesn't mean that their experiences and perspectives were not included. "I think that even if they didn't necessarily have free reign, there are still areas of expression that can be witnessed. This is a witness to what they have gone through or know that somebody went through . . . there are other ways . . . to read the tapestry and of seeing the embroiderers within it." She called attention to a scene where an Anglo-Saxon woman is holding a child's hand as Norman soldiers set fire to her home. "Whether that was chosen freely by the embroiderers or not, that is still a commentary and if you think of women embroidering that, and you never know what they may have witnessed or had done to them. That's a harrowing scene." Similarly, the borders show the bodies of dead Anglo-Saxon soldiers having their armor pulled off or being devoured by animals. "That kind of thing happened and . . . you can imagine someone stitching that and going, 'oh my god, that happened to my brother, my cousin, my dad, my husband.' " Whether or not the women chose any of the tapestry's content, they stitched it, and prior to that, they may have lived it. The tapestry is a testament to their experience preserved in a language they spoke.

In our interview at the Bayeux Tapestry Museum, Verney stated that the genius of the tapestry was that it was the first known graphic representation of a current event in northern Europe, adding that if it was not captured in this object, the history may be lost today. He said that the technique of embroidering wool yarn on linen cloth was likely chosen because it was a relatively quick method and made it easy to share the story of the event on both sides of the English Channel to a largely illiterate public. It may have also served a political purpose. It was a way to integrate the Anglo-Saxon tradition of needlework into the story of the Norman conquest of England and assure the English that their traditions were valued and would be preserved under this new rule.

French historian R. Howard Bloch calls the embroidery of the Bayeux Tapestry "a powerful vehicle for cultural memory at a time when even the most powerful lords were illiterate."[57] Janet Catherine Berlo wrote in response to Bloch's statement, "I position it as 'a powerful vehicle for cultural memory' of a different sort—a cultural memory for those of us who seek to understand the long history of the poetics of embroidery, and our places in it."[58] It is clear which history was thought valuable to preserve at the time—the content of the tapestry—and which was not—the process of its creation. Women looking to find their place in the "long history of the poetics of embroidery" often discover that it is a game of hide and seek. Even when the work remains, the hands that made it are so often invisible. Like so many stories of women throughout history, the creation story of the Bayeux Tapestry seems indelibly lost.

Still, much can be learned about the sociocultural role of women's textile work by following the many threads of the Bayeux Tapestry. Whether the embroiderers of the original tapestry were men or women, had any creative control or not, the Bayeux Tapestry has inspired several re-creation projects that have been produced by women and have sociocultural importance for preserving history and evolving our understanding of it.

Eight hundred years after the original Bayeux Tapestry was finished, a group of women in Victorian England created a full-scale replica of it, now on display at Britain's Reading Museum. The effort was spearheaded by Elizabeth Wardle, who in 1885 organized thirty-nine members of the Leek Embroidery Society so that Britain could have its own copy of this important historic artifact. It took just one year for the women to re-create the entire tapestry, working from pictures that had been hand-colored by archivists at what is now the Victoria and Albert Museum in London. It seems that these women were working to find their own place in embroidery history grounded in the Victorian-era "medieval revival," which spurred a renaissance of medieval art and architecture. Their focused effort reflects an interest in their British heritage, the tradition of English needlework, and a wish to meaningfully contribute to those legacies. Unlike the anonymous stitchers of the original tapestry, these women added their names below the sections they worked on, escaping the obscurity of their medieval counterparts. Their signatures show that some women worked alone for long stretches of the tapestry, while others worked closely together on a section. Seeing three women's names running the length of a four-foot section, we can imagine them huddled together talking and stitching.

Another difference between the Victorian re-creation and the original tapestry reflects the cultural mores of the time. In the original tapestry, there are several naked men, and male horses are depicted with anatomical accuracy. The Leek embroiderers omitted these "racy" details, though through no fault of their own. The men working in the museum archives felt it was improper to send such images to a group of British ladies. They "cleaned up" the photos that the women then faithfully copied.

More recently, a community project on the island of Alderney, in the British Channel, took inspiration from the tapestry but had a different aim: to finish it. The last panel of the original work is famously missing, its story lost to time. Historically, what naturally follows the Battle of Hastings, where the tapestry currently ends, is the coronation of William the Conqueror as William I of England. Kate Russell, the librarian on Alderney, spearheaded the project and together with artist Pauline Black imagined the ending and created the plan for the tapestry in 2012. Four hundred and sixteen people ranging in age from four to one hundred contributed stitches to the final piece. Along with a large contingent of Alderney islanders and notably King Charles III, then Prince of Wales, stitchers came from nearly every continent of the world. Russell told me not a day went by that there wasn't at least one person stitching while the library was open and often several people working together: "During that entire year, there was never any rancor, tension, disagreement, squabbling or any other sort of discord. Lots of stitching; no bitching. I imagine it must have been similar for the original stitchers, too, though the trauma they were living through in that torn-up country that England had become must have meant an entirely different atmosphere."[59]

Russell noted that there is not much to do on the island given its small size (just three miles long and a mile and a half wide) and relative isolation as the northernmost inhabited island in the English Channel, so it was particularly meaningful for the community to have an activity that brought people together.[60] When they finished the panel, one year from beginning it, she said that people on the island begged her to start another project, though Russell has not thought of another project that could so captivate the community. Fran Harvey, a local resident and principal stitcher, said: "England was never the same after the Norman invasion. And I don't think Alderney, as a community, will ever be the same again after so many people came forward and put their stitches into this amazing work. It is a landmark in Alderney's modern history, and I feel sure that everybody involved in it, just like us, is very proud. . . . The Tapestry . . . is like a thread that runs between Normandy and Alderney. It is almost a thousand years long, and today it brings us closer together."[61] Russell was awarded a British Empire Medal by Queen Elizabeth II for services to history and culture. Now, as a tourist destination on Alderney, the tapestry illustrates the cultural heritage of the community and carries the legacy forward.

Today, Mia Hansson, a Swedish seamstress living in England, is working to single-handedly re-create the Bayeux Tapestry. While most Bayeux Tapestry projects reflect a connection to British and French culture, Hansson's embroidery pieces are motivated by her connection to a culture of needlework—an answer to Berlo's call "to understand the long history of the poetics of embroidery" and her place in it.[62] As a young child, Hansson often complained of boredom to her grandmother, who gave her cross-stitch projects to complete. Idle fingers are not to be tolerated in Scandinavian culture, where needlework has long been a way of life. Hansson's grandmother and mother were both stitchers, and textile classes were a regular part of school in Sweden. Boredom similarly motivated Hansson to take on the Bayeux Tapestry re-creation project. After years of working as a schoolteacher and then in elder care, Hansson left paid employment to care for her stepson. She needed a project to keep her occupied at home, and it had to be something equal to her drive—equivalent to a full-time job but with the flexibility she needed for caretaking, a role that textile work has so often fulfilled for women. Stitching the Bayeux Tapestry is her decade-long endeavor, set to be completed in 2027, and Hansson knew that as long as she had this project to work on, she would never be bored.

In Scandinavia, it was customary to re-create an embroidered item when it was worn beyond repair. This practice maintained the visual language of Scandinavian textiles, resulting in patterns and color combinations so distinctive that they marked not only the region or town but even the family someone came from.[63] Hansson plans to finish her Bayeux Tapestry replica just in time for a major restoration of the original tapestry, which the French Ministry of Culture has scheduled to begin in 2028. The restoration effort has been led thus far by a team of seven female textile conservationists who have assessed the areas in need of repair. A one-thousand-year-old tapestry presents unique challenges. Because no one has worked on anything like this before, restorers will have to learn as they go. Hansson is helping to keep this object of cultural memory alive and in circulation even if the original can no longer be displayed for a time.

While stitching the tapestry, she was "forced to learn the history, almost against [her] will," noting that history is the only subject she ever fell asleep in.[64] But her real connection to the work is with the original stitchers and her grandmother, who, though deceased, is always looking over her shoulder to make sure the back side of the work is neat. She has come to know the original stitchers of the tapestry quite well through her close study and faithful re-creation of their work: "Although I often get frustrated with them and the way they chose to stitch, which I now have to replicate, I feel strangely protective over them. There were reasons why they did things in a certain way and I don't always understand. . . . I can complain and want to put my veto in, ask questions and want to suggest other ways of doing things, but . . . I want to give the women the benefit of doubt."[65]

Hansson said she can feel the tensions between the embroiderers who worked closely together and likely for long hours with poor lighting, as though there are ghosts in the fabric. Their varying skill levels are clear from the stitching. Some appear less patient than others: "There are places where stitches overlap, where none of the women wanted to give in. In other places, there is a gap, where the women have failed to connect their work. Why? Was there an argument? Was it a simple oversight?"[66] Unlike the harmonious working environment depicted in the stitching of the Alderney panel or the Victorian re-creation, Hansson imagines "the air being thick with emotion at times" while stitching the original tapestry. If it was in fact made by Anglo-Saxon women, many would have lost loved ones and been displaced during the bloody conquest in which over one hundred thousand lives were lost. These women could have been in mourning, angry, or ambivalent over the political upheaval. They may have found community and support in stitching together or had bitter arguments over political differences. Hansson's close study of the stitches and her efforts to re-create them help to carry forward the memory of these embroiderers and their experience of making the tapestry.

Choosing to re-create the Bayeux Tapestry has connected Hansson to a community of people interested in the tapestry and given her a role in a broader cultural and historical conversation. She gives talks to schoolchildren, women's groups, historical reenactors, and embroidery guilds. She has a designated dress for many of these talks; the material was handwoven by a friend, and she sewed the garment with her mother. She added a seventeenth-century pocket to wear on top of the dress, which she embroidered with images from the tapestry. During these talks, Hansson said, "I step into a role and kind of become part of the tapestry. I live and breathe it with every ounce of my body and soul. It's quite magical."[67] She jokes that her gravestone will read, "The woman who became the Bayeux Tapestry," as though she herself had become a carrier of cultural memory, an embodiment of the original embroiderers' hands and minds a thousand years later.

CHAPTER 6

Homespun Opportunities

For over five hundred years, cloth formed the backbone of Iceland's economy. Not only was the traditional Icelandic woven cloth *vaðmál* a commodity to be sold and exchanged, but it was also used as a unit of currency. There was an established system of legal standards and exchange values for cloth, allowing it to be used to pay taxes and tithes and traded or sold for other necessities. One eyrir (approximately an ounce, usually of silver) was equivalent to a length of *vaðmál* two ells wide by six ells long (an ell is an Icelandic unit of measurement equivalent to 49.2 centimeters or 19.4 inches) often woven in a 2/2 twill pattern. The 2/2 pattern meant that each weft thread passed over two warp threads, then under two. Prior to the use of *vaðmál* as currency, weft threads could be spun in either direction, but standardization made them counterclockwise (S-spun).

Of course, it was women who made the cloth. Archaeologist Michèle Hayeur Smith, who studies the textile record of Iceland and Greenland, thinks it likely that women, due to their knowledge of weaving, either created the legal standards around *vaðmál* or collaborated closely with men to determine the specifications of the cloth.[1] The use of *vaðmál* as currency indicates women's involvement in governmental affairs in Iceland as far back as the twelfth century. *Vaðmál* challenges the notion that women's work, or work done in the home, was not income producing. Women were quite literally *making* the money, and their financial wealth depended on their industry and tenacity.

Cloth also facilitated the greatest opportunity of all—human survival. The ability to keep people warm in harsh climates represents significant power over nature. Icelandic woven cloth was made to withstand the harsh climate. The warp threads were made from the coarse outer guard hairs of the sheep, which were strong enough to bear the tension of being stretched on the loom and created a waterproof core for the cloth. The weft threads were made from the soft, fluffy inner coat of the sheep that felted together to create a barrier from the cold. Together, they made a warm, waterproof garment.

Textiles in traditional cultures remained surprisingly consistent over centuries—unless a major event prompted a change. The Little Ice Age, which impacted Greenland in the fourteenth century and Iceland in the sixteenth, caused a drastic lowering in temperature. During this period, weavers more densely packed weft threads in Greenlandic textiles and added plies to the yarn in Icelandic textiles to create warmer garments. Hayeur Smith correlated the ratio of weft to warp threads in textile samples from Greenland with published records of climate data and found that weft-dominant cloth increased as temperatures dipped in the 1300s. She observed that "weft-dominant cloth represents a vital female statement in a world where female expression was suppressed. How frequently do archaeologists have the privilege to observe such human responses and decisions firsthand in the archaeological record?"[2] It was like she was seeing women's thought processes: "It's getting colder and we need to change the way we weave our cloth."

As archaeologist Elizabeth Wayland Barber writes: "So powerful, in fact, is simple string in taming the world to human will and ingenuity that I suspect it to be the unseen weapon that allowed the human race to . . . move out into every econiche on the globe during the Upper Paleolithic [from 50,000 to 12,000 years ago]. We could call it the String Revolution."[3]

The Homeworker Economy

Up until the industrial age, the home was the center of economic activity for much of human history. Families profited from their labor, their land, and the various skills of household members. All work contributed to the family's sustenance, so there was greater interdependence between men and women in economic pursuits. Cloth itself was a form of wealth, in some cases legal tender, as with *vaðmál*, and in many others a valuable trade commodity. The Rumpelstiltskin tale of spinning flax into gold has both alchemical and economical significance. Through textile production, women possess the ability to, quite literally, transform materials readily found in nature into a product of monetary value.

Women were constantly spinning yarn and making cloth, combining it with their childcare and housework responsibilities, which may have obscured the amount of labor textile work required. In the context of manual labor, work that could be done sitting down was often not considered "real" work and was devalued compared with plowing or harvesting. Barber explains the reality of women's work:

The women spun while they tended the flocks, fetched water, or walked to the market; they wove while they tended the children, the oven, and the cooking pot. Men could rest when the crops were in; but where making the cloth was the woman's chore, as it generally was, woman's work was never done. . . . We may justly surmise from all available data that not only did a woman spend far more hours per year working at the cloth industry than a man did at any one of the men's tasks, but the women also formed considerably more than half the work force in not a few of these societies.[4]

Icelandic historian Helgi Þorláksson calculated the annual needs of small preindustrial farm households in Iceland to be seventy to one hundred kilograms of wool. It provided for clothing, bedclothes, sails, taxes, and land rent. Of course, all of this wool had to be spun and woven to be useful. Based on records on the style of dress at the time, to spin the three kilograms of wool needed to produce one adult outfit took around four hundred hours, or fifty days, if we assume an average of eight hours of spinning a day. Þorláksson estimated twelve kilograms of wool were needed to produce the *vaðmál* required for yearly taxes and tithes, which would have taken sixteen hundred hours in spinning time alone.[5] The high demand for cloth and the exorbitant amount of time it took to make it indicates that every female in a household would have devoted the majority of her time to cloth production.

In rural Britain, from the seventeenth century until industrialization, the textile industry was structured around home-based work, which facilitated women's participation in the economy and allowed capitalist merchants to profit from the large rural labor force. Largely organized as a putting-out system, in which supplies were delivered to homes in rural areas and finished products were then put out to be collected by the merchants, it gave women a way to produce textiles at home for profit. Still, their earnings were often suppressed. Sometimes the work was contracted directly to male farmers looking to earn additional income. The men worked in cooperation with their wives and children, who were treated as "helpers" and paid low wages, even if they were the ones doing the majority of the work.[6] In effect, women could work for profit because they were theoretically under the management of their husbands.

The fact that work was done "on the side" of regular farmwork and alongside childcare made the income appear auxiliary rather than essential and was compensated as such. In urban areas, male embroiderers organized into guilds and workshops and sought to exclude women from profiting financially from this work to eliminate the competition and drive up prices. Their efforts resulted in a 1609 bylaw of the Worshipful Company of Broderers, a professional association of embroiderers in London, that stated that women should not be taken on as apprentices and outlined punishment for female embroiderers who sold their work, naming them as "unlawful workers."[7]

Yet women's home-based labor *was* essential to the European expansion of textile production from the medieval period until industrialization and provided substantial wealth, primarily to the merchants involved in its trade.[8] While some women were able to make a livable wage and support themselves independently, others toiled in utter poverty, struggling to make enough to survive.

Poet Thomas Hood's "The Song of the Shirt," published in 1843, poignantly describes a seamstress's continued destitution despite working her fingers to the bone—no time to sleep or even to cry lest it disrupt her production. The poem ends,

> With fingers weary and worn,
> With eyelids heavy and red,
> A woman sat in unwomanly rags,
> Plying her needle and thread—
> Stitch! stitch! stitch!
> In poverty, hunger, and dirt,
> And still with a voice of dolorous pitch,—
> Would that its tone could reach the Rich!—
> She sang this "Song of the Shirt!"

In contrast, knitting in Shetland allowed some women to fully support themselves. It bolstered the remote island's economy until the oil boom in the last quarter of the twentieth century, bringing in supplemental income for the family to buy goods that they could not source on the farm, like tea and sugar. As Shetland knitter Hazel Tindall told me, when the National Health Service began in 1947, her single aunt set out to sell enough of her knitting to buy National Insurance so she would get a pension. She accomplished her goal and began receiving a government pension at the age of sixty. She died at ninety-seven. Tindall declared, "She had a very good return on her knitting."[9]

Today, handcraft continues to be the leading source of employment for women worldwide, with an estimated 300 million home-based workers forming a largely invisible but critical form of labor in the supply chain. For factories, homework is a way to outsource nonmechanized aspects of production and is almost necessarily handwork, since most homeworkers do not have access to machinery beyond a sewing machine in their homes. Baskets cannot be woven on machines. Pom-poms are handsewn onto hats, and some tags are handstitched onto garments.

Meanwhile, the rise in awareness of the impact of fast fashion on our environment and the factory conditions for textile workers has fueled consumer interest in the way goods are made and pressured many companies to raise their standards of production. In response to this shift, the nonprofit organization Nest, which focuses on supporting and promoting the work of artisans around the world, worked with the United Nations to create standards for ethical handcraft that are now followed by major retailers such as Target, Madewell, Patagonia, and West Elm. Still, the dispersed supply chain created by homework can be difficult to oversee and regulate.

I spoke with Rebecca van Bergen, founder of Nest, about her research to develop these standards, which included a visit to the Philippines, where there are about six thousand basket weavers over five islands making baskets for big-box retailers. A version of the traditional putting-out system persists, where materials are delivered to homes via moped. Van Bergen shared that, on average, there are six people between the factory and the homeworker, with each person in the chain earning income through their role. Homeworkers are paid by the piece, which can make their income inconsistent and often well below the country's minimum wage. In some cases, they can make as little as $1.80 per day, an estimated 50 percent less than wages at factories.[10] Most businesses work backward from the item's price to figure out what they will pay per object, often resulting in low wages, rather than ensuring that workers are able to make enough pieces to earn a livable wage. While problematic economically, piece-rate work can give flexibility to the workers, who can decide how often and for how long they work based on the other demands of the home. This is especially important when household income is inconsistent, such as during the COVID-19 pandemic, when many workplaces closed, and in the case of agriculture, which is seasonal and can vary due to weather and the effects of climate change. Piecework can provide extra income to buffer the impact of difficult economic times.

Together with the companies they have partnered with, as of 2023 Nest has impacted 174 supply chains in 30 countries, ensuring the ethical treatment of 52,713 handworkers. For those companies, there has been a 100 percent increase in businesses paying their workers at least minimum wage by conducting time-motion studies to determine fair piece-rate pay, a 295 percent increase in the ability of businesses to show evidence that there is no child labor in their supply chain, and a 183 percent increase in systems to report, investigate, and resolve cases of abuse. In the marketplace, the Nest Seal of Ethical Handcraft is the only consumer-facing certification signaling that a product is ethically made in a home or small workshop by an individual whose rights and well-being are being protected by their employer. Nearly all of the homeworkers affected reported an improvement in their decision-making role in the home since earning a fair wage and stated that their income supports their children's formal education.[11]

Doing handwork that is rote and repetitive is a different experience than that of an artisan working through the full creative process from the inception of the idea to the finished product. Even women who had historically spent the majority of their time making cloth usually had some variety in their tasks, as they likely scoured, carded, spun, dyed, and wove, or at least engaged in a few of these steps. When I asked van Bergen about the meaning of this kind of production-scale handwork for women, she responded, "I think even when you're talking about the most rote of it—sewing a sole on a bottom of a shoe—it's still so much better than doing work in a factory. . . . Even when it's rote there's a level of autonomy and peace building that happens when you're doing handwork."[12]

While continued improvement in the ethics and economics of this system is still needed, women can control their own production and work together with other family and community members. Most homeworkers prefer to work from home in order to care for their children and do necessary housework, and many would be unable to work at all if they could not work from home.[13] Anthropologist Jane Schneider explains that in noncapitalist societies, women's reproductive process is often represented as an analogue to dyeing or weaving, as it is among the Kodi, whose indigo dyeing practices have paralleled women's reproductive functions. But capitalist, industrial societies pit the goals of production against the goals of reproduction, suggesting that they are inherently contradictory, which they often are when work must be done outside the home.[14] Indeed, the shift from home-based labor to factory work deters some women from having as many children as they would like, because working outside the home can make it difficult to care for them without other childcare support in place. A study of the impact of homework versus factory work on children found that in Bangladesh, homeworkers breastfed their children an average of 19.3 months, whereas factory workers breastfed for an average of 9.9 months. In China, only 10.5 percent of homeworkers said that their children are left at home unattended regularly, compared with 23.9 percent of factory workers.[15]

Even when children are not a factor in women's choice to work at home, other considerations weigh in favor of homework over factory work. Women in rural areas may not have a way to get to a place of employment, and even if they do, commuting may be unsafe and expensive. Also, factories can be crowded and, as during the pandemic, can expose women to illnesses. Women should be able to earn a living wage in a safe environment, whether at home or outside of it.

Factory Hands

Textile factories provide some advantages in that they give women opportunities to work outside of the home, live independently, and delay marriage. But they often also subject them to horrific and exploitative working conditions. Over the past two centuries, there have been well-documented accounts of crowded workhouses, long hours, and exposure to chemicals, dust, and dangerous machinery. The Triangle Shirtwaist Factory fire of 1911 killed 146 garment workers in New York City; 123 were women and girls. Many jumped eight to ten stories to their death to escape dying by fire. Management had locked the doors to keep workers from stealing supplies and to keep union organizers out. Other exits had been blocked by machines to maximize working space in the cramped factory. While the fire sparked some efforts at factory reform, dangerous working conditions have persisted worldwide. The collapse of the Rana Plaza garment factory in Bangladesh in 2013 killed 1,134 people, many of them women and children, and again raised global awareness of the unethical working conditions in the garment industry.

Child labor, sexual harassment and assault, and below-minimum wages have also been endemic to industrial textile production. Ten years after the Rana Plaza collapse, a *New York Times* investigation found middle-school-aged migrant children, largely from Central

America, working full-time shifts after school in garment facto-ries in Alabama and California.[16] Textile factories have employed a similar payment structure to that of the putting-out system, pay-ing women and children significantly less than men, despite often similar levels of output and hours worked. Currently, the apparel industry is the largest employer of women globally, yet fewer than 2 percent of women working in this industry earn a living wage.[17] In Dhaka, Bangladesh, which is home to nearly five thousand garment factories, workers typically earn half the estimated living wage.[18]

To protect garment workers in factories requires recognizing their humanity. While most aspects of factory work are mecha-nized, an understanding of garment construction and skill in textile production is needed to operate the machines, and in many cases, handwork is still a valuable and necessary part of factory-based gar-ment production. To get a behind-the-scenes look at a factory that does value the humanity of their employees, I took a tour of Ate-lier Saint James, a clothing factory in Normandy, France, famous for the classic striped sailor sweater that once kept cod fishermen warm and now conjures images of seaside vacations. Over the whir of the machines, my guide, Caroline Collin, described the design and manufacturing process and introduced me to women working in all areas of production. Saint James employs four hundred people, with women comprising the majority at every level of the company, including management, and forming 80 percent of the total work-force. Since the start of the COVID-19 pandemic, there has been an influx of young women (and some men) seeking jobs, eager to work with their hands and wanting to learn to sew. Staff members are trained on-site, and each person has a few different jobs to avoid repetitive strain injuries and boredom.

Even though machines are used to assist with most aspects of production, a lot of handwork goes into the creation of the garments. Master knitters program the knitting machines and check each piece as it comes out. Most of the sewing is done by seamstresses who specialize in either wool or cotton garments. Any piece with an imperfection is sent to menders, who fix each one by hand using tiny hooks and illuminated magnifiers. Following the initial design process, the menders deconstruct each piece of a collection to see exactly how it was made so they can plan how to fix any mistake made by the machines. Each piece presents its own intellectual puzzle, and menders shared with me the satisfaction they feel in figuring out how to fix a garment. Menders must train for two years before working on their own, and by the end they have "golden hands," as Collin expressed it.[19]

Mechanized assembly-line work has a different feel than making custom-made textiles by hand or even the rote production-scale tasks of homeworkers. Still, the women I spoke to at Saint James experienced it as meaningful work. Each person has autonomy over their work and can decide when to switch jobs. They often work collaboratively. The designers work closely with the fabricators to determine how each new design is best constructed. A member of the design team mentioned how much she enjoyed engaging in this problem-solving task with the seamstresses and knitters. In addition to earning an income, the workers feel valued for their skill and have a sense of community.

Staff are also welcome to use textile leftovers to make their own projects, and some stay after hours to sew together. Collin showed me a picture of a dress that some of the knitters made for the head of quality control when she retired. They programed the knitting machine to knit the words "Miss Quality" into the dress in the style of a beauty pageant sash. One woman made a sensory play mat for her grandchild using scraps of different-textured materials. While Saint James is unfortunately not representative of factory-based garment work more broadly, it provides insight into how—when people's skills are valued and working conditions are humane and ethical—women can continue to experience the satisfaction of making things with their hands in a factory setting.

Taking Matters into Our Own Hands

While home-based work and factory work are the two main revenue streams for women in textile production, some women found ways to take matters into their own hands to create their own economic security. Until the nineteenth and twentieth centuries, women were forbidden from inheriting land in many parts of Europe, leaving even those who had been formerly wealthy destitute following their husband's or father's death. But women generally owned the textiles they made, allowing these goods to serve as a means for them to hold personal wealth that could be sold or passed on to female relatives. In early modern England, women who could afford the supplies embroidered gold threads into their clothing to display their wealth, but also as an insurance policy in case their husband or father died or left them without money. Certain stitches were even designed to look like traditional embroidery stitches but required extra thread to add more gold per unit area and increase their value.[20] It was unlikely that the men of the household would notice the extra thread that was ordered and hidden in these garments, since men knew so little of the crafts (or the craftiness) of women.

Embroidery had long been a marker of luxury and leisure time that had been reserved for the wealthy, until the Industrial Revolution popularized factory-made textiles, freeing up artisan and peasant women's time from the laborious processes of spinning and weaving. In Italy, women of even modest means were able to then dedicate time to the intricate and prestigious art of whitework embroidery, which consisted of white embroidery thread sewn on white linen fabric. Creating their *corredo*, an elaborate embroidered dowry traditional in Italian culture from the nineteenth to mid-twentieth century, was often a girl's best chance of influencing her financial future. Italian girls learned to embroider at a young age, often before they turned seven, and spent much of their adolescence creating their corredo. Its value was appraised prior to marriage and reflected the technical and aesthetic skills of the woman who created it. It was also a direct reflection of the financial status of the family, since wealthier families could spare more time and resources for the corredo's creation. As anthropologist Anna Chairetakis writes, "a girl's linens not only announce her capacities and wealth, but also draw to her the man she wants—weaving and needlework were implicated in the practice and beliefs of love magic."[21] Girls could make their romantic interests known by providing their desired partner with an embroidered handkerchief or other such personal item.[22] Once married, the corredo served both practical and aesthetic functions. The sheets, towels, and underclothes were used daily but also added to the beauty and status of a home. During times of financial hardship, women could sell the linens to help their families or support themselves in widowhood, and in many cases, those who emigrated funded their journeys with these sales.[23]

While many women and girls did textile work in their homes amid other household tasks, others worked long hours in workshops, convents, orphanages, and schools. Although these institutions provided social protection and food and shelter for them, they often curtailed their freedom and kept them economically dependent. In sixteenth- and seventeenth-century Venice, for example, at a time when the city led the world in lacework, most Venetian lace was produced by nuns in convents. Lacework was considered an appropriate activity for the cultivation of female virtue but also provided an important means of economic support for convents. For most nuns, this work was unpaid. The proceeds generally profited the institution, though in many instances, nuns accepted commissions for needlework, executing the work in private and retaining the earnings for themselves. But it was often merchants and middlemen who profited most from the nuns' labor. Sometimes these middle*men* happened to be women, such as Arcangela Tarabotti, a nun who lived in the early seventeenth century and acted as a lace broker. Tarabotti secured commissions for lacework and functioned as an intermediary between her clients and the nuns who produced the pieces.

Born with a clubfoot that made her family view her as unmarriageable, Tarabotti was sent to a convent at the age of thirteen.[24] Her sense of injustice over this life sentence is evident in the titles of the books she wrote about convent life, including *Monastic Hell* and *Paternal Tyranny*. In these texts, she exposed the oppressive conditions of convents and called for equal treatment for women and men. Nuns were meant to be entirely separated from the larger world. In the sixteenth century, Italian cardinal Agostino Valier described convents as "fortresses against the forces of evil," invoking Saint Bernard's words, "What business does a married woman have with a virgin who is dedicated to God? . . . The worldly woman is often an instrument of Satan."[25] In reality, the convent walls were more permeable, especially between nuns and the elite. Tarabotti's published letters show that she was quite active in Venetian society and provide a glimpse into the way in which lacework was contracted, executed, and renumerated.

Tarabotti had a conflicted relationship with lace, deriding the people who wore it as frivolous and ostentatious while also expressing jealousy. She compared the nuns who were "condemned to a lifetime passed in a habit of rough cloth" with their more fortunate sisters who were "adorned with pearls, ribbons, and lace."[26] Whatever her views were on wearing lace, she and her lacemakers made good money for creating and distributing it. She records receiving 360 ducats (roughly $54,000 today) for six braccia of lace (approximately thirty-six feet) for one Madame d'Amo. For comparison, the annual salary of an unskilled laborer at the time was around 30 ducats. Tarabotti appears to have taken a larger share of the payment for brokering the deal than was given to the lacemakers. She also used her mercantile role as a means of furthering her literary ambitions, parlaying the connections she made with wealthy women in search of lace into the circulation of her books. Tarabotti's participation in the lace trade may not have freed her from the confines of her "monastic hell," but it gave her a voice in the world as a businesswoman and writer.

In the Victorian era in the United States, some women were able to earn enough money through textile production that they could afford not to marry and, through their industry, became merchants and businesspeople instead of wives. Mercy Jane Bancroft Blair, a traveling dressmaker in rural upstate New York, spent many years depending only on her own industry for income. Her diaries provide detailed accounts of her business dealings and daily life that challenge the notion of "separate and distinct spheres" of female existence during this period.[27] Her entries depict her as an independent woman—traveling alone, working in various homes, and even lending substantial amounts of money to men, which they had to pay back with interest. She spent anywhere from a few hours to a few weeks in a family's home making their attire. She did more cutting and fitting than sewing, as the cutting of a gown required skill that many women who could sew did not possess. Beginning in the 1850s, women could buy patterns drafted by professional dressmakers or through women's magazines, but they generally came in one size. It is likely that Bancroft Blair had the skill to adapt such patterns to fit her clients. Whatever sewing she did was done by hand, as she does not mention a sewing machine in her diaries until late in her life. From 1859 to 1863, she worked an average of two hundred days per year and earned an annual income of $50 for her work as a dressmaker, including room and board when employed in a family's home for more than a day. Including the interest earned on the money she lent and "in kind" trades, her income is estimated at around $75 per year, roughly $35,000 in today's dollars.[28] By comparison, an American woman working six days a week in a cloth mill at the time likely netted about $65 annually.[29]

After spending many years making money and spending it as she pleased, Bancroft Blair decided to marry at the age of thirty-eight. She noted, "how strange that seems" that she consented to marry.[30] When she entered the Blair household, it included Mr. Blair's parents and a young son from his previous marriage. His mother, Mary Robinson Blair, ran the household, and Bancroft Blair's diaries show her working side by side with her mother-in-law. Despite being solidly in the industrial era in the latter half of the nineteenth century, Robinson Blair still processed flax grown on the family farm and spun and wove her own linen thread.

There was much work to be done to maintain the farm and tend to the needs of the family, and Bancroft Blair's diaries depict her weary from her engagement in many tedious household tasks. On Saturday, September 1, 1866, she writes, "We have so much housework to day that I get but little time to spin," and later that month she writes, "I am toiling away at the loom as usual."[31] That same year, her husband bought a butter churning machine, and she began making butter to sell. She records earnings from 1868 to 1877 for butter at an average of $327.24 per year, more than twice what her father-in-law earned annually from farming. She used this income together with her savings from her seamstress work to pay off the mortgage on her husband's family farm. Through her industry, Bancroft Blair made it possible for her husband to become a landowner, something her own father had never achieved, though the property she helped to purchase was never in her name. She traded the social and economic freedoms afforded to poorer working women for a solidly middle-class social position. Her tombstone reads, "She Hath Done What She Could," an epitaph that seems to underestimate her considerable accomplishments in life, particularly given her time and place.

Much like the Icelandic *vaðmál*, cloth has long served as a form of currency in Indonesia.[32] While women have controlled textile production on the island of Sumba, they have generally been excluded from the larger economic system, which traditionally centered on the exchange of goods.[33] The rise of tourism and women working outside of the home, and therefore not weaving their own cloth, created an opportunity for some women to profit financially from handmade textiles.

Marta Mete, occasionally referred to as the "indigo queen," is the most successful textile entrepreneur in the Sumban district of Kodi.[34] She was the youngest of the five wives of the last Dutch-appointed raja, who she married in the 1960s when she was a teen-ager and he was nearly sixty. During his lifetime, the raja allowed Mete to control his finances and important paperwork because she was the most educated of his wives. In the 1980s, in the midst of the raja's failing health and subsequent death, Mete established a local textile cooperative in collaboration with the raja's fourth wife and six other local women. These women invested in store-bought thread and looms and recruited younger women to work with them in a cash-based production system. The work of tying the threads to create an ikat pattern was valued at around 5,000 rupiah, dye-ing the threads in the indigo bath was around 8,000 rupiah, and weaving the threads on a backstrap loom could be 4,000 rupiah. Expertise and artistry were valued over the time required to com-plete these tasks. Although weaving is the most time-consuming, taking from two weeks to a month of labor, it is the most rote and unskilled part of the process and therefore the least compensated, while tying the design rarely takes more than a week and dyeing takes just four or five days once the bath is prepared. The value assigned to these stages of the weaving process go back centuries, when only the aristocratic women would dye the thread and tie the designs while the weaving was carried out by poor or enslaved women.[35] Mete traveled to Java and Bali to exhibit Kodi textiles at fabric shows and sell them to merchants who catered to tourists willing to pay high prices for local cloth.

When the raja died in 1985, his pension was halved—a major blow to a household still supporting twelve children in school. His eldest surviving wife received the pension and therefore controlled the only regular income in the household. Mete's youngest son was only twelve when his father died and still had many years of schooling ahead of him. She also had a daughter, a recent high school graduate who was hoping to continue her education. In an apparent act of retribution for Mete's control over the household finances during the raja's life, the older co-wives seemed determined to take back the economic power that had been bestowed on her, restricting her access to the family's funds.[36] Mete took matters into her own hands and sought out new markets to sell her textiles and make a living for herself, telling anthropologist Janet Hoskins, "I will leave these old gossips behind and find my own way."[37] By selling Kodi textiles, Mete was able to support her daughter's continued education, and she became the first Kodi girl to finish college.

FINDING FREEDOM

It took a long time before the women of Gee's Bend, Alabama, earned an income from their now-famous quilts, but along the way, the practice of quilting has been an act of survival and liberation in the face of oppressive systems of race and gender. After the Civil War, Gee's Bend was developed by the descendants of the enslaved people from the Pettway plantation, who were brought from North Carolina by foot in 1845. By law, they took the last name of the plantation owner, Pettway, and most residents still share it. For decades after slavery was abolished, they worked as sharecroppers or tenant farmers. This system put them in a state of perpetual debt, especially because of dishonest landlords and merchants.

Generations of women in Gee's Bend made quilts to keep their families warm and to survive winters in drafty houses with usually only one fireplace. Fabric was hard to come by and was almost never new. Women repurposed the cloth from worn-out clothes and bags that seeds, flour, and sugar came in. They carefully pulled out the thread that held these bags together and wrapped it around a stick to save for sewing. To make the best use of the fabric they had, they used strips and blocks—round or curved pieces wasted fabric—to make geometric designs that were often aesthetically striking. When the quilts were too worn out to be used as blankets, they were repurposed as sanitary pads, rugs, saddle blankets, and insulation around pipes to keep them from bursting in the winter.

Quilting was also a source of pleasure—"the only pleasure women had at that time," said quilter Arlonzia Pettway, who was born in 1916.[38] Women worked in the field all day and then quilted at night. Many of them planned their quilts while they worked, looking forward to staying up late to quilt. When they finished one, they wanted to show it off. Sitting on the couch in front of her sewing table, third-generation quilter Tinnie (pronounced "tiny") Pettway recalled her mother's (Malissia Pettway's) experiences quilting when Tinnie was a child in the 1930s and '40s:

> My mama was very competitive. She loved to sew. . . . If she saw pieces of fabric by the side of the road, she'd get it and wash it, and anybody who had old clothes, she'd find something good in it and make a quilt with it. . . . Sometimes she'd lay up in the bed and she'd dream of something, a pattern, and she'd get up out of bed and had a little piece of paper and she'd mark it. . . . She'd [piece] the quilt and then they'd quilt them and hang them out on that fence for people to pass by to see them.[39]

Though physically isolated due to the surrounding river and farmland and socially and politically isolated through segregation, the people of Gee's Bend have long had an impact on the larger world. Quilter Marlene Bennett Jones, who we met in chapter 5, recalled a story she heard that her great aunt Minder Coleman had woven blue and white striped material to make President Franklin Roosevelt a suit. In fact, in addition to the suit material and together with Gee's Bend residents Mattie Ross and Patsy Mosely, Coleman wove draperies for the Roosevelt White House.[40] The people of Gee's Bend were also part of the fight for voting rights during the civil rights era in the South. Black people in Alabama were being evicted from their homes, fired from their jobs, and beaten or killed for trying to register to vote or protesting for voting rights. The cable ferry that ran between Camden and Gee's Bend, a wooden raft poled by a Gee's Bend resident, had been stolen in 1962 to keep Black people from coming to Camden to register to vote, but it also kept people from going to stores and work in town. It made what was once a five-minute river crossing into more than an hour-long drive for a community where most people did not have a car. Wilcox County Sheriff Lummie Jenkins reportedly said at the time, "We didn't close the ferry because they were Black, we closed it because they *forgot* they were Black."[41] Ferry service was not restored until 2006.

In February 1965, Martin Luther King Jr. spoke in Gee's Bend to encourage people to protest for voting rights. Just a few weeks later, protesters, including Gee's Bend residents, were brutally beaten by law enforcement officers as they tried to cross the Edmund Pettus Bridge in Selma on what became known as "Bloody Sunday." Later that year, Francis Xavier Walter, a white Episcopal priest formerly from Alabama but living in New Jersey, visited Wilcox County to support the civil rights efforts in the region. He drove through the area west of Montgomery seeking people to give testimony regarding their experiences trying to register to vote and facing repercussions such as eviction, job loss, and bank foreclosures. He got lost and ended up in Possum Bend, just across the river from Gee's Bend on the Camden side. He came upon a home with quilts hanging outside. He was struck by the similarity between the designs of the quilts and the modern op art works that hung in galleries in New York City and thought that liberal white people in the North, especially those in the art world, would like to buy these quilts. He tried to speak to the woman who created them, but seeing a white man in her yard, Ora McDaniel ran out of her house and hid in the woods. When he was able to speak to her later, accompanied by one of her neighbors, he suggested auctioning off the quilts to fund civil rights efforts and asked about other quilters in the area. She directed him across the river to Gee's Bend. With a $700 grant he had received from the Episcopal Society for Cultural and Racial Unity, he bought quilts from the women in the area for $10 each. The average family income at the time in Gee's Bend was just over $1,000 per year, so a single sale meant a 1 percent increase in a family's earnings. He recalled that women were lined up alongside the road with armfuls of quilts to sell to him.[42]

Walter arranged two quilt auctions, which took place in New York City in 1966. The sale of about seventy quilts netted $2,065 which went toward washing machines, telephones, and indoor bathrooms for the quilter's homes, as well as college tuition for the great-granddaughter of an enslaved person. The auctions were covered by *The New York Times* and caught the attention of influential artists, including painter Lee Krasner. Bloomingdale's and Saks Fifth Avenue soon bought quilts to sell to their customers.

Minder Coleman, who had been the president of the Gee's Bend

Farms cooperative, saw an opportunity and suggested that the women could create a similar quilt cooperative to earn money and help the community. On March 26, 1966, sixty women gathered at the Antioch Baptist Church in Camden to establish the Freedom Quilting Bee. Estelle Witherspoon, who had marched with Martin Luther King Jr. from Selma to Montgomery, was its first president. She described her motivation: "I wanted things to be well with us and not only well with me and my husband and my children but well with people and if I could do anything to help, I always try."[43]

The Freedom Quilting Bee began with members working out of their homes or meeting at Witherspoon's house to sew together. Initially they filled small, individual orders from ads they placed in mail-order catalogs. Each quilt was one of a kind and continued the tradition of using scraps of the fabrics they had available, which had expanded due to donations. But to make a livable income, they needed to quilt on a larger scale. The Bee's first major order was from Bloomingdales—$20,000 worth of quilts. They later secured a long-term contract making pillowcase covers for Sears, Roebuck & Co.[44] The women learned to conduct business and scaled up from making custom-made "my way" quilts to a mass-production approach by piecing the quilt tops using sewing machines instead of by hand and standardizing their methods of production. For the first time, they earned an income. The Freedom Quilting Bee even spurred a nationwide quilting revival.

In 1969, through grants and loans, the Gee's Bend community raised enough money to build a new, communal workplace, which they called the Martin Luther King Jr. Memorial Sewing Center. Founding member and later president of the Bee, Nettie Young, expressed their common feeling: "My days was happy because I had some place to go to work. . . . I had never had a job out of my home, you see, and I was happy to get up to go to work. They was happy days. Joyful, glad to go, ready to go."[45] The women also established a day care program at the sewing center, and generations of children grew up in that space as their mothers sewed.

This shift to employment outside of the home challenged the community's ideas about work and gave the women an opportunity to determine the economic value of their labor for the first time. Third-generation quilter and Navy veteran Delia Pettway Thibodeaux said, "The men had to give away some of that control. I'd say the women had to take that freedom because men were in control. Women just stayed home.... During that time when the women left, it was a big deal."[46] The men of Gee's Bend didn't consider anything but manual labor as work. Quilting, though necessary for survival, didn't count. Housework, no matter how strenuous, didn't count. Childbirth and childcare didn't count. Many women had to work in the fields as long as the men, even while pregnant or within days of giving birth, in addition to taking care of the children and doing the cooking, canning, washing, cleaning, and quilting. Tinnie Pettway said, "My daddy was crazy. He never got tired. He worked all the time," and he expected her mother Malissia and the kids to work right alongside him from dawn until dusk.[47] Afterward, Malissia had to cook dinner when the family came home after nightfall. According to Tinnie, Malissia lamented that she did not get as much time to quilt as some of the other women, whose husbands were less demanding. Tinnie's daughter, fourth-generation quilter Claudia Pettway Charley, reflected on Malissia's life at that time:

> My grandmother never went to the Freedom Quilting
> Bee so she never had the opportunity to earn the money

because her husband took care of her. . . . Those men back then, they were very prideful. They were like, 'that little bit of stuff that you're doing ain't nothing. Let's see how long that's going to last until you start doing just what you were doing before . . .' When we had the Freedom Quilting Bee, that was the first time that women actually owned their own income because the men back then, they weren't sharing.[48]

By the mid-1990s, many of the founding members of the Freedom Quilting Bee had retired, passed away, or taken steadier jobs outside the county, and the Bee lost momentum. In 1999, folk art collector William Arnett saw a photograph of Gee's Bend quilter Annie Mae Young with one of her quilts in Roland Freeman's 1996 book, *A Communion of the Spirits: African-American Quilters, Preservers, and Their Stories*. He paid a visit to Gee's Bend to find her, showing up at her door late one night. Not unlike Walker's reception in the area some thirty years earlier, Young did not open the door for him. But Arnett returned the next day and began purchasing quilts from members of the community. Tinnie recalled that at the time, white people who came to Gee's Bend to buy quilts never paid more than $20 to $25 for one. Arnett helped the quilters see the value of their work both artistically and economically. As Tinnie recalled:

> When those guys came down here and started telling us about the quilts it was kind of unbelievable, but they was telling us how much we could get but they didn't tell us a lot of facts because they got a lot of our stuff before we knew how valuable it was. They were just going up under

the bed buying every quilt that didn't look like nothing to us and pulling the quilts out of one of the horse stalls, and they had people refurbishing those quilts and we didn't really know the value of them because we definitely hadn't dealt with no art world before that.[49]

Arnett organized the *Quilts of Gee's Bend* exhibit, which debuted in 2002 at the Museum of Fine Arts Houston and traveled to museums in New York City, San Francisco, Milwaukee, Cleveland, and Washington, DC. The exhibition featured over sixty quilts created by forty-four artists and brought new fame to the women of Gee's Bend. Many of the quilters toured with the exhibit, including Tinnie. "We got a lot of fun out of it. . . . Going to places I had never gone, eating things I'd never eaten, seeing things I never would have seen," she said. It spurred a sort of renaissance for the quilters, some of whom had experienced the empowerment of the Freedom Quilting Bee and some who had not yet had their quilting recognized by the larger world.

During this time, the quilters gained popularity as artists because their work toured major museums. Their quilts were compared to works by Henri Matisse and Paul Klee.[50] Delia described her surprise at the recognition of the quilts as art: "My views of the quilts changed. I could see the artistry. . . . I thought well, then what I'm doing is not just for necessity, I'm actually creating a piece of art."[51] The quilters and the art world continue to reconcile the artistic and historical contexts of the quilts and their creators. There was a palpable divide in the way the quilts were treated as art in the high modernist tradition, while the quilters themselves were treated as "naive artisans" and "anthropological subjects."[52] Tinnie Pettway recalled her sense of Arnett's complicity in that divide while they

were touring with the exhibit: "Every dinner they had people looking at us like we was totally stupid, helpless, and all that stuff. So I
think that's how they got a whole lot of support. Because the people
wanted to help out the poor people."[53]

Still, the *Quilts of Gee's Bend* exhibit provided the quilters with
an artistic platform that created new opportunities. For Claudia,
while the experience with Arnett showed her the value of the quilts,
she realized that they needed to take ownership of their own production in order to make the most of this opportunity. As Claudia
explained, quilting "allowed us to be free in our choices. To know
that I can decide something for myself."[54] Tinnie and Claudia went
into business together selling their quilts and quilted pot holders
to local stores. Other quilters in the community followed suit. But
despite having their work in major art museums around the world,
the quilters of Gee's Bend remained in poverty.

In 2019, Rebecca van Bergen's organization, Nest, saw an opportunity to help the women translate their artistic success into economic success. At the time, the national median per capita income
was $34,103 annually, and the median per capita income in Alabama
was $27,928, almost 20 percent lower. Wilcox County had one of
the lowest median per capita incomes in the state at $16,841, which
falls within the lowest 1 percent of counties nationally. The quilters' median income was 11 percent lower than this figure at $15,000
per year.[55] Some quilters were living without the basic amenities of
phone and Internet access, limiting their ability to expand the sale
of their goods.

There were about forty active quilters in the community of under
three hundred residents. Increasing the income of the quilters would
have a significant impact on the average income of Gee's Bend and

uplift the community economically. Nest interviewed ten of these quilters to assess the economic needs of the women prior to developing their approach. Of the ten surveyed, 40 percent reported a total cost of living that was higher than their monthly household income, with most of their expenditures going to meet essential needs of food, shelter, healthcare, and clothing. Half had part-time or full-time employment besides quilting, and half received income from social welfare, including SSI, SNAP, and Medicare/Medicaid. Most felt they had not achieved the optimal earning potential from quilting, primarily because they were not compensated proportionately to the time and effort they put into making the quilts. Regardless, they were dedicated to quilting and preferred it to other occupations, even if they were to receive the same or higher compensation. All of the quilters expressed pride in their work and hoped the next generation would continue to quilt as a profession. For many it felt integral to their personal and collective identity. Claudia explained:

> It is very important to be able to be expressive, take an art form that's pretty much made from scraps . . . discarded like the rags that they are and be able to make something of value to myself and my family but also to my community. . . . Being a woman, and then being a Black woman in society, this particular art form is something that we're very proud of. . . . Because of our isolation and our roots, we were able to take just what we know and hone those skills to the point where they've become world-renowned. . . . In a time that we were forgotten about, we were able to take something which was pretty much nothing and change the outlook of our community.[56]

In partnership with Nest, the quilters of Gee's Bend received guidance on pricing and product photography to create Etsy shops. For some, this required setting up bank accounts for the first time and learning how to utilize technology platforms. Prior to creating nineteen shops, the average three-month income of Gee's Bend residents was $4,210. Within three months on Etsy, the average three-month income rose to $17,625. Gee's Bend quilts now sell for thousands of dollars apiece.

The quilters now value their time and skills differently than before and have taken financial ownership over their artistic production. Claudia said, "What I love about quilting is it allows you to determine your worth." She continued, "When you're able to set your price according to your own value, your own time spent, your creativity, your thought, your heart for it and say what you think you're worth, that's on a whole 'nother level. They can now say 'I deserve this. I am good enough. I am somebody. . . .' [T]hat brings more life, more opportunity, more advancement, and more girl power to all of us that have felt some ways in our life neglected, downtrodden, and not real at all. These quilts, they've done a whole lot for the Gee's Bend women."

The quilters also established brand collaborations with fashion designers like Chloé, Greg Lauren, and Marfa Stance, which, together with the Etsy sales, brought over half a million dollars into the community in 2021. This income has enabled Claudia to pay for the college education of her daughter. While studying anthropology and forensic science, Francesca Charley makes quilts and pot holders to sell along with her mother's and grandmother's. She designed some of the garments in the Marfa Stance X Gee's Bend collection. Of quilting, she said it "definitely makes me feel really free in a way that I feel like is different compared to other people's way of art.

Mostly because in Gee's Bend . . . we have no rules, we just do stuff and whatever comes out of it, comes out of it. It's always so much fun to have such a good free rein for what I want to do."[57]

Arnett's nonprofit organization, Souls Grown Deep, continues its investment in Gee's Bend, working to secure the intellectual property rights of the quilters and place quilts in the permanent collections of major national and international art museums. The organization began sponsoring the annual Airing of the Quilts Festival in 2022 to directly promote the work of new generations of quilters and invest in the community. Nest continues to support the financial independence of the quilters, with Claudia as community manager, partnering with brands and looking for ways to improve the Gee's Bend quilters' economic future. "We live by our own design," Claudia said, aptly describing both the free-form nature of Gee's Bend quilts and how quilting creates a space for women to form their own lives. She added that "quilting is a freedom for myself."

Freedom is a loaded word for the women of Gee's Bend. It speaks to a search for freedom from a racist legacy and its devasting economic, political, and social impact that continues to reverberate throughout the United States. It also encompasses the freedom for women to earn an income and have a voice in their family and community. But even more so, it encompasses personal freedom—the ability to choose what your quilt looks like and, in the process, to choose what your life looks like.

CHAPTER 7

Hands to Power

In 1910, the United Kingdom's Women's Social and Political Union made a suffragist banner designed by Ann Macbeth, an instructor at the Glasgow School of Art, that included the embroidered signatures of eighty women who were imprisoned for protesting for women's right to vote. These women, some of whom were still imprisoned at the time, signed their names in thread to testify to their experience and unite in solidarity. The signatures reflect each woman's struggle to be recognized as a person with a voice and to combat the dehumanization they experienced in prison, which included force-feeding as a punishment for hunger strikes, solitary confinement, and being left for days in handcuffs. The banner was carried in the From Prison to Citizenship procession through Glasgow in June 1910, a march of approximately ten thousand women that stretched for two miles.[1]

Between 1908 and 1913, a British organization called the Artists' Suffrage League embroidered over 150 protest banners in support of women's suffrage. They were carried many times over in the marches that ultimately resulted in women's right to vote.[2] Many commemorated accomplished women, including Mary Somerville, a scientist and mathematician who signed the women's suffrage petition in 1866, and Elizabeth Blackwell, the first American woman to qualify as a medical doctor, who worked both in Britain and the United States. Mary Lowndes, founder of the Artists' Suffrage League, described her rationale for making banners in a 1909 pamphlet: "A banner is not a literary affair, it is not a placard: leave such to boards and sandwichmen. A banner is a thing to float in the wind, to flicker in the breeze, to flirt its colours for your pleasure, to half show and half conceal a device you long to unravel: you do not want to read it, you want to worship it."[3] Speaking through textiles was a way for pro-suffrage women to thread the needle—performing their gender role while pushing the boundaries to expand their freedoms.

Playing with Paradoxes and Pushing Boundaries

Textile work has brought women together and given them power in numbers. In the Western feminist movement, women have used textile work as a tool of liberation and eschewed it as a tool of oppression. Interestingly, both the embrace and rejection of needlework has broadened the space for women's self-expression and moved women's voices beyond the walls of the home into the streets and onto the walls of museums. Female artists have worked at the intersections of art and craft, public and private, masculine and feminine, individual and collective to try to reconcile these binaries and expand the spaces in between them.

In *Quilting Lessons*, discussed in chapter 4, art historian Janet Catherine Berlo draws parallels between the crazy quilting trend of the 1880s and the rise of the first wave of feminism in the United States:

> Some women held meetings, signed petitions, and formed women's rights organizations. Other women felt an inarticulate longing, a restlessness in their controlled, circumscribed lives. It was premature for most of them to recognize that these feelings were widely shared, that soon they would be marching, that there would be hunger strikes. . . . They would break free from their constricted, repetitive patterns. Crazy, rich, freewheeling, individualistic, unpredictable designs: first they have to work it out in fabric. Only then could they put it into action in their own lives.[4]

As Ruth McEnery Stuart's letter "To Her Crazy-quilt . . . A Study of Values" showed in chapter 3, making crazy quilts was a way that some women first found a means of self-expression and began to work out their desire for greater freedom. The crazy quilters of the late 1880s realized they had something to say, and crazy quilts gave them a way to say it. By the early 1900s, McEnery Stuart's voice had wide reach as a writer. She believed that women had "serious public obligations to perform" and was an enthusiastic supporter of women's suffrage. Making her crazy quilt was a catalyst for personal transformation—her first full expression of self.

Making something of their own design helped women bridge the divide from the private "feminine" world, for which textile work was a marker, to the public "masculine" world of writing and speaking.[5] It created a space between these spheres, or a reconciliation of them that was reflected in the way that textiles were used in activism to further integrate women into public life. While expanding the boundaries of women's roles in society, many female activists were careful not to veer too far outside the lines of respectability. The use of embroidery and appliqué to protest for women's suffrage was a calculated one, given how inextricably tied textile work was with ideals of femininity. It was intended to reassure men that even if granted the right to vote, women would not stop being women. Anti-suffrage propaganda expressed people's fears that if granted the right to vote, women would act and dress like men, refuse to clean and cook, and even become infertile. Women's magazines "separated 'real' women—those who continued to sew or knit—from those wanting the vote."[6] The nonthreatening "feminine" nature of needlework may have made women's fight for the full rights of citizenship appear more palatable.

The use of art in activism during the British suffragette movement was in part the result of a larger effort to manage what was considered the problem of the rise of "spinsters" in late nineteenth-century Britain. To deal with this surplus of unmarried young women, art schools accepted more women so they could teach them skills that could lead to respectable professions. The Arts and Crafts Movement created opportunities for women to work in the "domestic arts" of embroidery and tapestry for designers like William Morris.[7] During the fight for women's suffrage, female illustrators had a means of making their work visible on posters, banners, cartoons, and pamphlets, while selling their designs for postcards and publications.

Women's struggle to have their creative expression recognized as art has also been intertwined with the feminist movement. Following the first wave of feminism, many of the female artists who had gained prominence during the women's suffrage movement found that they no longer had a platform for their work in the art world. Multimedia artist Faith Ringgold, most known for her narrative art quilts depicting the experiences of Black Americans, recalled protesting at the Whitney Museum in New York City in 1970 for the inclusion of female artists in the Whitney Annual exhibit (now the Whitney Biennial). In 1969, only about 5 percent of the work shown had been made by women. A group of feminist artists, including Ringgold, called for equal representation. They submitted the names of talented female artists and left eggs and tampons outside of the museum to make their point. Female representation rose to 23 percent in 1970, still too low. So, they demonstrated during the exhibition's opening to drive their point home.[8] Only, finally, in 2010 did women represent 55 percent of the artists exhibiting in the Whitney Biennial.

Most feminist artists had to operate outside of the mainstream art world. Many mid-century female artists used knitting, crochet, and embroidery to express their rage at domestic oppression. Through these mediums they carved out a space for women's voices beyond the traditional artistic spheres and engaged in consciousness-raising to organize activism. In doing so, they drew on the long history of women expressing their ideas and principles through textiles. "There was more than one man of Tory persuasion who slept unknowingly under his wife's 'Whig Rose Quilt,' " wrote Patricia Mainardi, a pioneer in women's studies.[9] The Whig Rose quilt is a repeating red rose design that originated around 1840 and was a way for women to, perhaps covertly, signal their political views, even when in opposition to those of their husbands. Given that the particulars of women's lives were often deemed unworthy of documentation and preservation, to stitch your ideas and beliefs into cloth, even in private, could be an act of resistance.

Kate Walker and Sally Gollop, artists, neighbors, and friends in South London, eschewed the male-dominated fine arts world and instead built a community for women like themselves—women who were also stay-at-home mothers and whose art was concerned with everyday life. It began with just the two of them. When Gollop moved to the Isle of Wight in 1974, they started sending each other art objects through the mail to share something of their daily routine, as they had as neighbors, and to continue supporting each other in their artistic expression. The art they exchanged was restricted to what they could make at home and what could be sent through the mail. One of the first works Gollop sent was a miniature kitchen dresser with shelves across the window like prison bars. As Walker described it, "This was the only kind of art one can do during children's TV."[10]

In 1975, Walker attended a women's art history conference in London and spoke up during a presentation to recruit more members to the art exchange. Su Richardson, who was in the audience and was inspired to join the project, paraphrased Walker's call to arms: "Look aren't there any housewives here who want to make some art, and who are fed up with all this fine art business? Aren't there any of you making things at home that you'd like to show each other?"[11] Walker proposed looking sideways to each other rather than up the male-dominated chain of the fine arts hierarchy.[12] What resulted was the Postal Art Event, an exchange of over three hundred art pieces shared between dozens of women, mostly white and middle-class, in different cities, towns, and villages in England.[13] The participants often used traditional women's craft techniques and depicted feminine and domestic imagery. Walker knitted a panel that read "Not Art, Heart—Homemade I'm Afraid" with a knitted fetus in the birthing position. Richardson crocheted a full English breakfast with burnt edges and a series of crocheted plants—she sent a blooming African violet to Walker for Mother's Day and a cactus prickled with metal pins to a less supportive friend.[14] Each work was imbued with the stuff of their daily lives and came to reflect the personal relationships between the women. Monica Ross, another participant, describes the event as "a nonstop process, new work constantly emerges as a visual conversation develops. The aim is communication, not perfect aesthetics." These conversations broke through the isolation of the home by offering connections to other women and a chance to explore and express their own experiences of domestic life, beyond the identity of mother, wife, or caregiver. "We have the common enemy—a vast indifference to our creativity—to unite us," Ross adds.[15]

Like the crazy quilts of first-wave feminism, projects like the Postal Art Event provided an outlet for expression and dialogues between women that spurred them to action. These women worked in the spaces in between the domestic and artistic spheres using what they had available, "the broken and discarded bits," to make their experiences visible to themselves and each other.[16] The use of traditional craft techniques both validated the pleasure there is in knitting and crochet while also drawing attention to the ways women's time has been consumed by the demands of the domestic economy.[17] Ross recalls that it was after the Postal Art Event began that they started reading books and becoming more aware of feminist ideology.[18] It was part of the consciousness-raising process that led women to take action in the feminist movement.

Though intended as a private art exchange, the Postal Art Event resulted in several exhibitions in the United Kingdom, including *Feministo* and *Portrait of the Artist as a Young Woman/Housewife* in 1976 and 1977, respectively.[19] The endeavor was an example of the developing feminist ideology that "the personal is political," which became a slogan of second-wave feminism. Ironically, the Northwest Arts Association, which housed the first *Feministo* installation, included signs reading "Unsuitable for Children," even though much of the work had been made in the presence of young children and out of the materials of domestic life. Many felt that the "portrait of a housewife" depicted in the works was unsettling—perhaps because it hit "dangerously close to home."[20] It turned the interiority of the production of domestic life outward, exposing the reality behind closed doors and subverting materials traditionally made to signal domestic comfort into a means of revealing women's domestic discomfort. This in itself was a critical moment of consciousness-raising. If mothers' artistic expressions of domestic life were not suitable for children to see, if it was uncomfortable to glimpse the daily reality of women's unpaid labor in the home, something needed to change.

Notably, Sally Gollop opted not to have her contributions to the project exhibited, as she considered the postal exchange a strictly personal affair.[21] The participants did not expect their artifacts to enter the gallery space at the outset of the project, so the exchange was about the process of communicating with other women through making art, not the art product itself.[22] The individual bonds and mutual support formed a community of women, which is perhaps another work of art in this story.

These women aimed to challenge the traditional values of the fine arts world and create a new art to replace the old, in this case one that challenged the division between art and craft and corresponding divisions between masculine and feminine, public and private. Reflecting on their use of "craft," Kate Walker states, "Although we respect the skills passed on to us, they stink of poverty . . . your work was used, trodden on, or worn out, like you yourself."[23] Ross presents a more positive view of their methods and materials: "Our creativity derives from non-prestigious folk traditions. It is diverse and integrated into our lives; it is cooked and eaten, washed and worn. Contemporary standards either ignore our creativity or rate it as second-class. We communicate, we don't compete. . . . Our creativity is valid."[24] The two perspectives reveal the range of women's experience of domestic creativity—celebrating its power while also revealing its limitations.[25]

On the heels of *Feministo*, Kate Walker, Monica Ross, Suzy Varty, and Su Richardson created the FENIX collective (1978–1980), which highlighted the difficulties female artists faced in finding the space and time to make art—the conflict between domestic and artistic life. The artists worked in a gallery space that was open to the public throughout the entire creative process, providing the women protected time and space for artistic work and revealing the process of art making alongside the finished product. Working collectively in a shared space addressed issues that plagued female artists and women more broadly, such as isolation and childcare needs. The children played together while their mothers created art and visitors surveyed the projects in progress.[26] Working this way drew on feminist traditions of mutual support and consciousness-raising and was in direct contrast to male artists, who tended to have independent, dedicated studios.[27] To show women working harmoniously together was meant as a political statement as well, a counter to the stereotypes of jealousy and infighting that often mischaracterized relations between women and kept them from uniting toward a shared goal. Working together also emboldened the women to present art that expressed vulnerable feelings about being women, artists, and mothers. Richardson says, "One of the things that people have often said is . . . 'How can you go in public and put all your dirty washing out?' We're all very scared of that, but people don't realise that fear is overcome by group support."[28]

The FENIX artists used materials from daily life—buttons, bedsheets, household items, in line with the concept of femmage. Richardson made a soft sculpture of a work apron and pair of pants on a hanger, the many pockets overflowing with granny squares, a crochet hook, tools, and kitchen cutlery—the stuff of middle-class housewives' lives. The apron has the words "bear it in mind," spelled out in buttons as a nod to what we would now call the mental load or women's invisible labor. A silhouette of a hand is embroidered on one of the apron's pockets, and a pair of gloves hangs from the bottom, suggesting the many hands needed to accomplish these daily tasks.

Their art spoke directly to other women. Rather than waiting for the mainstream art movement to recognize women's modes of creative expression, women could recognize it among themselves. In their paper on femmage, artists Miriam Schapiro and Melissa Meyer declare that "the culture of women will remain unrecognized until women themselves regard their own past with fresh insight."[29] Choosing to communicate with each other rather than seek the approval of men shifted the balance of power for women in the feminist movement. Making and exhibiting the forms of art that women have made for generations was an effort to democratize self-expression, creating opportunities to unite women through a shared language and expand the possibilities for how we can live. It also exposed the inaccuracy of viewing "women's work" as only a tool of oppression and showed that it has been and continues to be a symbol of both women's subservient position in the home *and* an empowered and vital contribution to family, community, and culture.[30]

Feminists of the third wave sought to amplify the empowering aspect of needlework. We tend to think that objects like knitted blankets belong at home, much like women traditionally, but what happens when we move both blankets and women outside of it? We no longer have to hide or obscure our creative power—we can boldly assert it through a variety of acts, from knitting in public to yarn-bombing in the streets. But beyond taking public actions, these feminists endeavored to shift the mindset about what textile work means and has meant for women as an expression of our value and influence. Writer and maker Betsy Greer, who coined the term *craftivism*, says: "It's about making your own creativity a force to be reckoned with. The moment you start thinking about your creative production as more than just a hobby or 'women's work,' and instead as something that has cultural, historical and social value, craft becomes something stronger than a fad or trend."[31] In the Western world, needlework has increasingly become a hobby for women, men, and non-binary people of all ages and is integrated into their lives alongside their careers and family, but generally outside of their specific roles in either of these realms. The Stitch 'n Bitch movement of the early 2000s shifted the aesthetics of knitting "from rocking chair to riot grrrl,"[32] altering the cultural conception of what it means to be a knitter today. These cultural changes further disentangle textile crafts from ideas of "women's work" and misogynistic gender divisions.

The practice of yarn-bombing, also known as guerilla knitting or knitted graffiti, was started in 2005 by Texas-based artist Magda Sayeg. A sort of renegade activity, like graffiti, though one that is more "grandma than gangster," yarn-bombing inserts feminist messages into the commercial spaces of everyday life.[33] Sayeg began by wrapping the door handle to the boutique she owned with a piece of knitted fabric to make something she touched every day a bit warmer and more inviting. Her first large-scale piece was a knitted and crocheted covering for a bus in Mexico City, which enhanced the bus's beauty, making it colorful and soft to the touch, but not interfering with its function. Yarn-bombing has now spread, resulting in frequent sightings of knitting and crochet "in the wild" in many urban settings. Some are done as forms of political protest, like a combat tank in Copenhagen that artist Marianne Jørgensen covered in bright pink knitted and crocheted squares as a statement against Danish involvement in the war in Iraq in 2006. Others are acts of artistic expression, like the Wall Street *Charging Bull* sculpture in New York City that was covered in bright pink and purple yarn in 2010 by artist Agata Oleksiak, aka "Olek." And many are community projects, like the 7,800 crocheted afghans that covered the steps of Finland's Helsinki Cathedral in 2011 before being donated to local shelters. To have knitting and crochet hit the streets in this way plays with the idea of where this traditionally domestic craft belongs. People take notice of its incongruity in the setting and perhaps wonder why it's there and what it means, making us all look at the world a little differently and see new possibilities.

Textiles can also be used conceptually in ways that may even obscure the materials and transform them into something else. Portuguese artist Ana Martins, aka Aheneah, is a "graphic embroiderer," making what she refers to as "urban cross stitch" displayed on city streets—think graffiti with thread instead of spray paint. She integrates her education in art and graphic design with the embroidery techniques that her grandmothers taught her as a child after realizing how cross-stitches function as pixels do in digital design. The images that she creates appear computer generated, but they are rendered by wrapping wool around a series of closely placed screws on wooden boards to mimic the look of cross-stitch, merging digital and analog ideas of a pixel.[34] She affixes these boards to the sides of buildings to bring cross-stitch into public spaces. Blending wool with nails transforms traditional associations with fiber as something that is soft and yielding to something that can also be hard and sharp.

In the gallery space, artist Zoë Buckman's 2018 exhibit *Every Curve* displayed vintage lingerie embroidered with misogynistic rap lyrics. Using women's undergarments as a canvas to be displayed as artwork in a gallery, she plays with what is private and what is public, integrating the two spheres. By overlaying male rap artists' words on these delicate garments, she also explores what belongs to women and what is put upon them. The words themselves are forceful, violent, and dismissive of women's subjectivity, but they are written in gentle cursive loops of thread on silk and lace, highlighting the vulnerability of women's position in a male-dominated world. A sheer mint-green negligee trimmed with beige lace has the words "I like 'em cute, round tits and fat asses. Educated, so I can bust off on they glasses," a line from Notorious B.I.G.'s song "Big Booty Hoes," scrawled across it in bright pink thread. The anachronistic clash between the use of embroidery on vintage lingerie to depict modern rap lyrics ultimately underscores the timelessness of women's subjugation as well as the use of textiles to bring it to light. Taking textile practice and its products into many different spaces from the home to the pub, from the streets to the museum, adds complexity and texture to the meaning of textile work and humanizes the people who engage in it, which is itself a form of activism.

THE EMOTIONAL IS POLITICAL

In the 1970s, a team of social workers and psychologists from the Child Development Project at the University of Michigan intervened with families of children whose parents had suffered abuse in childhood, identifying the children as at high risk for abuse and neglect themselves. They wrote of their experience in an article called "Ghosts in the Nursery," where they explored why some parents repeat the abuse that was inflicted upon them while others vow to protect their children. In their work with previously abused parents, the therapists found that the parents' ability to remember the emotional pain of their own abuse, not just the actual events, was the key to ending the intergenerational repetition of childhood abuse.[35] The same theory can apply to social justice issues; when we intellectualize the issues, rather than connect to people's pain and their lived experiences, it becomes easier to maintain inequality and discrimination. Experiencing our own feelings around injustice, resonating with the hurt it causes others, creates the possibility for collective action to change the source of the problem.

Embroidery artist and activist Heather Scholl aims to bridge this divide by portraying issues like racial and gender inequality in an emotionally accessible and deeply personal way. For her, it means connecting systems of power and oppression to lived experiences, often her own as a queer white woman. She makes the emotional toll of living within a racist, sexist, and homophobic culture visible for others to see and relate to. She believes that "art has a way to speak to us that bypasses those intellectual blockades."[36] Scholl's *White-work* series draws on traditional European white-on-white embroidery to reflect the sometimes subtle yet often violent ways that white women have maintained white supremacy. A piece called *The Hero-ine's Veil* depicts a white woman with a halo and wings standing on a Black woman's torso while offering an arm as if to help the woman up. Another, called *Cleanliness Is Next to Godliness*, is a white apron embroidered with hands holding a noose, in reference to white women's complicity in the lynching of Black people in the Jim Crow era South. The ties of the apron are embroidered with "I was afraid" on one side and "I am not to blame" on the other.

Scholl chose embroidery as an artistic medium because it "felt like home" to her, having learned needlework as a child. The small scale of embroidery also draws people in to examine and explore the work in an intimate way, which allows for the kind of close, personal engagement she is looking for through her work. A friend said of her art, "It forces you to put your face right up to the work and then it slaps you." The pieces in the *Whitework* series are pretty and delicate. Their initial approachability makes their message even more power-ful by the contrast between the medium and the content, reaching people who might not otherwise seek out this subject matter.

The *Whitework* series prompted Scholl to co-found Confront White Womanhood, an anti-racist education initiative for white women. She conducted workshops at the 2017 US Women's March and in university settings to explore the intersections of trauma and white supremacy and to learn how to engage in deeper, emo-tionally centered conversations about ways that white women are both victims and perpetrators of oppression. While she found these workshops to be a meaningful parallel to her art practice, Scholl was motivated to engage in this more didactic form of activism out of the fear that her art was not enough.

Activism through art has been discounted by some as a luxury, but it can make emotional and human connections in a way that other forms of activism struggle to do. In her essay "Poetry Is Not a Luxury," feminist and poet Audre Lorde writes, "Within living structures defined by profit, by linear power, by institutional dehumanization, our feelings were not meant to survive." To continue to care for our feelings and the feelings of others in the face of dehumanization is itself a form of resistance. Lorde also writes, "There are no new ideas. There are only new ways of making them felt."[37] The power of art is in finding new ways to help people *feel* ideas, like the suffrage banners whose movement was meant to stir emotion, not just communicate a message.

Scholl's latest series, *Resurrection of a Victim*, lays bare her own experience of processing the trauma of intimate partner violence and the ending of a long-term romantic relationship. She began to embroider images related to this pain to keep her hands busy and to begin to make sense of her experience. "The repetitive nature of the work takes some of the sting out of it," she said. Sometimes the motion soothed her and other times she felt the pain but could experience it from a more grounded place through the stitching. She chose to use religious forms, such as illuminated manuscripts and wooden triptychs, to imbue the work with a sense of weight and importance. Having diminished her experiences in the past, "simply that act of saying my story deserves to take up all this space . . . has been very therapeutic," she said.[38] One piece, *A Warrior's Birth*, is a wooden triptych with intricately embroidered scenes in each of the three parts. The central figure is a mermaid who appears to be in agony, holding two large sewing needles that pierce through feminine forms in the shapes of a pig and a fox kneeling at her feet. Flanking the central figure are embroidered nude female bodies, one hanging upside down with blood gushing from her neck and the other who appears to be liquefying, losing her form. While

clear expressions of pain and violence, the images are also beauti-
fully rendered in thread. Another piece, *Paper Dolls*, looks like a
page from an illuminated manuscript, with embroidered flowers and
butterflies surrounding text—a poem about an idealized love story
after the illusion has been shattered. A doll-like figure in the corner
near the gilt frame appears to cry out in pain and protest against the
loss of this fantasy.

Stitching details of her abuse claimed a physical space for healing
and helped Scholl trust her experience. When one's identity reflects
multiple layers of oppression, such as female and queer in Scholl's
case, it can be even more difficult to speak out against instances
of violence and discrimination. In *Resurrection of a Victim*, Scholl
hopes to break her own and others' silence and isolation, which are
all entangled in dynamics of abuse and domination:

> I'm seeking connection through the work in ways that I
> can . . . to affect other people, connect to them on a more
> emotional level, and hopefully inspire some amount of
> empathy and change. I hope that through the intimacy
> of my work that it will inspire somebody to investi-
> gate something in themselves or approach the issue in a
> slightly different way.[39]

She noted that many people have responded to the work with
a similar level of openness and intimacy, sharing their own stories
of trauma to break the silence and connect around shared experiences. By generating conversations about intimate partner violence
in LGBTQ+ relationships, she hopes her work can contribute to
building a safer community from within.

Meaningful connection is possible when we allow ourselves to be vulnerable to others, and connection with others is necessary for collective action. Lorde writes: "My silences had not protected me. Your silence will not protect you. But for every real word spoken, for every attempt I had ever made to speak those truths for which I am still seeking, I had made contact with other women while we examined the words to fit a world in which we all believed, bridging our differences. And it was the concern and caring of those women which gave me strength and enabled me to scrutinize the essentials of my living."[40] Sharing our stories—full of as much complexity, imperfection, contradiction, and emotion as possible—helps us battle the dehumanization that is at the root of systemic oppression.

La Federación de Mujeres de Sucumbíos (Women's Federation of Sucumbios, or FMS), is a feminist organization founded in 1987 aiming to eradicate gender-based violence and support women survivors in Sucumbios Province, Ecuador. Amparo Peñaherrera Sandoval, an activist and advocate for survivors of gender-based violence, is the coordinator of several programs within FMS, including Casa Amiga, a shelter for women healing from gender-based violence, and the Common Threads Project group therapy program, which I described in chapter 4. FMS aims to heal survivors and help them raise their voices against gender-based violence in their communities.

In 2015, Sandoval worked with a group of thirty-five mainly Indigenous women from Puerto El Carmen, the poorest and most remote city in Ecuador, and guided them through the Common Threads Project treatment where they made story cloths depicting their experiences of gender-based violence. Many of these women had to travel seven hours by canoe to reach the workshop. The group included members of the same family, including three generations of women who had suffered incest. Through the therapy process, they were able to confront and heal the intergenerational cycle of violence, exorcising the ghosts that had perpetuated it. After completing the therapy program, the women in the group exhibited their story cloths for local authorities and presented a law enforcement plan for the protection of their right to be free from sexual abuse and gender-based violence.

In a project with transgender women called *Vestidas para la Resistencia* (Dressed for Resistance), the women made dresses symbolizing their resistance to oppressive gender-identity norms and violence against the LGBTQ+ community. After embroidering dresses with their stories and hopes for the future, they wore them in runway shows to share their experiences with each other and with members of their communities. Sandoval said, "Every dress was a demand for their rights, and showed not only a personal story but a collective story of a group of trans women that were coming out empowered. Through sewing and art we found a way to resist that gives us better chances to get together, recognize each other and be empathetic."[41]

In all of these therapy groups, and many more that followed them, using story cloths to process the emotional pain of traumatic experiences connected women on a deep level and joined their voices together in speaking out against gender-based violence. And every year on November 25, the FMS holds a vigil in the city of Lago Agrio, Ecuador, where women sew together throughout the night in memory of the victims of femicide. They "come together through that invisible web that connects us through sewing and through story cloths," said Sandoval, and they invite anyone who passes by to join them. "We embroider and sew together an arpillera to keep the memory of this moment and to spread a message about freedom, collective freedom because we can only be free when we are together," she explained. "Together we built a strong and clear message that we are not going to be silenced, we demand justice for every victim and survivor of gender-based violence . . . because where there aren't collective actions, there lies the patriarchy."[42]

In November 2022, the participants at the vigil washed each other's clothes to symbolically wash the hearts and bodies of the victims of gender-based violence and to clean the memory of their ancestors, many of whose voices remained silent and are now lost to time. Participants hugged each other, wishing they could hug every victim of gender-based violence, including those who have died. For many survivors of trauma, processing painful personal experience becomes the basis for activism against the broader social and political injustices that contributed to their traumatic experiences. When we identify an injustice and the pain it causes, we want to rip it open, expose it, and then stitch it back together to make something new. Sandoval credits the Common Threads Project therapy program for creating such an opportunity for activism, calling the arpilleras "the seed that allowed a possibility of transformation for all women"—to heal, to recognize themselves as survivors, and to rebuild their personal and collective power.[43]

HOLDING OUR GROUND

We live in a world in motion, where acts of creation arise in the face of acts of destruction; a world where we strive to preserve and protect, resist and remember. This is apparent in the creativity and art that occurs during times of war, subjugation, and natural disasters as we try to combat loss of land or a way of life. Making textiles can help us expose these devastating changes and hold onto what we can of our culture, our rights, our voices, our homes. We can engage in art as an act to preserve culture and as a form of resistance to threats of oppression and colonization. Textiles are often reflective of human culture as a daily practice and as a symbolic language. By preserving traditional textile practices and donning traditional dress, people show their opposition to efforts to eradicate their way of life. As Iranian artist Shirin Neshat said, "Art is our weapon. Culture is a form of resistance."[44]

Mahatma Gandhi understood this. In the early part of the twentieth century, he initiated a spinning movement to promote rural self-employment and self-reliance as part of the Indian independence struggle. The khadi cloth woven from it became a national symbol of an economy free from British cloth and foreign clothing. As something made in India, by the people of India, and for the people of India, khadi was integral to the Swadeshi movement to reduce reliance on imported products. It held great importance for promoting gender egalitarianism in India, since women were the main producers of khadi and could earn an income through this work. It also broke down socioeconomic barriers, as khadi was worn by everyone from rural villagers to politicians. "Gandhian India poetically turned to the music of the spinning wheel," wrote Peruvian writer and Marxist philosopher José Carlos Mariátegui, highlighting the centrality of khadi cloth in Ghandi's movement to resist Britain's colonial rule.[45] Even today, the Indian flag must be made of khadi. Both serve as symbols of India's national identity.

For those living in exile or in the diaspora, maintaining a connection to traditional textile practices can serve as a critical tie to cultural identity and a powerful tool for resistance. The practice of Palestinian embroidery, known as *tatreez* in Arabic, has been a way for Palestinian women to express their cultural identity for over three thousand years. They use many tiny stitches in elaborate patterns such as olive trees, birds, and stars to adorn garments and household textiles and imbue them with meaning, such as commemorating an event or expressing an idea. Tatreez stitches look much like the European cross-stitch but are sewn differently, often by holding a waste canvas with an open grid structure, similar to the Aida cloth typically used in cross-stitch, on top of the garment cloth without the use of an embroidery hoop. The waste canvas is later picked away from the thread, leaving only the stitches on the underlying fabric. Practitioners of tatreez use the sewing method where the needle goes in and out of the fabric in one motion instead of the stab stitch method typically used in European cross-stitch. Unlike other cultural traditions that are tied to the land, Palestinians have been able to continue to practice tatreez while displaced. As a result, the preservation of tatreez garments and techniques are particularly meaningful for Palestinians living in refugee camps and in the broader diaspora.

Tatreez sessions have traditionally been a time for mothers and grandmothers to impart their wisdom and skill to their daughters and granddaughters. In the diaspora, they have also become a time to transmit cultural identity, history, and traditions that might otherwise be lost to future generations.[46] The motifs, their placement, and their colors tell the wearer's story—where they're from and who they are. The use of deep red embroidery on white or black linen in geometric and floral designs is a distinguishing feature of the *thobes* (dresses) in Ramallah. Bethlehem is known for its "tree of life" pattern that often runs along the side panels of a thobe. Bedouin women embroider their thobes in shades of red and pink when they are married and in blue, the color of mourning, when they are widowed.

Palestinian dress historian, educator, and activist Wafa Ghnaim learned tatreez from her mother, Feryal Abbasi-Ghnaim, when she was just two years old. During an embroidery class I took with Ghnaim in October 2023, she shared how meaningful embroidery is to her mother's sense of personal and cultural identity. To continue this important cultural tradition, Abbasi-Ghnaim taught tatreez in Palestinian refugee camps before moving to the United States, where Ghnaim was raised. Ghnaim credits her mother with inspiring her to carry on tatreez: "I grew up admiring her and her stitches. . . . I want people to see the power of Palestinian hands . . . and ultimately our humanity."[47]

Ghnaim views tatreez as a connection to home, as part of the cultural inheritance embedded in the muscle memory of Palestinian women, just waiting to be activated by instruction. To that end, she teaches anyone interested in learning, while working to collect Palestinian oral history, rescue tatreez garments from thrift stores and personal collections for study and preservation, and properly identify and catalog pieces of tatreez in museum collections to maintain the history of the region and its rich embroidery tradition. It is critical to Ghnaim that the motifs and color combinations do not lose their cultural meaning and regional significance.[48]

Tatreez took on national and political meaning in 1948, when over seven hundred thousand Palestinians were displaced as a result of the establishment of Israel, an event that Palestinians refer to as the *Nakba* (the "catastrophe"). Tatreez has since provided economic opportunities for Palestinian women whose refugee status makes it difficult to seek employment in countries where they are encamped. Women can work as embroidery teachers and sell their work, though many are unable to earn enough to justify the intensive labor involved and therefore view the primary function of their work as preserving the tradition. Maryam Malakha, an embroidery teacher originally from Jaffa, says, "I felt we are not doing our heritage justice. How among all the things that Palestine has lost, we're also losing our material culture. . . . So, I got excited about working with embroidery. I told myself, I am unable to fight with a rifle so I will fight with a needle."[49] Randa Yousef Al Miyari, a tatreez artist in a Palestinian refugee camp in Lebanon, believes: "Tatreez is also an excellent teacher of patience and perseverance—two values that are much needed when you're a refugee. . . . It's a long and arduous process that takes significant patience, but once you're done and are able to look back at your beautiful creations and know that you have contributed to preserving the heritage of your people—nothing is more rewarding."[50]

While maintaining the tradition of tatreez is a form of cultural resistance, it is also used directly as a political tool. During the First Intifada (uprising) from 1987 until 1993, the Israeli army confiscated symbols of Palestinian national identity, such as flags, at protests. Palestinian women responded by creating the "Intifada dress," a traditional Palestinian thobe covered in tatreez depicting Palestinian flags, maps, and phrases such as, "We will return," in defiance of Israeli bans on the public exhibition of Palestinian nationalism. Women throughout the diaspora made Intifada dresses as a way of holding their ground in unity even when separated by great distances. It serves as a tool of peaceful resistance and is proof of the long history of Palestinians in the region.[51] In her book *Tatreez and Tea*, Ghnaim shares one of her mother's designs. It is meant to represent their family garden. It can no longer be a single family tree because their "strong roots" in Palestine cannot be contained by one tree. Instead, she writes, "we blossomed into a family garden with our flowers and seeds planted in a sprawl across the earth," which is the Palestinian diaspora.[52]

Textile artist Sonya Clark also explores issues of cultural identity and social justice in her work, using flags to symbolically unravel the long history of racism in the United States and collectively weave reparative justice. In 2015, in the context of Black Lives Matter and the 150th anniversary of the end of the Civil War, Clark unraveled a Confederate flag by hand in the gallery space. It was a slow and tedious process, with some threads easier to pull out than others—a fitting metaphor for undoing the legacies of racial injustice that these flags have represented.[53] In a piece titled *Unraveled*, she showed the Confederate flag taken down to piles of red, white, and blue thread. A second piece titled *Unraveling* is a Confederate flag partially unraveled and hung on the wall with its tattered ends. She turned it into a community project with fifty volunteers taking turns working with Clark to further unpick the threads of the flag on opening night of the gallery exhibit. They managed to undo only about an inch in an hour and a half.

Clark explained the purpose of her project: "We are all wearing cloth. But we actually don't understand how it is made. We live in the United States of America and we are used to a kind of injustice because it is part of the fabric of our nation. There's a way in which unraveling a cloth—using that metaphor . . . helps us understand that."[54] To make a Confederate flag, the cloth is woven in separate colors and then pieced together so that the white cloth is stitched to the blue cloth that is stitched to the red cloth, and then stars are stitched on top. Clark noted, "When people were unraveling it with me, they were . . . understanding the complexity of cloth itself which I think is akin to understanding the complexity of the history of racism in our nation."[55] Deconstructing the flag is a metaphor for understanding the social construction of racial inequality—it was woven in a particular way for a particular reason. From its unraveled state, the flag could be rewoven into anything and raises the question of what transformation we would like to see.

Clark appears to address that question in her 2019 exhibit *Monumental Cloth, The Flag We Should Know*. In it, she focuses on a different flag: the Confederate Flag of Truce. It is nothing more than a handwoven white linen dishcloth with three thin red stripes at each end. This cloth was carried by a staff officer to signal the surrender of the Confederate army at the Battle of Appomattox Court House on April 9, 1865. In an interview during her exhibit, Clark asked the question, "What if this cloth, the Flag of Truce, was the symbol of the Civil War rather than one of the many Confederate battle flags?" And, by extension, "did the truce actually happen?"[56] If it did, would the Confederate flag still be such a prominent symbol of the Southern United States? Would we have seen the systematic racism—Jim Crow laws, voter suppression, and mass incarceration of Black people—in the years following this "truce"?

For the exhibit, Clark wove a large-scale version of the Flag of Truce, measuring fifteen by thirty feet—ten times the size of the original flag—a monument reflecting the scale of its importance as a symbol for peace and unity that is inherent in the word *truce*. She also invited visitors to participate in weaving replicas of this flag at the exhibit, symbolizing a collective effort at reparative justice. The act of weaving brings individual threads together to create something stronger—offering a vision for what the United States could have been and could still be if we collectively take a stand against systemic racism.

Clark's work vividly demonstrates how creative and destructive forces are interwoven. Unraveling the Confederate battle flag shows how acts of destruction offer new possibilities for creation—a pile of red, white, and blue thread that could be reworked into something new. Weaving the Confederate Flag of Truce shows how acts of creation arise to counter acts of destruction. A symbol of peace and harmony can offer an alternative to violence and inequality.

Rilla Marshall's weaving is driven by a different political purpose. In an almost literal effort to hold her ground and not have it swept to sea from under her feet, Marshall began tackling the impact of climate change on Prince Edward Island (PEI), Canada, through handweaving. PEI has been experiencing coastal erosion at a rate of around one foot per year for decades, but Hurricane Fiona in 2022 caused a loss of thirty to eighty feet in some areas.[57] Marshall shared her interest in taking "hard data, dehumanized, and rehumanizing it through textiles."[58] The tactile, approachable nature of the textiles she weaves softens the "hard" data and, she hopes, makes this important topic approachable and engaging to people.

Marshall works from drone aerial footage to gather before and after images of the coastline as well as changes in wrack lines that, as sea levels rise, creep higher and higher onto the land. By showing lines on her weaving that reflect the amount of land lost to erosion, Marshall wants people to notice the changes in their landscape that they may not otherwise observe. You can stand on a beach and think it feels different, but you might not realize that three feet of shoreline have been lost. By looking at before-and-after images, you can understand these spatial differences more clearly. Marshall hopes her work strikes viewers at both the visceral and cerebral levels in a way that makes them feel the value of the land that is being lost.

Her artistic process reflects the unpredictability of nature as well as the climate data that quantify and describe environmental changes. Marshall paints her warp prior to weaving. How the warp threads absorb the paint depends on their thickness, the quality of the fiber, and the humidity of the air, so she does not have full control over where the colors go or how dark they become. She has more control over the weaving, which is technical and precise and allows her to depict where the shoreline once was compared with where it is now through the use of different patterns. The effect is rich and layered in color and texture, made more beautiful by the element of chance, much like the waves on the shore themselves.

Marshall expresses her interest in the physical processes at work in this changing landscape but also in the poetic and metaphorical ideas expressed in the shifting space of the shoreline. She understands that people could become depressed by dealing with the effects of climate change but does not want them to end up in despair: "By examining this liminal space of the shoreline, this transitional space that's always in flux and always changing, I think existentially it's a little reassuring that life keeps changing and mostly it's at these very slow, incremental levels that we can only see in hindsight when a lot of those little incremental changes have happened and we see, oh there's a big change."

In life we tend to concentrate on the beginnings and endings, but most of the time we're somewhere in between. Things are often in flux, and if you take time to really observe, you may notice how they evolve and change. As Marshall explained, "Examining shorelines the way I do in my artwork, there's a certain element of taking the time to really pay attention. . . . I think the act of paying attention is really valuable."

So much about textile work, whether weaving, crocheting, knitting, or quilting, is about paying attention: to the materials, to the skills, to the traditions, to the stories. We learn from others and then pass on their knowledge. In this way, textiles are often the common thread that connects us to our heritage. But while the creators of cloth maintain skills and traditions, they can also incorporate change by imbuing their own sense of style, color, and personality into the cloth, which evolves these practices and, in turn, our culture. Making something by hand reminds us of the slow pace of transformation—that change requires sustained, cooperative effort—one stitch at a time. Through these crafts, we find ways to organize ideas, accomplish goals, and connect with others, which sets the stage for how to do that in activism as well. We feel empowered through our projects, which can lead to empowering acts in other areas of life. Amid oppression, war, and climate change, the methodical and intricate work of making textiles can help us to pay attention, raise awareness, maintain our traditions, hold our ground, and change the world.

Epilogue: Crafting a Purpose

In all of my research for this book, one particular woman's story stands out as exemplifying the process of making a meaningful life using textile work—that of Olutosin Oladosu Adebowale, who seeks to empower women through sewing in her community of Owo, in southwestern Nigeria. I was struck by the beauty she creates both in textiles and in building communities of women who know their worth. As a survivor of domestic violence, her own empowerment was hard won. Adebowale earned a master's degree in English language from the University of Lagos prior to getting married. One night she asked her husband to help her with their newborn. Her body was still healing from a difficult childbirth, and she was tired from carrying her baby and trying to sing her to sleep. Instead of helping his wife, he beat her. Her family told her to stay quiet about the incident and accept the fact that all Nigerian men beat their wives. But a doctor she visited to treat her wounds had a different perspective. He told her to either divorce her husband or join the fight for women's rights and demand better treatment.

Following the abuse, she felt she had reached the lowest point in her life. She told me, "If nothing changed, I would have preferred to die. . . . When you get to a point that you choose death, the only thing that can help you survive [is] radical change."[1] Adebowale thought of her daughters: "If I can't make change happen, how will

I teach these girls how to make change happen. . . . So, I said, okay I have to brace it because of my daughters."

That was when she started sewing, which she described as "a fight for my life." She began by using discarded textiles because she had no money to buy new fabric. "I said, I am going to start with trash because I was treated like trash." She made practical items like purses and phone cases. After a while, she began making gorgeous fabric paintings from scraps too small to sew with. Transforming trash into things that are beautiful and useful became a metaphor for her own life. She said, "When you create things you become alive. When you create beautiful things, you don't want to die. You don't think about death. You think about growth. . . . You want to create more, and you can see yourself as adding to the beauty of the world." Adebowale sewed for survival and in the process found a reason to live.

Transforming her own life by creating beauty with her hands motivated Adebowale to help others do the same. Research shows that a sense of meaning can motivate action and the pursuit of goals. When people view their lives as meaningful, they are more likely to connect with others and offer help by volunteering or giving to charities.[2] In 2011, Adebowale set out to raise the voices of women in southwestern Nigeria by founding the Star of Hope Transformation Centre to empower women and girls to fight against child sexual abuse and gender-based violence. She teaches women skills like sewing, knitting, farming, and carpentry, which are accessible to everyone regardless of their education level, so they can earn an income and become independent.

Because of her own experience of domestic violence, Adebowale realized that education does not equal empowerment. She stated with passion and clarity, "Any certificate that you have and you remain voiceless, it is a useless certificate." She said of her programs, "We don't use certificates, we use stories" to empower women. Group members are encouraged to look deep within themselves for what they can create from their experiences of gender-based violence. She described how women share these experiences as they stitch: "There are some stories that when you hear them you just have to lift your whole body and place it on the floor and you hug another person so that you [both] know you are not alone. . . . Most of the time our issues are almost the same. If it is not violence, it is emotional, it is financial, it is psychological . . . you know, different shades of colors for the same violence." The women experience emotional transformation and deep personal connection through the act of sewing together and crafting a personal narrative for their lives. They are also transforming their narrative by coming together, learning skills, and writing a new chapter for themselves.

In her program Tosin Turns Trash into Treasure, Adebowale draws parallels between the abuse of women and the abuse of our earth by teaching women how to transform trash in the environment into useful goods that they can sell to earn their own income. They collect fabric scraps, which would otherwise end up in the tailor's dustbin, to make slippers, sanitary pads, hair accessories, and quilts. From discarded Styrofoam padding, they make bags for storing and insulating food, Wonderbag slow cookers, and laptop bags. "The more you create beautiful things, your self-esteem grows. If I can create such beauty and treasure and they're saying I'm useless, is that not a contradiction?" she asked.

Adebowale was raised by a single mother after her father died when she was three years old. Her father's family blamed her mother for his death and accused her of being a witch. Her mother was very poor and worked as a farmer to feed her children but was not able to provide the family with a home, and she died in poverty. Her mother's struggles have inspired many of Adebowale's efforts. Beyond her skills-based programs, Adebowale has also built Sisters City, a community of homes for unhoused women, and started a farm and food bank called Free Farm for Females to feed women in the community in a self-sustaining way. She has focused many of her efforts on poor elderly women who have been accused of witchcraft and ostracized from the community. For her birthday in 2022, she sewed 315 dresses for these women using local Ankara (West African wax print) fabric. She told me that wearing clothes is not just about covering our nakedness, it is a form of dignity, so she used only the highest-quality textiles for the dresses.

Adebowale has also been accused of witchcraft. "Who builds a whole city if not a witch? Who can sew [that] many dresses for abandoned women? It's only a witch who does that," she said as she laughed. "I know I am not a witch and my mother was not a witch. So those people had nobody to speak for them. We are their voices and we speak for them. We stand for them, we protect them, we feed them. We make them feel as if yes, they are human beings and they have somebody." Through these actions she stands up for what she believes in, humanizing people whose humanity has been denied.

Adebowale continues to make beautiful fabric paintings out of scraps; the finished art resembles a hybrid of painting, mosaic, and quilting, often depicting women or local wildlife. She noted that she has no formal training as an artist and taught herself to make these paintings in order to avoid wasting any cloth. She wanted to ensure that nothing would go to the dump to become a problem for the environment. Each sale supports a local woman's education or business venture. In this way, her fabric paintings have a purpose both in transforming trash into artwork and transforming a woman's life into something equally beautiful and powerful: "When I look at trash, I see it as a woman who needs help. When I look at the artwork, eventually it becomes an empowered woman who is ready to fly." The money goes to pay the rent on a woman's shop for two years and provide her with sewing equipment and forty different kinds of fabrics to start her business. Adebowale explained, "Before you know it, she has other women in her locality learning from her. She becomes the boss. She teaches others, she spreads the knowledge and you know, you are a different person when you acquire knowledge, you become a different person." Adebowale's efforts to empower women have created a chain reaction that ripples through the social fabric in her community. Women she taught to sew have gone into business together and have empowered their daughters, and some, like Adebowale, have even helped their husbands take a stand against domestic violence.

Survival in difficult circumstances depends on one's ability to find meaning in one's suffering. Adebowale took a painful experience and made a purpose out of it, transforming her life through her textile art. She said, "I was treated like trash. I actually felt like trash. . . . I began to use trash to create beautiful things so that I can convince myself that if I can make beautiful things out of nothing, I can equally make beautiful things out of my life. . . . I am happy that I am alive, that I did not choose death." She has made beautiful textiles and a beautiful life in the process, helping hundreds of other women to do the same. Adebowale marveled at the experience of translating an idea in her mind to a canvas that everyone could see: "It is like creating a dream. . . . It is like giving birth to what is inside of me for the whole world to see and to admire." She described the feeling she gets when she makes a fabric painting as being "like a miracle. Like transformation. It's something I cannot really explain. I can't explain it."

Through writing this book, I set out to understand the personal meaning of textile work for women across time and place. I have discovered that this meaning runs deeper than I ever could have imagined—so deep that it is difficult to put it into words. Like Adebowale, so many of the women I spoke to found words insufficient for describing what their textile practices mean to them. It is possible to experience a feeling through touch and express it in a visual product but be unable to verbalize it. Many women express the unspeakable through their craft—just like Philomela, in Ovid's *Metamorphoses*, who could not tell the story of her rape in spoken words but could weave it. Artist Michelle Kingdom said that she aims to evoke some kind of truth in her embroidery "that we can't really put into words."[3] She said that if she could put these ideas into words, she'd be a writer. Instead, she embroiders metaphorical images meant to evoke a feeling beyond words. Angela Maddock said of Bloodline, her joint knitting project with her mother, "Some things are beyond words but not beyond making."[4]

The rich meaning of this work to the women who engage in it can also elude us at times. Gee's Bend quilter Claudia Pettway Charley said of continuing the quilting tradition of her ancestors, "Just the idea of being able to carry on and appreciate the heritage that they left for us is beyond imaginable. If there was a word, I don't even know what that word would be."[5] Marlene Bennett Jones, also a quilter from Gee's Bend, shared her sense of awe at having one of her quilts hanging in the Royal Academy of Arts in London. When asked what it means to her to have her work recognized at this level, she said, "I am so ecstatic, I am speechless. I don't know what to say. . . . I just, I don't have the words."[6]

Gabina Sicus Mamani, an avid weaver in the remote mountain community of Quiswarani, in Peru, spun wool constantly during the hour that we spoke at her house. When asked what she would do if she could not weave anymore, a sudden silence struck in what had been a lively conversation. She looked at me blankly while continuing to spin. My translator interpreted the silence, which we all understood: "Sometimes there are no words."[7]

Acknowledgments

I set out to write this book in search of the meaning of textile work for women throughout history and found that my search became a source of meaning for me as well. It fulfilled me intellectually, creatively, and personally, but, most significantly, it connected me with people around the world, mostly women, who share my passion for creating textiles. When I began my research during the COVID pandemic, I was isolated. In crafting this book, I have also crafted a community that I am exceedingly grateful for. I will take these pages to express my appreciation for their contributions to this book and to my life.

Thank you to my editors, Amy Cherry and Huneeya Siddiqui, for moving me away from my usual academic style of writing to find my own voice and ensure that the women's stories come shining through. From our very first meeting, it was clear that you shared my vision for this book, and I am so appreciative that this has remained the case throughout. A special shout-out to Huneeya for taking up crochet while editing this book.

To my agent, Kendall Berdinsky, for believing in the project when it was nothing more than a ball of yarn and an idea for a sweater. Thank you for seeing the possibilities from the start and for checking in on both my writing progress and my knitting projects, knowing as you do the importance of each.

To Carole Zimmer, for pointing me in the right direction when I was stumbling in the dark not knowing quite what to do with an idea for a book, and to Constance Rosenblum, who took me by the hand and guided me as I wrote the proposal.

To Anna Emerson for providing citation support and life support so I could devote time to writing.

A special thanks to my textile-crafting friends for nerding out about projects with me, often over cocktails. And to many other friends who took a genuine interest in the topic, listened to me talk through ideas, connected me with people to interview, and provided support and encouragement every step of the way.

To my parents, Russ and Gail, for acting as satellite reporters during their travels—taking pictures of textiles and asking women around the world about what textile work means to them. And to my brother, Max, for deeming my handknits fashionable enough to integrate into his dapper wardrobe.

The warmest, most heart-bursting appreciation to my husband and children for taking an interest in these passions of mine. To Jerome for listening to me talk endlessly about knitting for eighteen years, spending countless hours waiting inside yarn and fabric stores, and deigning to entertain questions like, "Do you think I should knit a few extra rows of this yoke to raise the neckline?" You have been a true partner to me as I wrote this book—deeply engaging in conversations about my research, drawing on your knowledge of history, math, and classics to guide and fact-check me. Thank you for reading nearly every draft of every chapter and reminding me of what I'm trying to say when I lost my way. To Eleanor for sharing my love of handwork and eagerly trying every fiber craft we can think of. You bring such beauty and warmth into this world, and I know you will make it a better place with all that you create. To Ari for embroidering monsters, designing the most interesting creations for me to construct with yarn, and learning to knit so you can make a linen chain mail vest. The products of your mind and your hands never cease to amaze me.

Finally, thank you to the forty-five people who took the time to share their research, opinions, artwork, and stories in interviews with me. Most of these interviews lasted over two hours, and I spoke with many people multiple times. While I came to these interviews prepared with questions, they inevitably took me to places I could not have foreseen, and I delighted in the discovery of our dialogues. Similarly, many people I interviewed connected me with other inspiring artists and scholars, and following this thread of personal connections broadened my awareness of the textile field and introduced me to people I would not have known otherwise. Some helped more than I ever could have expected, and I want to extend a special thank-you to Janet Catherine Berlo for reading the first couple of chapters and reassuring me that I was on the right track and then surprising me with a box of her handspun yarn; Rebecca van Bergen for answering many follow-up emails about Nest and connecting me with the Gee's Bend quilting community; Juan Carlos Auccapuma Ccorqhua for helping me navigate Peru and being an endless source of knowledge on Andean culture and religion; and Lilly Marsh for welcoming me into her studio and teaching me how to weave. This book would not exist without:

Diana Greenwold

Rosa Pomar

Flora Collingwood-Norris

Lilly Marsh

Josh Faught

Deborah Valoma

Sarah Mosteller

Anastasiia Bytko

Sarah Confer

Juan Carlos Auccapuma Ccorqhua

Marcela Salas Calcina

Anita Quispe Apaza

Juana Huaman Willca

Gabina Sicus Mamani

Mari Luz Aranzabal Sicus

Nilda Callañuapa Alvarez

Haley Pierson-Cox

Elena Kanagy-Loux

Ghada Amer

Adeyinka Akinsulure-Smith

Rilla Marshall

Rachel Cohen

Chantal James

Antoine Verney

Fanny Garbe

Véronique Thomazo

Caroline Collin

Michelle Kingdom

Rebecca van Bergen

Janet Catherine Berlo

Lindsay Degen

Hazel Tindall

Heather Marie Scholl

Gertrude Banda

Claudia Pettway Charley

Delia Pettway Thibodeaux

Janet Hoskins

Tinnie Pettway

Marlene Bennett Jones

Francesca Charley

Olutosin Oladosu Adebowale

Kate Russell

Mia Hansson

Alexandra Lester-Makin

Annamarta Dostourian

Notes

INTRODUCTION

1. Girija Kaimal, Adele M. L. Gonzaga, and Victoria Schwachter, "Crafting, Health and Wellbeing: Findings from the Survey of Public Participation in the Arts and Considerations for Art Therapists," *Arts & Health* 9, no. 1 (January 2, 2017): 81–90.
2. C. G. Jung and Aniela Jaffé, *Memories, Dreams, Reflections*, rev. ed. (Vintage Books, 1989), 340.
3. Julia Kristeva, "Is There a Feminine Genius?," *Critical Inquiry* 30, no. 3 (March 2004): 493–504.
4. Kristeva, "Is There a Feminine Genius?," 493–504.
5. Carolyn G. Heilbrun, *Reinventing Womanhood* (W. W. Norton, 1979), 34.
6. Heilbrun, *Reinventing Womanhood*, 37.
7. Elizabeth M. Brumfiel, "Cloth, Gender, Continuity, and Change: Fabricating Unity in Anthropology," *American Anthropologist* 108, no. 4 (December 2006): 862–77.

CHAPTER 1. TO LIVE AND DYE

1. Marcela Salas Calcina (Peruvian weaver) in discussion with the author, December 10, 2022.
2. Elizabeth Wayland Barber, *Women's Work: The First 20,000 Years: Women, Cloth, and Society in Early Times* (W. W. Norton, 1994).
3. Michèle Hayeur Smith, *The Valkyries' Loom: The Archaeology of Cloth Production and Female Power in the North Atlantic* (University Press of Florida, 2020).
4. Véronique Dasen, "Childbirth and Infancy in Greek and Roman Antiquity," in *A Companion to Families in the Greek and Roman Worlds*, ed. Beryl Rawson (Wiley, 2010), 291–314.
5. P. M. Dunn, "Aristotle (384–322 BC): Philosopher and Scientist of Ancient

Greece," *Archives of Disease in Childhood: Fetal and Neonatal Edition* 91, no. 1 (September 20, 2005): F75–77.

6. Ami Ronnberg and Kathleen Rock Martín, eds., *The Book of Symbols: Archetypal Reflections in Word and Image* (Köln: Taschen, 2010).

7. Barber, *Women's Work*.

8. Ann Futterman Collier, *Using Textile Arts and Handcrafts in Therapy with Women: Weaving Lives Back Together* (Jessica Kingsley Publishers, 2013).

9. Janet Hoskins, "Why Do Ladies Sing the Blues? Indigo Dyeing, Cloth Production, and Gender Symbolism in Kodi," in *Cloth and Human Experience*, ed. Annette B. Weiner and Jane Schneider (Smithsonian Books, 1989).

10. Janet Hoskins, "The Menstrual Hut and the Witch's Lair in Two Eastern Indonesian Societies," *Ethnology* 41, no. 4 (2002): 317.

11. Janet Hoskins (anthropologist) in discussion with the author, September 20, 2023.

12. Hoskins, "The Menstrual Hut and the Witch's Lair."

13. Yang Qi-yue et al., "From Natural Dye to Herbal Medicine: A Systematic Review of Chemical Constituents, Pharmacological Effects and Clinical Applications of Indigo Naturalis," *Chinese Medicine* 15, no. 1 (December 2020): 127; Ning Liu et al., "Anti-Inflammatory and Analgesic Activities of Indigo through Regulating the $IKK\beta/I\kappa B/NF$-κB Pathway in Mice," *Food & Function* 11, no. 10 (2020): 8537–46.

14. Hoskins in discussion with the author.

15. Hoskins, "Why Do Ladies Sing the Blues?," 167.

16. Traci Ardren, "Mending the Past: Ix Chel and the Invention of a Modern Pop Goddess," *Antiquity* 80, no. 307 (March 1, 2006): 25–37.

17. William K. Mahony, *The Artful Universe: An Introduction to the Vedic Religious Imagination*, SUNY Series in Hindu Studies (State University of New York Press, 1998), 23.

18. Janet Catherine Berlo, "Dreaming of Double Woman: The Ambivalent Role of the Female Artist in North American Indian Myth," *American Indian Quarterly* 17, no. 1 (1993): 31.

19. Berlo, "Dreaming of Double Woman."

20. The etymology of the word *siren* in Greek comes from the word *rope* or *cord* and effectively means one who binds or entangles.

21. E. Goldwater, "What Do Men Fear?," *Modern Psychoanalysis* 23, no. 2 (1998): 211–24.

22. Magnus Magnusson and Hermann Palsson, trans., *Njál's Saga* (Penguin Books, 1960).

23. Magnusson and Palsson, *Njál's Saga*.

24. Smith, *The Valkyries' Loom*.

25. Smith, *The Valkyries' Loom*.

26. Lotte Hedeager, *Iron Age Myth and Materiality* (Routledge, 2011).

27. Max Dashu, *Witches and Pagans: Women in European Folk Religion, 700–1100* (Velona Press, 2016).

28. Nancy Chodorow, *The Reproduction of Mothering: Psychoanalysis and the Sociology of Gender* (University of California Press, 1978).

29. Dan Jorgensen, "Preying on Those Close to Home: Witchcraft Violence in a Papua New Guinea Village," *Australian Journal of Anthropology* 25, no. 3 (December 2014): 267–86; Shamsher Alam and Aditya Raj, "Witchcraft and Witch Hunting in India: An Assessment," Emerging Challenges of Violence Against Women, Odisha State Women Commission, February 22, 2018; Adinkrah Mensah and Adhikari Prakash, "Gendered Injustice: A Comparative Analysis of Witchcraft Beliefs and Witchcraft-Related Violence in Ghana and Nepal," *International Journal of Sociology and Anthropology* 6, no. 10 (October 31, 2014): 314–21.

30. David Cressy, *Birth, Marriage and Death: Ritual, Religion and the Life-Cycle in Tudor and Stuart England* (Oxford University Press, 1997).

31. Sheilagh C. Ogilvie, *A Bitter Living: Women, Markets, and Social Capital in Early Modern Germany* (Oxford University Press, 2003).

32. H. C. Erik Midelfort, *Witch Hunting in Southwestern Germany, 1562–1684: The Social and Intellectual Foundations* (Stanford University Press, 1972).

33. Linda Stone-Ferrier, "Spun Virtue, the Lacework of Folly, and the World Wound Upside-down: Seventeenth-Century Dutch Depictions of Female Handwork," in *Cloth and Human Experience*, ed. Annette B. Weiner and Jane Schneider (Smithsonian Books, 1989).

34. Alison G. Stewart, "Distaffs and Spindles: Sexual Misbehavior in Sebald Beham's Spinning Bee," in *Saints, Sinners, and Sisters: Gender and Northern Art in Medieval and Early Modern Europe*, ed. Jane Louise Carroll, (Routledge, 2003), 127–54.

35. Stewart, "Distaffs and Spindles."

36. Rozsika Parker, *The Subversive Stitch: Embroidery and the Making of the Feminine* (Women's Press, 1984), 119.

37. Sigmund Freud, *The Standard Edition of the Complete Psychological Works of Sigmund Freud*, ed. James Strachey (Hogarth Press, 1999).

38. Goldwater, "What Do Men Fear?"

39. Traude Gavin, *The Women's Warpath: Iban Ritual Fabrics from Borneo* (UCLA Fowler Museum of Cultural History, 1996).

40. Euripides and Diane J. Rayor, *Euripides' Medea: A New Translation* (Cambridge University Press, 2013).

41. Froma I. Zeitlin, *Playing the Other: Gender and Society in Classical Greek Literature* (University of Chicago Press, 1996), 351.

42. Ann Bergren, *Weaving Truth: Essays on Language and the Female in Greek Thought*, Hellenic Studies; 19 (Center for Hellenic Studies, Harvard University Press, 2008).

43. Hoskins, "Why Do Ladies Sing the Blues?"

44. Hoskins in discussion with the author.

45. Hoskins, "Why Do Ladies Sing the Blues?"

46. Hoskins in discussion with the author.

47. Hoskins, "Why Do Ladies Sing the Blues?"

48. Hoskins in discussion with the author.

49. Ruth Clifford, "Textiles, Language and Metaphor," *Threads Unpicked* (blog), June 30, 2015.

50. Michaela Cabrera, "Tribe Brings Back Dead with 'Clothing' Ritual," *Reuters*, February 1, 2010.

51. S. Hyland, C. Lee, and R. Aldave Palacios, "Khipus to Keep Away the Living Dead: Andean Funerary Khipus Resurge During the COVID-19 Pandemic," *Anthropology News* 64, no. 5 (2021).

52. Catherine Allen, "The Sadness of Jars: Separation and Rectification in Andean Understandings of Death," in *Living with the Dead in the Andes*, ed. Izumi Shimada and James L. Fitzsimmons (University of Arizona Press, 2015), 304–28.

53. Allen, "The Sadness of Jars."

54. Allen, "The Sadness of Jars."

55. Hyland, Lee, and Aldave Palacios, "Khipus to Keep Away the Living Dead."

56. Deborah Valoma (textile artist) in discussion with the author, November 11, 2022.

CHAPTER 2. WEBS OF KNOWLEDGE

1. Barbara J. Toth, "The Gift of Spider Woman," *Early American Review* 15, no. 1 (Winter/Spring 2011).

2. Marcela Salas Calcina and Anita Quispe Apaza (Peruvian weavers) in discussion with the author, December 10, 2022.

3. Denise Y. Arnold et al., eds., *The Andean Science of Weaving: Structures and Techniques of Warp-Faced Weaves* (Thames & Hudson, 2015).

4. Hazel Tindall (Shetland knitter) in discussion with the author, August 31, 2023.

5. Elizabeth Zimmermann, *Knitting Without Tears: Basic Techniques and Easy-to-Follow Directions for Garments to Fit All Sizes* (Fireside Books, 1995).

6. Suzanne B. Butters, "From Skills to Wisdom: Making, Knowing, and the Arts," in *Ways of Making and Knowing: The Material Culture of Empirical Knowledge*, ed. Pamela H. Smith, Amy R. W. Meyers, and Harold J. Cook (University of Michigan Press, 2014), 48–85.

7. Butters, "From Skills to Wisdom."

8. Bruce Metcalf, "Replacing the Myth of Modernism," *American Craft* (blog), 1993.

9. Yonas Geda, "Exercise Your Brain to Prevent Memory Loss" (61st Annual Meeting of the American Academy of Neurology, Seattle, WA, 2009).

10. Betsan Corkhill et al., "Knitting and Well-Being," *TEXTILE* 12, no. 1 (March 2014): 34–57.

11. Lucette Toussaint and Aurore Meugnot, "Short-Term Limb Immobilization Affects Cognitive Motor Processes.," *Journal of Experimental Psychology: Learning, Memory, and Cognition* 39, no. 2 (2013): 623–32; Kelly Lambert, "Do or DIY," *RSA Journal* 161, no. 5561 (2015): 20–23.

12. Matthew B. Crawford, *The Case for Working with Your Hands, or, Why Office Work Is Bad for Us and Fixing Things Feels Good* (Penguin Books, 2010).

13. Rye Dag Holmboe, "Anna Freud's Loom," *International Journal of Psycho-Analysis* 102, no. 5 (October 2021): 932–49.

14. Ann Hamilton, *Habitus*, Fabric Workshop and Museum, September 17, 2016, Exhibition Catalog, 11, 15.

15. Elena Kanagy-Loux (lacemaker and lace scholar) in discussion with the author, February 25, 2023.

16. Nilda Callañuapa Alvarez (director of Centro de Textiles Tradicionnales del Cusco) in discussion with the author, December 16, 2022.

17. "Natural Dyes of Peru," *Threads of Peru*, 2024.

18. Cameron J. Menezes et al., "Mechanisms for Falling Urine pH with Age in Stone Formers," *American Journal of Physiology: Renal Physiology* 317, no. 7 (July 1, 2019): F65–72.

19. William DeFooR et al., "Results of a Prospective Trial to Compare Normal Urine Supersaturation in Children and Adults," *Journal of Urology* 174, no. 4, part 2 (October 2005): 1708–10.

20. Pamela H. Smith, Amy R. W. Meyers, and Harold J. Cook, eds., *Ways of Making and Knowing: The Material Culture of Empirical Knowledge* (University of Michigan Press, 2014).

21. Janet Hoskins, "Why Do Ladies Sing the Blues? Indigo Dyeing, Cloth Production, and Gender Symbolism in Kodi," in *Cloth and Human Experience*, ed. A. Weiner and J. Schneider (Smithsonian Books, 1989).

22. Dominique Cardon, *Natural Dyes: Sources, Tradition, Technology and Science* (Archetype, 2007).

23. Alicia Weisberg-Roberts, "Between Trade and Science: Dyeing and Knowing in the Long Eighteenth Century," in *Ways of Making and Knowing: The Material Culture of Empirical Knowledge* (University of Michigan Press, 2014).

24. Paracelsus, *The Hermetic and Alchemical Writings of Aureolus Philippus Theophrastus Bombast, of Hohenheim, Called Paracelsus the Great: Now for the First Time Faithfully Translated into English*, ed. Arthur Edward Waite (Martino Publishing, 2009).

25. Margaret Swanson and Ann Macbeth, *Educational Needlecraft* (Longmans, Green and Co., 1911).

26. Swanson and Macbeth, *Educational Needlecraft*, 1, 2.

27. Kanagy-Loux in discussion with the author.

28. Judith A. Tyner, *Stitching the World: Embroidered Maps and Women's Geographical Education* (Routledge, 2018).

29. Henry Albers, ed., *Maria Mitchell: A Life in Journals and Letters* (College Avenue Press, 2001).

30. Rozsika Parker, *The Subversive Stitch: Embroidery and the Making of the Feminine* (Women's Press, 1984).

31. Parker, *The Subversive Stitch*, 207.

32. Su Hui's "Xuanji Tu" or "Star Gauge" has been re-created by Michéle Métail.

33. David Hinton, trans., *Classical Chinese Poetry: An Anthology* (Farrar, Straus and Giroux, 2010).

34. Hinton, *Classical Chinese Poetry*.

35. Hinton, *Classical Chinese Poetry*.

36. Janet Catherine Berlo, "Suturing My Soul: In Pursuit of the Broderie de Bayeux," in *Stitching the Self: Identity and the Needle Arts*, ed. Johanna Amos and Lisa Binkley (Bloomsbury Visual Arts, 2020), 167.

37. Haley Pierson-Cox (cross-stitch designer) in discussion with the author, February 13, 2023.

38. Carrie Brezine, "Algorithms and Automation: The Production of Mathematics and Textiles," in *The Oxford Handbook of the History of Mathematics*, ed. Eleanor Robson and Jacqueline Stedall (Oxford University Press, 2008), 468–92.

39. Giovanni Fanfani et al., "(Micro-)Performing Ancient Weaving in the PENELOPE Project," *Performance Research* 25, no. 3 (April 2, 2020): 123–30.

40. Virginia I. Postrel, *The Fabric of Civilization: How Textiles Made the World* (Basic Books, 2020).

41. Ellen Harlizius-Klück in Postrel, *The Fabric of Civilization*, 80.

42. Postrel, *The Fabric of Civilization*.

43. Ellen Harlizius-Klück, "Weaving as Binary Art and the Algebra of Patterns," *TEXTILE* 15, no. 2 (April 3, 2017): 176–97.

44. Ada Lovelace in Harlizius-Klück, "Weaving as Binary Art," 177.

45. Harlizius-Klück, "Weaving as Binary Art," 192.

46. Harlizius-Klück, "Weaving as Binary Art."

47. Lovelace in Harlizius-Klück, "Weaving as Binary Art," 191.

48. Postrel, *The Fabric of Civilization*.

49. *Crocheting Hyperbolic Planes*, TEDxRiga, 2014.

50. Margaret Wertheim, *The Beautiful Math of Coral*, TED Talk, filmed April 2009 at TED2009, Long Beach CA.

51. *Crocheting Hyperbolic Planes*.

CHAPTER 3. STITCHING A SELF

1. Elizabeth Zimmermann, *Knitting Without Tears: Basic Techniques and Easy-to-Follow Directions for Garments to Fit All Sizes* (Fireside Books, 1995).

2. Maureen Lilly Marsh, "Knitting Rebellion: Elizabeth Zimmermann, Identity, and Craftsmanship in Post War America," Open Access Dissertations, Purdue University, 2016.

3. D. W. Winnicott, *Home Is Where We Start From* (W. W. Norton, 1986).

4. Kate Lampitt Adey, "Understanding Why Women Knit: Finding Creativity and 'Flow,' " *TEXTILE* 16, no. 1 (January 2, 2018): 84–97.

5. D. W. Winnicott, *Winnicott on the Child* (Perseus Publishing), 78.

6. Sara Bauer, "Elizabeth Zimmermann and the Emergence of Critical Knitting," interview with Lilly Marsh; *Yarns at Yin Hoo*, podcast audio, episode 269, June 6, 2021.

7. Whitney Chadwick, *Militant Muse* (Thames and Hudson, 2017).

8. Whitney Chadwick, "Leonora Carrington: Evolution of a Feminist Consciousness," *Woman's Art Inc.* 7, no. 1 (1986): 37–42.

9. Gabriel Weisz and Jonathan Paul Eburne, *The Invisible Painting: My Memoir of Leonora Carrington* (Manchester University Press, 2021).

10. Luis Buñuel in Leonora Carrington, *The Hearing Trumpet* (Exact Change, 1996), Luis back cover.

11. Rosa Pomar (knitwear designer and yarn producer) in discussion with the author, August 9, 2022.

12. Mihaly Csikszentmihalyi, *Flow: The Psychology of Optimal Experience* (Harper & Row, 1990), 3.

13. Mihaly Csikszentmihalyi and Reed Larson, *Flow and the Foundations of Positive Psychology*, Vol. 10 (Springer, 2014), 8.

14. Arne Dietrich, "Neurocognitive Mechanisms Underlying the Experience of Flow," *Consciousness and Cognition* 13, no. 4 (December 2004): 746–61.

15. Rozsika Parker, *The Subversive Stitch: Embroidery and the Making of the Feminine* (Women's Press, 1984), 84.

16. Parker, *The Subversive Stitch*, 49.

17. Parker, *The Subversive Stitch*.

18. Colette, Robert Phelps, and Helen Beauclerk, *Earthly Paradise—Colette: An Autobiography Drawn from Her Lifetime Writings* (Sphere, 1970), 205.

19. Christine Zinni, "Stiches in Air: Needlework as Spiritual Practice and Service in Batavia, New York," in *Embroidered Stories: Interpreting Women's Domestic Needlework from the Italian Diaspora*, ed. Edvige Giunta and Joseph Sciorra (University Press of Mississippi, 2014), 74.

20. D. W. Winnicott, "Transitional Objects and Transitional Phenomena—A Study of the First Not-Me Possession," *International Journal of Psychoanalysis* 34 (1953): 90.

21. Winnicott, *Home Is Where We Start From.*

22. Rilla Marshall (weaving artist) in discussion with the author, March 22, 2023.

23. Flora Collingwood-Norris (knitwear designer) in discussion with the author, October 3, 2022.

24. Patricia J. Cooper and Norma Bradley Allen, *The Quilters: Women and Domestic Art: An Oral History* (Texas Tech University Press, 1999), 20.

25. Parker, *The Subversive Stitch.*

26. Parker, *The Subversive Stitch,* 89.

27. Haley Pierson-Cox (cross-stitch designer) in discussion with the author, February 13, 2023.

28. Judith Butler, *Undoing Gender* (Routledge, 2004), 1.

29. Csikszentmihalyi, *Flow: The Psychology of Optimal Experience.*

30. Virginia Woolf, *A Room of One's Own* (Penguin Books, 2000), 113.

31. Joseph McBrinn, " 'Knitting Is the Saving of Life; Adrian Has Taken It Up Too': Needlework, Gender, and the Bloomsbury Group," in *Stitching the Self: Identity and the Needle Arts,* ed. Johanna Amos and Lisa Binkley (Bloomsbury Visual Arts, 2020), 67–79.

32. Sandra L. Bem, "The Measurement of Psychological Androgyny," *Journal of Consulting and Clinical Psychology,* 42, no. 2 (1974): 155–62.

33. Woolf, *A Room of One's Own,* 88.

34. Anne Bradstreet, *The Works of Anne Bradstreet,* ed. Jeannine Hensley (The Belknap Press of Harvard University Press, 2010).

35. Janet Catherine Berlo, "Beyond Bricolage: Women and Aesthetic Strategies in Latin American Textiles," in *Textile Traditions of Mesoamerica and the Andes,* ed. Margot Blum Schevill, Janet Catherine Berlo, and Edward B. Dwyer (University of Texas Press, 1996), 437–79.

36. Lev Semenovič Vygotskij, "Thinking and Speech," in *The Collected Works of LS Vygotsky: Problems of the Theory and History of Psychology,* Vol. 3 (Springer Science & Business Media, 1987), 157.

37. Parker, *The Subversive Stitch,* xx.

38. D. W. Winnicott, *Playing and Reality* (Routledge, 1997).

39. Cherri M. Pancake, "Communicative Imagery in Guatemalan Indian Dress," in *Textile Traditions of Mesoamerica and the Andes,* ed. Margot Blum Schevill, Janet Catherine Berlo, and Edward B. Dwyer (University of Texas Press, 1996), 45–62.

40. Jane Przybysz, "The Victorian Crazy Quilt as Comfort and Discomfort," *The Quilt Journal* 3, no. 2 (1994): 11.

41. Przybysz, "The Victorian Crazy Quilt as Comfort and Discomfort," 10.

42. Claire E. Reynolds, " 'Featherbed Resistance' and 'A Dozen Proofs of Woman's Superiority,' " *CEA Critic* 67, no. 2 (2005): 43–61.

43. Reynolds," 'Featherbed Resistance' and 'A Dozen Proofs of Woman's Superiority.' "

44. Przybysz, "The Victorian Crazy Quilt as Comfort and Discomfort," 11.

45. "Crazy Work and Sane Work," *Harper's Bazaar*, 1884, 578.

46. "Crazy Work and Sane Work," 578.

47. Przybysz, "The Victorian Crazy Quilt as Comfort and Discomfort," 11.

48. Przybysz, "The Victorian Crazy Quilt as Comfort and Discomfort," 11.

49. Przybysz, "The Victorian Crazy Quilt as Comfort and Discomfort," 11.

50. Margaret Swanson and Ann Macbeth, *Educational Needlecraft* (Longmans, Green and Co., 1911), x.

51. Ghada Amer (multimedia artist) in discussion with the author, March 2, 2023.

52. Maura Reilly, "D as in Drips: A Conversation with Ghada Amer," Ghada Amer, Exhibition Catalog (Cheim & Reid, 2010).

53. Reilly, "D as in Drips: A Conversation with Ghada Amer."

54. Amer in discussion with the author.

55. Amer in discussion with the author.

56. Ricia A. Chansky, "A Stitch in Time: Third-Wave Feminist Reclamation of Needled Imagery," *Journal of Popular Culture* 43, no. 4 (July 19, 2010): 681–700.

57. Michelle Kingdom (embroidery artist) in discussion with the author, July 13, 2023.

CHAPTER 4. UNRAVELING EMOTIONS

1. Janet Catherine Berlo, *Quilting Lessons: Notes from the Scrap Bag of a Writer and Quilter* (University of Nebraska Press, 2001), 3.

2. Berlo, *Quilting Lessons*, 6.

3. Berlo, *Quilting Lessons*, 14.

4. Berlo, *Quilting Lessons*, 6.

5. Berlo, *Quilting Lessons*, 68.

6. Janet Catherine Berlo, "Suturing My Soul: In Pursuit of the Broderie de Bayeux," in *Stitching the Self: Identity and the Needle Arts*, ed. Johanna Amos and Lisa Binkley (Bloomsbury Visual Arts, 2020).

7. Harry Harlow and Robert Zimmerman, "The Development of Affectional Responses in Infant Monkeys," *Proceedings of the American Philisophical Society* 102, no. 5 (1958): 501–9.

8. Ann Futterman Collier, *Using Textile Arts and Handcrafts in Therapy with Women: Weaving Lives Back Together* (Jessica Kingsley Publishers, 2012).

9. Sinikka Pöllänen, "Elements of Crafts That Enhance Well-Being: Textile Craft Makers' Descriptions of Their Leisure Activity," *Journal of Leisure Research* 47, no. 1 (March 2015): 68.

10. Barry L. Jacobs, Francisco J. Martín-Cora, and Casimir A. Fornal, "Activ-

ity of Medullary Serotonergic Neurons in Freely Moving Animals," *Brain Research Reviews* 40, nos. 1–3 (October 2002): 45–52.

11. Jill Riley, Betsan Corkhill, and Clare Morris, "The Benefits of Knitting for Personal and Social Wellbeing in Adulthood: Findings from an International Survey," *British Journal of Occupational Therapy* 76, no. 2 (February 2013): 50–57.

12. Stephanie Pearl-McPhee, *At Knit's End: Meditations for Women Who Knit Too Much* (Storey Publishing, 2005).

13. Kelly Lambert, "Do or DIY," *RSA Journal* 161, no. 5561 (2015): 20–23.

14. Kelly G. Lambert et al., "Contingency-Based Emotional Resilience: Effort-Based Reward Training and Flexible Coping Lead to Adaptive Responses to Uncertainty in Male Rats," *Frontiers in Behavioral Neuroscience* 8 (April 28, 2014).

15. Ann Futterman Collier, "The Well-Being of Women Who Create with Textiles: Implications for Art Therapy," *Art Therapy* 28, no. 3 (September 2011): 104–12.

16. Mihaly Csikszentmihalyi, *Flow: The Psychology of Optimal Experience* (Harper & Row, 1990).

17. Ann Hood, "Ten Things I Learned from Knitting," *Tin House*, 2013.

18. Sarah Mosteller (knitting artist and creative arts therapist) in discussion with the author, November 4, 2022.

19. Betsan Corkhill, *Knit for Health & Wellness: How to Knit a Flexible Mind & More . . .* (FlatBear Publishing, 2014).

20. Deborah Valoma, "Dust Chronicles," *TEXTILE* 8, no. 3 (November 2010): 260–68.

21. Christy Thompson, "Grieving for My Brother Lost in a Landslide, I Wove a Shroud Out of His Clothes," CBC Radio Doc Project, 2020.

22. Judith Butler, *Undoing Gender* (Routledge, 2004).

23. Carole Hunt, "Worn Clothes and Textiles as Archives of Memory," *Critical Studies in Fashion & Beauty* 5, no. 2 (December 1, 2014): 207–32.

24. Mark Epstein, *Going to Pieces Without Falling Apart: A Buddhist Perspective on Wholeness* (Alfred A. Knopf, 1998).

25. Philip M. Bromberg, "Standing in the Spaces: The Multiplicity of Self and the Psychoanalytic Relationship," *Contemporary Psychoanalysis* 32, no. 4 (October 1996): 509–35.

26. Sarah Mosteller, "Entangled and Unraveled: Navigating Internal and External Realities Through Disintegration and Integration" (unpublished master's thesis, New York University, 2019).

27. Mosteller, "Entangled and Unraveled," 37–38.

28. Emmanuel Ghent, "Masochism, Submission, Surrender: Masochism as a Per-

version of Surrender," *Contemporary Psychoanalysis* 26, no. 1 (January 1990): 108–36.

29. Mosteller, "Entangled and Unraveled," 58.

30. Publius Ovidius Naso, *Metamorphoses*, trans. Rolfe Humphries (Indiana University Press, 1960).

31. Rachel Cohen, "Sew to Speak: Common Threads Project Psychotherapy Circles," in *Groupwork with Refugees and Survivors of Human Rights Abuses: The Power of Togetherness*, ed. Jude Boyles, Robin Ewart-Biggs, Rebecca Horn, and Kirsten Lamb (Routledge, 2022).

32. Emily A. Holmes, Chris R. Brewin, and Richard G. Hennessy, "Trauma Films, Information Processing, and Intrusive Memory Development," *Journal of Experimental Psychology: General* 133, no. 1 (2004): 3–22.

33. Cohen, "Sew to Speak."

34. Cohen, "Sew to Speak," 215.

35. Lisa Raye Garlock, "Stories in the Cloth: Art Therapy and Narrative Textiles," *Art Therapy* 33, no. 2 (April 2, 2016): 58–66.

36. Judith Lewis Herman, *Trauma and Recovery*, rev. ed. (BasicBooks, 1997), 214.

37. Rachel Cohen (founder of Common Threads Project) in discussion with the author, March 24, 2023.

38. Cohen in discussion with the author.

39. Ruth Leys, *Trauma: A Genealogy* (University of Chicago Press, 2000).

40. Cohen, "Sew to Speak," 216.

41. Common Threads Project Annual Report 2022.

42. Alton Barron and Carrie Barron, *The Creativity Cure: A Do-It-Yourself Prescription for Happiness* (Scribner, 2014).

43. Judith Lewis Herman, *Trauma and Recovery: The Aftermath of Violence—From Domestic Abuse to Political Terror* (Basic Books, 2003), 70.

44. Robert Storr, *Intimate Geometries: The Art and Life of Louise Bourgeois* (Monacelli Press, 2022).

45. Elizabeth V. Spelman, *Repair: The Impulse to Restore in a Fragile World* (Beacon Press, 2002).

46. Sanem Odabasi, "The Hidden Potential of Textiles: How Do They Heal and Reveal Traumas?," *TEXTILE* 21, no. 2 (April 3, 2023): 409–21.

47. Esther Nisenthal Krinitz and Bernice Steinhardt, *Memories of Survival* (Art and Remembrance, 2005).

48. Helena Duffy, "The Silence of the Mothers: Art Spiegelman's *Maus* and Philippe Claudel's *Brodeck*," *Journal of Holocaust Research* 34, no. 2 (April 2, 2020): 138–54.

49. Hans W. Loewald, "The Experience of Time," *Psychoanalytic Study of the Child* 27, no. 1 (January 1972): 401–10.

50. Deborah Valoma (textile artist) in discussion with the author, November 11, 2022.

CHAPTER 5. THE SOCIAL FABRIC

1. Robert Harry Lowie, *Myths and Traditions of the Crow Indians*, Sources of American Indian Oral Literature (University of Nebraska Press, 1993).

2. Janet Catherine Berlo, "Dreaming of Double Woman: The Ambivalent Role of the Female Artist in North American Indian Myth," *American Indian Quarterly* 17, no. 1 (1993): 31–43.

3. Silvia Federici, *Caliban and the Witch: Women, the Body and Primitive Accumulation* (Autonomedia, 2004).

4. Elizabeth Wayland Barber, *Women's Work: The First 20,000 Years: Women, Cloth, and Society in Early Times* (W. W. Norton, 1994).

5. Virginia I. Postrel, *The Fabric of Civilization: How Textiles Made the World* (Basic Books, 2020), 46.

6. Rozsika Parker and Griselda Pollock, *Framing Feminism: Art and the Women's Movement, 1970–85* (Pandora, 1987).

7. Hazel Tindall, "Fruity Knitting Interview with Andrea Doig," Shetland Wool Week 2017. Fruity Knitting, podcast video, episode 39, October 10, 2017.

8. Jill Riley, Betsan Corkhill, and Clare Morris, "The Benefits of Knitting for Personal and Social Wellbeing in Adulthood: Findings from an International Survey," *British Journal of Occupational Therapy* 76, no. 2 (February 2013): 50–57.

9. Betsan Corkhill et al., "Knitting and Well-Being," *TEXTILE* 12, no. 1 (March 2014): 34–57.

10. Ann Hood, "Ten Things I Learned from Knitting," *Tin House*, November 12, 2013.

11. Jessica Benjamin, *The Bonds of Love: Psychoanalysis, Feminism, and the Problem of Domination* (Pantheon Books, 1988).

12. Kate Lampitt Adey, "Understanding Why Women Knit: Finding Creativity and 'Flow,' " *TEXTILE* 16, no. 1 (January 2, 2018): 84–97.

13. William S. Burroughs and Brion Gysin, *The Third Mind* (Seaver Books, 1982).

14. Burroughs and Gysin, *The Third Mind*.

15. Miriam Schapiro and Melissa Meyer, "Waste Not Want Not: An Inquiry into What Women Saved and Assembled-FEMMAGE (1977–78)," in *Heresies 1*, 1977, 66–69.

16. Marlene Bennett Jones (Gee's Bend quilter) in discussion with the author, October 13, 2023.

17. Roland L. Freeman, *A Communion of the Spirits: African-American Quilters, Preservers, and Their Stories* (Rutledge Hill Press, 1996).

18. Lilly Marsh (weaver) in discussion with the author, October 7, 2022.

19. Hazel Tindall (Shetland knitter) in discussion with the author, August 31, 2023.

20. Anne L. Macdonald, *No Idle Hands: The Social History of American Knitting* (Ballantine Books, 1990).

21. Debbie Stoller, *Stitch 'n Bitch: The Knitter's Handbook* (Workman, 2004).

22. Lindsay Degen (knitwear designer) in discussion with the author, August 12, 2023.

23. Angela Maddock, "Bloodline," *Angela Maddock* (blog), n.d.

24. Angela Maddock, "Bloodline: An Experiment in Knit and Proximity" (PhD thesis, Royal College of Art, 2018), 43.

25. Maddock, "Bloodline: An Experiment in Knit and Proximity," 51.

26. Maddock, "Bloodline: An Experiment in Knit and Proximity," 12.

27. Rozsika Parker, *The Subversive Stitch: Embroidery and the Making of the Feminine* (Women's Press, 1984), 213.

28. Rosa Pomar (knitwear designer and yarn producer) in discussion with the author, August 9, 2022.

29. Juana Huaman Willca (Peruvian weaver) in discussion with the author, December 12, 2022.

30. Bennett Jones in discussion with the author.

31. Martha Bebinger, "Alzheimer's Stopped Her from Finishing a Rug. A Stranger Stepped Up to Help," WBUR, radio broadcast, June 20, 2023.

32. Bebinger, "Alzheimer's Stopped Her from Finishing a Rug."

33. Bebinger, "Alzheimer's Stopped Her from Finishing a Rug."

34. Martha Swann-Quinn, "For Families Missing Loved Ones After Loss, This Company Is Making Miracles," *Parents Magazine*, November 27, 2023.

35. Barber, *Women's Work*.

36. Terence S. Turner, "The Social Skin," in *Reading the Social Body*, ed. Catherine B. Burroughs and Jeffrey Ehrenreich (University of Iowa Press, 1993).

37. Kathryn Sullivan Kruger, *Weaving the Word: The Metaphorics of Weaving and Female Textual Production* (Susquehanna University Press, 2001), 29.

38. Janet Catherine Berlo, *Quilting Lessons: Notes from the Scrap Bag of a Writer and Quilter* (University of Nebraska Press, 2001).

39. Donald Watson, "The Navajo Blanket. Mesa Verde Notes," *Mesa Verde National Park* 3, no. 3 (October 1932).

40. Bob Morgan and Jeanne Brako, "Conservation of Navajo Textiles," *WAAC Newsletter* 6, no. 1 (January 1984): 3–5.

41. *Shaped by the Loom: Weaving Worlds in the American Southwest*, Bard Graduate Center, New York, July 17, 2023.

42. *Shaped by the Loom.*

43. Claude Lévi-Strauss, *The Savage Mind*, The Nature of Human Society Series

(University of Chicago Press, 2000); Janet Catherine Berlo, "Beyond Bricolage: Women and Aesthetic Strategies in Latin American Textiles," in *Textile Traditions of Mesoamerica and the Andes*, ed. Margot Blum Schevill, Janet Catherine Berlo, and Edward B. Dwyer (University of Texas Press, 1996), 437–79.

44. Berlo, "Beyond Bricolage," 438.

45. Berlo, "Beyond Bricolage."

46. Kruger, *Weaving the Word*.

47. Kruger, *Weaving the Word*, 4.

48. Alexandra Lester-Makin, "The Making of the Bayeux Tapestry: Who Made It, How Long Did It Take, and How Has It Survived?," HistoryExtra, October 24, 2019.

49. Alexandra Lester-Makin, "Embroidery and Its Early Medieval Audience: A Case Study of Sensory Engagement," *World Archaeology* 52, no. 2 (March 14, 2020): 298–312.

50. Antoine Verney (Bayeux Tapestry Museum curator) in discussion with the author, June 16, 2023.

51. Alexandra Lester-Makin, "The Front Tells the Story; the Back Tells the History: A Technical Discussion of the Embroidering of the Bayeux Tapestry," in *Making Sense of the Bayeux Tapestry: Readings and Reworkings*, ed. Anna C. Henderson and Gale R. Owen-Crocker (Manchester University Press, 2016).

52. Turner, "The Social Skin" in *Reading the Social Body*.

53. Lester-Makin, "The Making of the Bayeux Tapestry."

54. Jan Messent, *The Bayeux Tapestry Embroiderers' Story* (Search Press, 2010).

55. Mia Hansson (re-creator of Bayeux Tapestry) in discussion with the author, January 10, 2024.

56. Alexandra Lester-Makin (medieval embroidery scholar) in discussion with the author, January 10, 2024.

57. R. Howard Bloch, *A Needle in the Right Hand of God: The Norman Conquest of 1066 and the Making and Meaning of the Bayeux Tapestry* (Random House, 2006), 42.

58. Janet Catherine Berlo, "Suturing My Soul: In Pursuit of the Broderie de Bayeux," in *Stitching the Self: Identity and the Needle Arts*, ed. Johanna Amos and Lisa Binkley (Bloomsbury Visual Arts, 2020), 156.

59. Katherine Russell to Nicole Nehrig, email message to the author, January 31, 2024.

60. Katherine Russell (creator of Alderney Island Bayeux Tapestry project) in discussion with the author, December 22, 2023.

61. Russell, email message to the author.

62. Berlo, "Suturing My Soul," 156.

63. "Scandinavian Needlework," *Nordic Needle*, needlery newsletter.

64. Hansson in discussion with the author.

65. Mia Hansson, email message to the author, January 10, 2024.

66. Hansson, email message to the author.

67. Hansson, email message to the author.

Chapter 6. Homespun Opportunities

1. Michèle Hayeur Smith, *The Valkyries' Loom: The Archaeology of Cloth Production and Female Power in the North Atlantic* (University Press of Florida, 2020).

2. Hayeur Smith, *The Valkyries' Loom*, 161.

3. Elizabeth Wayland Barber, *Women's Work: The First 20,000 Years: Women, Cloth, and Society in Early Times* (W. W. Norton, 1994), 45.

4. Elizabeth Wayland Barber Barber, *Prehistoric Textiles: The Development of Cloth in the Neolithic and Bronze Ages with Special Reference to the Aegean* (Princeton University Press, 1991), 4.

5. Hayeur Smith, *The Valkyries' Loom*.

6. Silvia Federici, *Caliban and the Witch: Women, the Body and Primitive Accumulation* (Autonomedia, 2004).

7. Rozsika Parker, *The Subversive Stitch: Embroidery and the Making of the Feminine* (Women's Press, 1984).

8. Constance H. Berman, "Women's Work in Family, Village, and Town after 1000 CE: Contributions to Economic Growth?," *Journal of Women's History* 19, no. 3 (September 2007): 10–32.

9. Hazel Tindall (Shetland knitter) in discussion with the author, August 31, 2023.

10. "The State of the Handworker Economy 2018" (Nest, 2018).

11. "The State of the Handworker Economy 2018."

12. Rebecca van Bergen (founder of Nest) in discussion with the author, July 14, 2023.

13. Canaria Gaffer and Ines Kaempfer, "In the Interest of the Child? Child Rights and Homeworkers in Textile and Handicraft Supply Chains in Asia" (Save the Children: Centre STC Study, 2019).

14. Annette B. Weiner and Jane Schneider, eds., *Cloth and Human Experience*, Smithsonian Series in Ethnographic Inquiry (Smithsonian Institution Press, 1989).

15. Gaffer and Kaempfer, "In the Interest of the Child?"

16. Hannah Dreier, "Alone and Exploited, Migrant Children Work Brutal Jobs Across the U.S.," *New York Times*, February 25, 2023.

17. Emma Ross, "Fast Fashion Getting Faster: A Look at the Unethical Labor Practices Sustaining a Growing Industry," George Washington University International Law and Policy Brief, October 28, 2021.

18. M. E. Khan et al., "Living Wage Report: Dhaka, Bangladesh and Satellite Cities," Series 1, Report 7 (Global Living Wage Institution, 2016).

19. Caroline Collin (tour director of Atelier Saint James) in discussion with the author, June 16, 2023.

20. Tricia Wilson Nguyen, "Scandal and Imprisonment: Gold Spinners of 17th Century England," *Hidden Stories/Human Lives: Proceedings of the Textile Society of America 17th Biennial Symposium, October 15–17, 2020.*

21. Anna Wood, "Tears of Blood. The Calabrian Villanella and Immigrant Epiphanies," in *Studies in Italian American Folklore* (Utah University Press, 2020), 1–51.

22. Edvige Giunta and Joseph Sciorra, *Embroidered Stories: Interpreting Women's Domestic Needlework from the Italian Diaspora* (University Press of Mississippi, 2014).

23. Giunta and Sciorra, *Embroidered Stories.*

24. Meredith Ray, "Letters and Lace: Arcangela Tarabotti and Convent Culture in Seicento Venice," in *Early Modern Women and Transnational Communities of Letters*, ed. Anne R. Larsen and Julie D. Campbell (Ashgate, 2009).

25. Ray, "Letters and Lace," 47.

26. Ray, "Letters and Lace," 57.

27. Melissa Jurgena, "By God's Grace and the Needle: The Life and Labors of Mercy Jane Bancroft Blair" (EDT Collection for University of Nebraska-Lincoln, 2006).

28. Jurgena, "By God's Grace and the Needle."

29. Paul E. Rivard, *A New Order of Things: How the Textile Industry Transformed New England* (University Press of New England, 2002).

30. Jurgena, "By God's Grace and the Needle," 70.

31. Jurgena, "By God's Grace and the Needle," 130.

32. Michael Hitchcock, *Indonesian Textiles* (Icon Editions, 1991).

33. Janet Hoskins, "In the Realm of the Indigo Queen Dyeing, Exchange Magic, and the Elusive Tourist Dollar on Sumba," in *What's the Use of Art?*, ed. Jan Mrazek and Morgan Pitelka (University of Hawaii Press, 2017), 100–26.

34. Hoskins, "In the Realm of the Indigo Queen Dyeing."

35. Christiane Brauer and Johann Borwin Luth, *Woven Messages—Indonesian Textile Tradition in Course of Time* (Roemer Museum, 1991).

36. Hoskins, "In the Realm of the Indigo Queen Dyeing," 111.

37. Hoskins, "In the Realm of the Indigo Queen Dyeing," 150.

38. *Quilts of Gee's Bend* exhibit, 2013.

39. Tinnie Pettway (Gee's Bend quilter) in discussion with the author, October 8, 2023.

40. "Minder Coleman," Souls Grown Deep, n.d.

41. Nancy Callahan, "Freedom Quilting Bee," *Encyclopedia of Alabama*, August 8, 2008.

42. Callahan, "Freedom Quilting Bee."

43. Callahan, "Freedom Quilting Bee."
44. Callahan, "Freedom Quilting Bee."
45. Callahan, "Freedom Quilting Bee."
46. Delia Pettway Thibodeaux (Gee's Bend quilter) in discussion with the author, September 13, 2023.
47. Tinnie Pettway in discussion with the author.
48. Claudia Pettway Charley (Gee's Bend quilter) in discussion with the author, September 11, 2023.
49. Tinnie Pettwayin discussion with the author.
50. Michael Kimmelman, "ART REVIEW; Jazzy Geometry, Cool Quilters," *New York Times*, November 29, 2002.
51. Delia Pettway Thibodeaux (Gee's Bend quilter) in discussion with the author.
52. Bridget R. Cooks, *Exhibiting Blackness: African Americans and the American Art Museum* (University of Massachusetts Press, 2011).
53. Tinnie Pettway in discussion with the author.
54. Claudia Pettway Charley in discussion with the author.
55. "Shared Prosperity Study with the Gee's Bend Quilters: A Mixed-Methods Analysis of Income and Cost of Living," Brief, Shared Prosperity Study with the Gee's Bend Quilters (Nest, May 2022).
56. Claudia Pettway Charley in discussion with the author.
57. Francesca Charley (Gee's Bend quilter) in discussion with the author, November 11, 2023.

Chapter 7. Hands to Power

1. Janice Helland, "From Prison to Citizenship, 1910: The Making and Display of a Suffragist Banner," in *Stitching the Self: Identity and the Needle Arts*, ed. Johanna Amos and Lisa Binkley (Bloomsbury Visual Arts 2021).
2. Krista McCracken, "Embroidery as Record and Resistance," *Contingent Magazine*, November 19, 2019.
3. Mary Lowndes, *Banners & Banner-Making*, pamphlet (Artists' Suffrage League, 1909).
4. Janet Catherine Berlo, *Quilting Lessons: Notes from the Scrap Bag of a Writer and Quilter* (University of Nebraska Press, 2001), 95.
5. Jane Przybysz, "The Victorian Crazy Quilt as Comfort and Discomfort," *The Quilt Journal* 3, no. 2 (1994).
6. Laura Elizabeth Sapelly, "Pedagogies of Historical and Contemporary American Sewing Circles" (dissertation in Art Education, The Pennsylvania State University, 2016).
7. Jessica Lack, "The Role of Artists in Promoting the Cause of Women's Suffrage," *Frieze Magazine*, September 2, 2018.

8. Faith Ringgold, *We Flew over the Bridge: The Memoirs of Faith Ringgold* (Duke University Press, 2005).

9. Miriam Schapiro and Melissa Meyer, "Waste Not Want Not: An Inquiry into What Women Saved and Assembled-FEMMAGE (1977–78)," in *Heresies 1*, 1977, 66–69.

10. Rozsika Parker and Griselda Pollock, *Framing Feminism: Art and the Women's Movement, 1970–85* (Pandora, 1987).

11. Kathy Battista, *Renegotiating the Body: Feminist Art in 1970s London* (I. B. Tauris, 2013).

12. Amy Tobin, "I'll Show You Mine, If You Show Me Yours: Collaboration, Consciousness-Raising and Feminist-Influenced Art in the 1970s," *Tate Papers* no. 25 (Spring 2016).

13. Monica Ross, "Portrait of the Artist as a Young Woman: A Postal Event," in *Framing Feminism: Art and the Women's Movement, 1970–85*, ed. Rozsika Parker and Griselda Pollock (Pandora, 1987).

14. Tobin, "I'll Show You Mine, If You Show Me Yours."

15. Ross, "Portrait of the Artist as a Young Woman," 211.

16. Monica Ross, "History or Not." Conference presentation at 347 minutes, Whitechapel Exhibition *Live in Your Head*, Conway Hall, London, March 24, 2000.

17. Parker and Pollock, *Framing Feminism*.

18. Ross, "History or Not."

19. Tobin, "I'll Show You Mine, If You Show Me Yours."

20. Alexandra Kokoli, "Undoing 'Homeliness' in Feminist Art: Feministo: Portrait of the Artist as a Housewife (1975–7)," *Paradoxa: International Feminist Art Journal, Domestic Politics* 13 (2004): 13.

21. Kokoli, "Undoing 'Homeliness' in Feminist Art."

22. Ross, "Portrait of the Artist as a Young Woman."

23. Kate Walker and Agnes Walker, "Starting with Rag Rugs: The Aesthetics of Survival," in *Women and Craft*, ed. Gillian Elinor, Su Richardson, and Kate Walker (Virago, 1987), 27.

24. Ross, "Portrait of the Artist as a Young Woman."

25. Phil Goodall, "Growing Point/Pains in 'Feministo' 1977," in *Framing Feminism: Art and the Women's Movement, 1970–85*, ed. Rozsika Parker and Griselda Pollock (Pandora, 1987).

26. Joanna Klaces, "Phoenix Arising," in *Framing Feminism: Art and the Women's Movement, 1970–85*, ed. Rozsika Parker and Griselda Pollock (Pandora, 1987), 37.

27. Kokoli, "Undoing 'Homeliness' in Feminist Art."

28. Su Richardson, " 'Fenix' Documents," in *Framing Feminism: Art and the Women's Movement, 1970–85*, ed. Rozsika Parker and Griselda Pollock (Pandora, 1987).

29. Schapiro and Meyer, "Waste Not Want Not."

30. Ricia A. Chansky, "A Stitch in Time: Third-Wave Feminist Reclamation of Needled Imagery," *Journal of Popular Culture* 43, no. 4 (July 19, 2010): 681–700.

31. Betsy Greer, "Craftivism in Three Parts," *Knitchicks* (blog), May 6, 2006.

32. Corey D. Fields, "Not Your Grandma's Knitting: The Role of Identity Processes in the Transformation of Cultural Practices," *Social Psychology Quarterly* 77, no. 2 (June 2014): 150–65.

33. Kristie Ramirez, "Magda Sayeg's Bedside Table," *Texas Monthly*, December 2011.

34. Chiara Barbagallo, "Cross Stitch as Pixels," *Indie Life Magazine*, July 8, 2021.

35. Selma Fraiberg, Edna Adelson, and Vivian Shapiro, "Ghosts in the Nursery," *Journal of the American Academy of Child Psychiatry* 14, no. 3 (June 1975): 387–421.

36. Heather Marie Scholl (embroidery artist) in discussion with the author, September 5, 2023.

37. Audre Lorde, *Sister Outsider: Essays and Speeches* (Crossing Press, 2007), 39.

38. Scholl in discussion with the author.

39. Scholl in discussion with the author.

40. Lorde, *Sister Outsider*, 41.

41. Ecuador webinar: *Celebrating 10 Years of Story Cloths with Sandoval Peñaherrer*, Common Threads Project, 2022.

42. Ecuador webinar: *Celebrating 10 Years of Story Cloths with Sandoval Peñaherrer*.

43. Ecuador webinar: *Celebrating 10 Years of Story Cloths with Sandoval Peñaherrer*.

44. Shirin Neshat, *Art in Exile*, TEDwomen, 2010.

45. José Carlos Mariátegui and Michael Pearlman, *The Heroic and Creative Meaning of Socialism: Selected Essays of José Carlos Mariátegui* (Humanity Books, 1999).

46. Alisha Roy, "3000-Year-Old Embroidery Art of Tatreez Tells the Story of Palestinian Identity," *Gulf News*, October 31, 2023.

47. Wafa Ghnaim, *Tatreez & Tea: Embroidery and Storytelling in the Palestinian Diaspora* (self-published, 2018).

48. Ghnaim, *Tatreez & Tea*.

49. *The Embroiderers* (Palestinian Museum, 2016).

50. Roy, "3000-Year-Old Embroidery Art of Tatreez."

51. Roy, "3000-Year-Old Embroidery Art of Tatreez."

52. Ghnaim, *Tatreez & Tea*.

53. Gabrielle Canon, "Here's One Confederate Flag That Shouldn't Be Taken Down," *Mother Jones*, June 27, 2015.

54. Canon, "Here's One Confederate Flag That Shouldn't Be Taken Down."

55. "Unraveling: An Artist's Take on the Confederate Flag," *Morning Edition*, WFAE, radio broadcast, June 22, 2015.

56. Sonya Clark, "On Truce and the Everyday Work of Dismantling Systemic Racism," podcast, Fabric Workshop and Museum, Philadelphia, March 2019.
57. H. Parnham et al., "Prince Edward Island State of the Coast Report," Canadian Centre for Climate Change and Adaptation, St. Peters Bay, Canada. Report submitted to the Department of Environment, Energy and Climate Action, Government of Prince Edward Island, 2023.
58. Rilla Marshall (weaving artist) in discussion with the author, March 22, 2023.

EPILOGUE. CRAFTING A PURPOSE

1. Olutosin Oladosu Adebowale (textile artist and activist) in discussion with the author, December 1, 2023.
2. Clay Routledge and Taylor A. FioRito, "Why Meaning in Life Matters for Societal Flourishing," *Frontiers in Psychology* 11 (January 14, 2021): 601899.
3. Michelle Kingdom (embroidery artist) in discussion with the author, July 13, 2023.
4. Angela Maddock, "Bloodline: An Experiment in Knit and Proximity" (PhD thesis, Royal College of Art, 2018).
5. Claudia Pettway Charley (Gee's Bend quilter) in discussion with the author, September 11, 2023.
6. Marlene Bennett Jones (Gee's Bend quilter) in discussion with the author, October 13, 2023.
7. Gabina Sicus Mamani (Peruvian weaver) in discussion with the author, December 12, 2022.

Image Credits

35 Drawing by Hannen Wolfe, adapted from Christine R. Franquemont's "Chinchero Pallays: An Ethnic Code," 1986.

IMAGE GALLERY

Andean weaver Marcela Salas Calcina: Nicole Nehrig

A Navajo wedding basket: Nicole Nehrig

A re-creation of Su Hui's "Star Gauge": Michèle Métail

"Pod World: Plastic Fantastic Too": Photo courtesy 58th Venice Biennale, by Francesco Galli

Knitwear designer Flora Collingwood-Norris: Flora Collingwood-Norris

Ghada Amer paints with thread: Courtesy of the artist and Marianne Boesky Gallery, New York and Aspen, and Kewenig Galerie

Michelle Kingdom's piece The Height of Folly: Michelle Kingdom

This story cloth, titled The Rosebush: Common Threads Project at Federacíon de Mujeres de Sucumbíos in Lago Agrio, Ecuador

Holocaust survivor Esther Nisenthal Krinitz: Art and Remembrance

In 10,000 Stitches with No Goal *(2022)*: Deborah Valoma

Navajo Germantown Eye-Dazzler blanket: Nicole Nehrig

Artist Mia Hansson: Joe Giddens / Alamy

Three generations of Gee's Bend quilters: Stephen Pitkin / Pitkin Studio

A suffrage banner created in 1908: © Newnham College, Cambridge, UK

Su Richardson, a participant in the Postal Art Event: Su Richardson

Switch-Over, a graphic embroidery installation: Aheneah (creative identity of Ana Martins)

Olutosin Oladosu Adebowale's fabric paintings: Olutosin Oladosu Adebowale

Index